Hawaiian Islands

must SEES

Chief Editor	Cynthia Clayton Ochterbeck
Senior Editor	M. Linda Lee
Writers	Diane Bair and Pamela Wright
Production Coordinator	Allison M. Simpson
Cartography	Peter Wrenn
Photo Editor	Brigitta L. House
Photo Research	Martha Hunt
Documentation	Doug Rogers, Martha Hunt
Proofreader	Margo Browning
Production	Octavo Design and Production, Inc.
	Apopka, Florida
Cover Design	Paris Venise Design
	Paris, 17e
Printing and Binding	Banta Book Group
	Salt Fork, UT

Michelin North America
One Parkway South
Greenville, SC 29615
USA
800-423-0485
www.michelin-us.com
email: TheGreenGuide-us@us.michelin.com

Special Sales:

For information regarding bulk sales, customized editions and premium sales, please
contact our Customer Service Departments:

USA – 800-423-0485 **Canada** – 800-361-8236

Manufacture française des pneumatiques Michelin

Société en commandite par actions au capital de 304 000 000 EUR
Place des Carmes-Déchaux – 63 Clermont-Ferrand (France)
R.C.S. Clermont-FD B 855 800 507

Note to the reader:

While every effort is made to ensure that all information in this guide is correct and up-
to-date, Michelin Travel Publications (Michelin North America, Inc.) accepts no liability
for any direct, indirect or consequential losses howsoever caused so far as such can be
excluded by law.

Admission prices listed for sights in this guide are for a single adult, unless otherwise
specified.

Welcome to the Hawaiian Islands

Table of Contents

Star List   6

Calendar of Events   8

Must Know: Practical Information   10

Introduction: The Hawaiian Islands   18

Pearls of the Pacific: The Hawaiian Islands   20

The Must Sees

Big Island★★   22

Beaches   26
Parks and Natural Sites   29
Scenic Drives   35
Gardens   40
Historic Sites   42
Museums   47
Musts for Outdoor Fun   48
Musts for Kids   52
Must Go: Performing Arts   52
Must Shop   53
Must Be Seen: Nightlife   54
Must Be Pampered: Spas   55

Maui★★   56

Beaches   60
Parks and Natural Sites   62
Scenic Drives   65
Museums   66
Gardens   67
Historic Sites   67
Musts for Fun   68
Musts for Outdoor Fun   70
Musts for Kids   73
Must Go: Performing Arts   74
Must Shop   74
Must Be Seen: Nightlife   78
Must Be Pampered: Spas   79

Kauai★★   80

Beaches   82
Parks and Natural Sites   85
Scenic Drives   89
Gardens   92
Historic Sites   94
Museums   94
Musts for Fun   95
Musts for Outdoor Fun   97

Table of Contents

Kauai *(continued)*
Musts for Kids	100
Must Shop	101
Must Be Seen: Nightlife	102
Must Be Pampered: Spas	103

Oahu★★   **104**
Cities	105
Beaches	109
Parks and Natural Sites	112
Scenic Drives	114
Gardens	116
Museums	119
Historic Sites	125
Musts for Fun	129
Musts for Outdoor Fun	131
Musts for Kids	135
Must Go: Performing Arts	138
Must Shop	140
Must Be Seen: Nightlife	143
Must Be Pampered: Spas	144

Lanai★   **146**
Beaches	148
Natural Sites	150
Scenic Drives	150
Gardens	152
Historic Sites	152
Musts for Fun	153
Musts for Outdoor Fun	154
Musts for Kids	156
Must Be Pampered: Spas	157

Molokai★   **158**
Beaches	159
Natural Sites	160
Scenic Drives	160
Historic Sites	161
Musts for Outdoor Fun	162
Musts for Fun	163

Kahoolawe and Niihau   **164**
Hawaiian Culture	165

Must Eat   **166**

Must Stay   **178**

Index   **190**

THE MICHELIN STARS

For more than 75 years, travelers have used the Michelin stars to take the guesswork out of planning a trip. Our star-rating system helps you make the best decision on where to go, what to do, and what to see. A three-star rating means it's one of the "absolutelys"; two stars means it's one of the "should sees"; and one star says it's one of the "sees" — a must if you have the time.

★★★   Absolutely Must See
★★   Really Must See
★   Must See

The following abbreviations appear in the list below: HAW Hawaii, The Big Island; KAU Kauai; LAN Lanai; MAU Maui; MOL Molokai; OAH Oahu; NHP National Historical Park; NP National Park; SRA State Recreational Area.

Three-Star Sights

Bishop Museum and Planetarium★★★(OAH)

Haleakala NP★★★(MAU)

Hana Highway★★★(MAU)

Hawaii Volcanoes NP★★★(HAW)

Hulopoe Beach★★★(LAN)

Kaunaoa Beach ★★★(HAW)

Kilauea Volcano★★★(HAW)

Na Pali Coast ★★★(KAU)

Waikiki Beach★★★(OAH)

Two-Star Sights

Chain of Craters Road★★ (HAW)

Crater Rim Drive★★ (HAW

Diamond Head★★ (OAH)

Foster Botanical Garden★★ (OAH)

Halemaumau Crater★★ (HAW)

Hanauma Bay Nature Preserve★★ (OAH)

Hanauma Bay Beach Park★★ (OAH)

Hanalei Bay★★ (KAU)

Hapuna Beach SRA★★ (HAW)

Hawaii, The Big Island★★

Hawaii Tropical Botanical Garden★★ (HAW)

Highway 44★★ (LAN)

Kokee State Park★★ (KAU)

Lahaina★★ (MAU)

Lanikai Beach★★ (OAH)

Laupahoehoe Point Beach★★ (HAW)

Hilo★★ (HAW)

Honolulu★★ (OAH)

Honolulu Academy of Arts★★ (OAH)

Iao Valley State Park★★ (MAU)

Iolani Palace★★ (OAH)

Kaanapali Beach★★ (MAU)

Kailua Beach Park★★ (OAH)

Kalalau Trail★★(KAU)

Kalalau Valley★★ (KAU)

Kalaupapa NHP★★ (MOL)

Kauai★★

Kawaiahao Church★★ (OAH)

Kilauea Visitor Center★★ (HAW)

Puuhonua o Honaunau NHP★★ (HAW)

Sea Life Park★★ (OAH)

Shipwreck Beach★★ (LAN)

Southeast Shore★★ (OAH)

Two-Star Sights *continued*

Limahuli Garden★★ (KAU)
Maui★★
Mauna Kea★★ (HAW)
McBryde and Allerton
    Botanical Gardens★★ (KAU)
Mission Houses
    Museum★★ (OAH)
Munro Trail★★ (LAN)
North Shore★★ (KAU)
Oahu★★
Oheo Gulch★★ (MAU)
Pearl Harbor★★ (OAH)
Poipu Beach Park★★ (KAU)
Polynesian Cultural
    Center★★ (OAH)

USS Arizona
    Memorial★★ (OAH)
Waikiki★★ (OAH)
Waimea Canyon★★ (KAU)
Waimea Canyon
    Drive★★ (KAU)
Waimea Canyon State
    Park ★★ (KAU)
Waimea Valley
    Audubon Center★★ (OAH)
Waipio Valley★★ (HAW)
World Botanical
    Garden★★ (HAW)

One-Star Sights

Aloha Tower★ (OAH)
Akaka Falls State Park★ (HAW)
Battleship Missouri
    Memorial★ (OAH)
Big Beach★ (MAU)
Chinatown★ (OAH)
Contemporary
    Museum★ (OAH)
Fern Grotto★ (KAU)
Green Sand Beach★ (HAW)
Grove Farm
    Homestead★ (KAU)
Hawaii Maritime
    Center★ (OAH)
Hawaii State Capitol★ (OAH)
Honolulu Zoo★ (OAH)
Hulihee Palace★ (HAW)
International
    Market Place★ (OAH)
Jhamandas Watumull
    Planetarium★ (OAH)
Kaunolu★ (LAN)
Kealakekua Bay★ (HAW)
Kee Beach★ (KAU)
Kohala Coast★ (HAW)
Koko Crater
    Botanical Gardens★ (OAH)
Kona Village Luau★ (HAW)
Kualoa Ranch★ (OAH)
Lanai★
Lumahai Beach★ (KAU)
Lyon Arboretum★ (OAH)
Make Horse Beach★ (MOL)
Maui Ocean Center★ (MAU)

Maui Tropical
    Plantation★ (MAU)
Mauna Loa★ (HAW)
Molokai★
Mookini Heiau★ (HAW)
Moomomi Dunes★ (MOL)
Murphy's Beach★ (MOL)
National Memorial Cemetery
    of the Pacific★ (OAH)
North Shore Beaches★ (OAH)
Paia★ (MAU)
Parker Ranch★ (HAW)
Pepeekeo Scenic
    Drive★ (HAW)
Polihale Beach★ (KAU)
Poipu★ (KAU)
Polihua Beach★ (LAN)
Punaluu Black Sand
    Beach★ (HAW)
Purdy's Macadamia
    Nut Farm★ (MOL)
Rainbow Falls★ (HAW)
Senator Fong's
    Plantation★ (OAH)
Shangri La★ (OAH)
Spouting Horn★ (KAU)
Swim with Rays★ (HAW)
Thomas A. Jagger
    Museum★ (HAW)
Thurston Lava Tube★ (HAW)
USS Bowfin Submarine
    Museum & Park★ (OAH)
Wahiawa Botanical
    Garden★ (OAH)
Wailea Beach★ (MAU)

Listed below is a selection of Hawaii's most popular annual events. Please note that the dates may change from year to year. For more information, contact the Hawaii Visitors and Convention Bureau *(808-923-1811; www.gohawaii.com)*.

January
Lunar New Year 808-521-4934
Chinatown, Honolulu, Oahu   www.chinatownhi.com

Molokai Makahiki 808-553-3673
Molokai (island-wide)   www.molokaievents.com

February
Waimea Town Celebration 808-338-9957
Waimea, Kauai   alohavisitkauai.com

Pro Bowl 808-486-9300
Aloha Stadium, Honolulu, Oahu   www.nfl.com

March
Cherry Blossom Festival 808-949-2255
All islands   www.cbfhawaii.com

East Maui Taro Festival 808-248-8972
Hana, Maui   www.tarofestival.org

Tahiti Fete of Hilo 808-935-3002
Afook Chinen Civic Auditorium, Hilo, Big Island
www.polynesia.com/tahiti_festival/information.htm

April
Merrie Monarch Festival 808-935-9168
Edith Kanakole Stadium, Hilo, Big Island
(week after Easter) www.merriemonarchfestival.org

May
Molokai Ka Hula Piko 808-552-2800
Papohaku Beach Park, Molokai
www.molokaievents.com

June
King Kamehameha Celebration 808-586-0333
All islands   www.hawaii.gov/dags/agencies/king_
kamehameha_commission

Puuhonua O Honaunau Festival 808-328-2288
Puuhonua O Honaunau National
Historical Park, Big Island   www.nps.gov/puho

Taste of Honolulu 808-536-1015
Civic Center Grounds
Honolulu, Oahu   www.taste808.com

July
Parker Ranch Rodeo 808-885-7311
Parker Ranch, Waimea
Big Island   www.parkerranch.com/events.html

Ukulele Festival 808-732-3739
Kapiolani Park
Waikiki, Oahu www.ukulele-roysakuma.com/uf.html

August

Hawaiian International Billfish Tournament
Kailua-Kona, Big Island   808-329-6155
www.konabillfish.com

Made in Hawaii Festival   808-533-1292
Neal S. Blaisdell Center
Honolulu, Oahu   www.madeinhawaiifestival.com

Red Bull World Cliff-Diving Championships
Kaunolu Point, Lanai   808-575-9151
www.redbullcliffdiving.com

September

Aloha Festivals   800-852-7690
All islands   www.alohafestivals.com

Mauifest Hawaii   808-573-5530
Maui Arts & Cultural Center
Hotel Hana-Maui, Hana   www.mauifest.net

October

Ironman Triathlon World Championship
Kailua-Kona, Big Island   808-329-0063
www.ironmanlive.com

Molokai Hoe Canoe Race   808-259-7112
Hale o Lono, Molokai   www.holoholo.org

Oktoberfest   808-955-4811
Ala Moana Hotel
Honolulu, Oahu   www.alamoanahotel.com

November

Kona Coffee Cultural Festival   808-326-7820
Kailua-Kona, Big Island   www.konacoffeefest.com

Slack Key Guitar Festival   808-239-4336
Maui, Molokai and Kauai
www.hawaiianslackkeyguitarfestivals.com

VANS Triple Crown Surfing Championships
North shore of Oahu   www.triplecrownofsurfing.com
(Nov–Dec)

World Invitational Hula Festival   808-735-7950
The Waikiki Shell, Oahu   www.worldhula.com

December

Anniversary Commemoration Pearl Harbor
USS Arizona Memorial   808-422-0561
Honolulu, Oahu   www.nps.gov/usar

Grand Slam   800-742-8258
Poipu Bay Resort Golf Course, Kauai   www.pga.com

Honolulu City Lights   808- 523-4834
Honolulu, Oahu

Waimea Christmas Parade and Festival   808-937-2833
Waimea, Big Island

Area Codes

To call between the islands, dial 1 + 808 + seven-digit number. To dial between different area codes on the mainland, dial 1 + area code + seven-digit number. It's not necessary to use the area code to make a local call.

The area code for all the Hawaiian Islands: **808**

PLANNING YOUR TRIP

Before you go, contact the following organizations to obtain maps and information about sightseeing, accommodations, travel packages, recreational opportunities and seasonal events.

Hawaii Visitors and Convention Bureau
2270 Kalakaua Ave., Suite 801, Honolulu (Oahu), HI 96815
800-464-2924; www.gohawaii.com

Big Island Visitors Bureau/Hilo
250 Keawe St., Hilo, HI 96720
808-961-5797; www.gohawaii.com

Big Island Visitors Bureau/West Hawaii
250 Waikoloa Beach Dr., Waikoloa, HI 96738
808-886-1655; www.gohawaii.com

Kauai Visitors and Convention Bureau
4334 Rice St, Suite 101, Lihue, HI 96766
808-245-3971; www.kauaivisitorsbureau.com

Destination Lanai
730 Lanai Ave., Suite 102, Lanai City, HI 96763
800-947-4774; www.visitlanai.net

Maui Visitors Bureau
1727 Wili Pa Loop, Wailuku, HI 96793
808-244-1337; www.visitmaui.com

Molokai Visitors Association
P.O. Box 960, Kaunakakai, HI 96748
808-553-3876; www.molokai-hawaii.com

Oahu Visitors Bureau
733 Bishop St., Suite 1875 Honolulu, HI 96813
808-524-0722; www.gohawaii.com

In The News

Hawaii's main daily newspapers are the morning *Honolulu Advertiser* (www.honoluluadvertiser.com) and the afternoon *Honolulu Star-Bulletin* (www.starbulletin.com). Both papers feature extended entertainment sections, including a calendar of weekend events, in Friday's editions. The alternative *Honolulu Weekly* (www.honoluluweekly.com) offers a peek into local happenings.

Other islands also have daily newspapers, including the *Hawaii Tribune-Herald* (www.hawaiitribune-herald.com) and *West Hawaii Today* (www.westhawaiitoday.com) on the Big Island; *Maui News* (www.mauinews.com) on Maui; and *The Garden Island* (www.kauaiworld.com) on Kauai.

You can pick up a copy *101 Things To Do* (http://hawaii.101thingstodo.com), which is published for Oahu, Maui, Kauai and the Big Island, at resorts and shopping centers. *This Week* magazine (www.thisweek.com), featuring travel tips, activities and discount coupons for each of the major islands is available free throughout the islands.

TIPS FOR SPECIAL VISITORS

Disabled Travelers – Federal law requires that businesses (including hotels and restaurants) provide access for the disabled, devices for the hearing impaired, and designated parking spaces. For further information, contact the Society for Accessible Travel and Hospitality (SATH), 347 Fifth Ave., Suite 610, New York, NY 10016 *(212-447-7284; www.sath.org)*.

Web Sites

Here are some additional Web sites to help you plan your trip:

www.thisweek.com
  (island activities)
www.travelsmarthawaii.com
www.mauivisitor.com
www.alternative-hawaii.com
www.hawaii.com

All national parks have facilities for the disabled, and offer free or discounted passes; contact the National Park Service *(Office of Public Inquiries, P.O. Box 37127, Room 1013, Washington, DC 20013-7127; 202-208-4747; www.nps.gov)*.

Passengers who will need assistance with train or bus travel should give advance notice to Amtrak *(800-872-7245 or 800-523-6590/TDD; www.amtrak.com)* or Greyhound *(800-752-4841 or 800-345-3109/TDD; www.greyhound.com)*. Make reservations for hand-controlled rental cars in advance with the rental company.

Local Lowdown – Contact the following agencies for detailed information about access for the disabled in Hawaii:

- The **Disability and Communication Access Board** publishes *Hawaii Travelers Tips*, including accessibility information at the five major airports *(available free; 919 Ala Moana Blvd., Room 101, Honolulu, HI 96814; 808-586-8121; www.hawaii.gov/health/dcab)*.

- **Access Aloha Travel** specializes in providing travel services for disabled travelers in Hawaii *(414 Kuwili St., Honolulu, HI 96817; 808-545-1143 or 800-480-1143; www.accessalohatravel.com)*.

- On Oahu, **Handicabs** *(808-524-3866)*, **The Cab** *(808-422-2222; www.thecabhawaii.com)* and **The Bus** *(808-848-5555 or 808-852-6080/TTY; www.thebus.org)* provide public transportation services for the disabled. **Kapalua Executive Transportation** *(808-669-2300)* provides similar services on the Big Island. Private van rentals (drive yourself) are the only options on Maui. Kauai has no accessible public transportation.

- For beach wheelchairs and other equipment rentals on Oahu, contact **Hawaiian Islands Medical** *(808-597-8087; www.wheelchairshawaii.com)*. Contact **Gammie** *(808-877-4032 on Maui, 808-632-2333 on Kauai)* for equipment rentals on those islands. No wheelchair rentals are available on the Big Island.

Senior Citizens – Many hotels, attractions and restaurants offer discounts to visitors age 62 or older (proof of age may be required). The AARP (formerly the American Association of Retired Persons) offers discounts to its members *(601 E St. NW, Washington, DC 20049; 202-434-2277; www.aarp.com)*.

Must Know: Practical Information

Important Numbers	
Emergency (Police/Ambulance/Fire Department, 24hrs)	**911**
Police *(non-emergency, Mon–Fri 9am–6pm)*	
Honolulu Police	808-529-3111
Kauai Police	808-241-1653
Big Island	808-326-4646
	(Hilo) 808-961-2213
Maui and Lanai	808-244-6445
Poison Control	800-222-1222
Medical Referral:	
Queen's Medical Center Referral Program, Oahu	808-547-4606
	or 800-342-5901, ext. 4606
Hilo Medical Center, Big Island	808-974-4700
Maui Memorial Hospital, Maui	808-244-9056
Lihue Wilcox Memorial, Kauai	808-245-1010
Lanai Community Hospital, Lanai	808-565-6411
Dental Emergencies: Hawaii Dental Hotline	(Oahu) 808-522-5904
	(other islands) 800-522-5904
24-hour Pharmacies: Long's Drugs in downtown Honolulu	
1330 Pali Hwy.	808-536-7302
2220 S. King St.	808-949-4781
Coast Guard Search and Rescue	800-552-6458
To report an injured turtle, dolphin or whale	800-853-1964

WHEN TO GO

There is no bad time to travel to the Hawaiian Islands. The busiest time is from mid-December through March, when mainlanders rush to the islands to cure their winter blues. Generally, you'll find the best lodging discounts from late September until about mid-December.

Weather is consistently warm throughout the year, with nighttime temperatures ranging about 10 degrees lower than during the day. The average water temperature is 74°F (23.3°C), with a summer high of 80°F (26.7°C). That said, you'll find diverse environments on each of the islands, from misty tropical rain forests, cool mountaintops, arid deserts and sunny beaches—all within a few short miles of each other.

What to Pack

Casual is the rule here, but if you plan to dine in high-end restaurants, dressy resort wear is a good idea. Bring sunglasses and sunscreen (you can buy those in Hawaii, of course, but most items cost about 18% more on-island), and a rain jacket and a sweater. It's cooler in the high country, and sudden showers are common. No need to bring big sports gear, like surfboards; everything is available for rent in Hawaii.

The major difference between winter *(Nov–Apr)* and summer *(May–Oct)* is the surf. You'll find the biggest waves during the winter months, the most popular time for surfers to head to Hawaiian beaches. The **wettest months** are from November through March; most of the rain falls in the mountains and valleys on the windward (northeastern) side of the islands.

Seasonal Temperatures in Hawaii

	Jan	Apr	July	Oct
Avg. high	79°F / 26°C	82°F / 28.9°C	88°F / 31°C	87°F / 30.6°C
Avg. low	64°F / 17.8°C	66°F / 18.9°C	70°F / 21°C	69°F /20.6°C

GETTING THERE

By Air – Honolulu International Airport (HNL), on **Oahu,** located about 3 miles west of downtown Honolulu, is where the majority of visitors to the Hawaiian Islands land *(808-836-6411; www.honoluluairport.com)*. From here, you can hop on flights to the other major islands *(see Island Hopping, p 14)*.

Airport Waikiki Express provides 24-hour transportation from the airport to any hotel in Waikiki for $14 round-trip. TheBus *(see p 14)* runs from the airport to major stops in Waikiki Beach and downtown Honolulu. Taxis and rental-cars *(see p 14)* are available at Honolulu International and at all the airports listed below.

Big Island – Hilo International Airport (ITO) is located 2 miles east of Hilo on the Big Island's eastern shore *(808-934-5840; www.hawaii.gov/dot/airports/hawaii/ito)*. There is no public bus service from the airport, and hotel shuttles are limited. Twenty **cab companies** operate on the Big Island and fares are not cheap. From the airport, it will cost you about $10 to go into Hilo; $20 to Keaau, $65 to Volcano National Park, and up to $200 to get to Kailua town.

Kona International Airport (KOA) at Keahole is located about 7 miles north-west of Kailua-Kona *(808-329-3423; www.hawaii.gov/dot/airports/hawaii/koa)*. **SpeediShuttle** *(808-329-5433; www.speedishuttle.com)* offers service to Big Island resorts.

Maui – Kahului Airport (OGG) is located on the northern edge of the land bridge between Haleakala and the West Maui Mountain Range on Maui *(808-872-3893, www.hawaii.gov/dot/airports/maui/ogg)*. **SpeediShuttle** *(above)* and **Kapalua Executive Express** *(808-669-2300)* offer shuttle services from the airport to resorts. **Maui Airport Taxi** *(808-877-0907)* charges about $60 to get to Kaanapali, $8 to Kahului town, and $50 to Lahaina.

Kauai – Lihue Airport (LIH) is located about 1.5 miles east of Lihue, on the southeast coast of Kauai *(808-246-1448; www.hawaii.gov/dot/airports/kauai/lih)*.

Lanai – Tiny **Lanai Airport (LNY)** is located about 3 miles southwest of Lanai City *(808-836-6417; www.hawaii.gov/dot/airports/lanai/lny)*. Its single runway primarily serves scheduled interisland and commuter traffic. The two major resorts on the island *(see Must Stay)* provide shuttle service from the airport.

Lei Greetings

As you step off the plane, a Hawaiian islander may greet you with "aloha" then place a fresh lei around your neck. But this isn't the norm anymore, so arrange it for yourself or a friend, through **Airport Lei Greetings** *(888-349-7888; www.getleidinhawaii.com)* or **Lei Greetings.com** *(800-665-7959; www.leigreetings.com)*. They need 24-hour notice; leis cost $20–$30 each, including delivery. Many hotels and resorts throughout the islands also offer fresh leis to their visitors upon check-in.

Molokai – Molokai Airport (MKK) is located about 4 miles west of Kualapuu on Maunaloa Highway *(808-567-6361; www.hawaii.gov/dot/airports/molokai/mkk)*. The airport has two runways that accommodate commuter/air taxi and general interisland flights.

By Cruise Boat – Cruises have become a popular way to see the Hawaiian Islands. Most cruises begin and end in Honolulu, but longer itineraries are available featuring round-trip tours from Los Angeles or including the French Polynesian islands. Major cruise companies include **Princess** *(800-PRINCESS; www.princess.com)*; **Carnival** *(800-CARNIVAL; www.carnival.com)*; **Holland America** *(800-724-5425; www.hollandamerica.com)*; **Norwegian Cruise Line** *(800-327-7030; www.ncl.com)*; and **Royal Caribbean** *(866-562-7625; www.rccl.com)*.

GETTING AROUND

Island Hopping – **Aloha Airways** *(800-367-5250; www.alohaairways.com)* and **Hawaiian Airlines** *(800-367-5320; www.hawaiianairlines.com)* offer daily service from western US gateway cities (San Francisco, Los Angeles, San Diego, Sacramento, Las Vegas, Portland and Seattle) and convenient and frequent interisland flights. Daily ferry service between Hawaii's four major islands is scheduled to begin in 2006 *(check www.hawaiisuperferry.com for updates)*.

By Car – Of course, if you want to drive on the islands, you'll need to rent a car. Alamo *(800-651-1223; www.alamo.com)*, Avis *(800-321-3712; www.avis.com)*, Budget *(800-526-6408; www.budget.com)*, Dollar *(800-367-5171; www.dollar.com)*, Hertz *(800-654-3011; www.hertz.com)* and National *(800-227-7368; www.nationalcar.com)* all offer services on Oahu, Maui, the Big Island and Kauai. Dollar is the only national affiliate that operates on Lanai. You'll find Thrifty *(800-847-4389; www.thrifty.com)*, Avis and Dollar on Molokai.

Honolulu is a big city with busy streets and traffic jams; other drivers and pedestrians are your biggest driving hazards here. On some of the other islands, you'll find plenty of narrow, twisty dirt roads, one-lane bridges and blind curves, so stay alert. On Lanai and Molokai, it's best to rent a four-wheel-drive vehicle to maneuver the muddy, dirt roads that cover much of the island.

By Public Transportation – Oahu is the only island with a public transportation system—and it's a great one. **TheBus** *(808-838-5555, www.thebus.org)* operates a fleet of 525 buses, with 93 routes covering the entire island of Oahu, and the airport. These buses are fast, efficient, convenient, safe and clean. You'll find well-marked stops and terminals near all major attractions and hotels in downtown Honolulu and Waikiki Beach, and in cities, neighborhoods and towns across the island. Fares are $2 for adults (one-way), $1 for children (ages 6-17).

By Taxi – You'll find taxis lined up at the major airports; some are readily available at large hotels and resorts. Generally you must call a cab when you need one. Rates on the islands are set at $2.25–$2.50 for first $1/8$-mile, 30¢ for each additional $1/8$-mile, and 30¢ for each 40 seconds of waiting time.

Here's a list of Hawaii's major cab companies. There is no taxi service on Lanai.

Oahu – **TheCab** *(808-422-2222; www.thecabhawaii.com)* and **Charley's Taxi** *(808-947-0077; www.charleystaxi.com)*.

Maui – **Sunshine Cabs** *(808-879-2220)* and **Islandwide Taxi** *(808-874-8294)*.

Big Island – **Laura's Taxi** *(808-326-5466)*, **C&C Taxi** *(808-329-6388)* and **SpeediShuttle** *(808-329-5433; www.speedishuttle.com)*.

Kauai – **Sue's Northside Taxi** *(808-652-1741)*, **Kauai Taxi Company** *(808-246-9554; www.lauhala.com/kauaitaxi)*, and **Akiko's Taxi** *(808-822-7588)*.

Molokai – **Molokai Off-Road Tours and Taxi** *(808-553-3369; www.molokai.com/offroad)*.

FOREIGN VISITORS

Visitors from outside the US can obtain information from the Hawaii Visitors and Convention Bureau on Oahu *(2270 Kalakaua Ave., 8th floor, Honolulu; 808-924-0246; www.gohawaii.com)* or from the US embassy or consulate in their country of residence. For a complete list of American consulates and embassies abroad, visit the US State Department Bureau of Consular Affairs listing on the Internet at: *http://travel.state.gov/links.html.*

Entry Requirements – Travelers entering the United States under the Visa Waiver Program (VWP) must have a machine-readable passport. Any traveler without a machine-readable passport will be required to obtain a visa before entering the US. Citizens of VWP countries are permitted to enter the US for general business or tourist purposes for a maximum of 90 days without needing a visa. Requirements for the Visa Waiver Program can be found at the Department of State's Visa Services Web site *(http://travel.state.gov/vwp.html)*.

All citizens of non-participating countries must have a visitor's visa. Upon entry, nonresident foreign visitors must present a valid passport and round-trip transportation ticket. Canadian citizens are not required to present a passport or visa, but they must present a valid picture ID and proof of citizenship. Naturalized Canadian citizens should carry their citizenship papers.

US Customs – All articles brought into the US must be declared at the time of entry. Prohibited items: plant material; firearms and ammunition (if not for sporting purposes); meat or poultry products. For more information, contact the US Customs Service, 1300 Pennsylvania Ave. NW, Washington, DC 20229 *(202-354-1000; www.cbp.gov)* or the **Hawaii Department of Agriculture** *(808-973-9560; www.hawaiiag.org)*.

• Because rabies doesn't exist in Hawaii, all animals entering Hawaii must be held for four months at the quarantine facility on Oahu.

• Hawaiian officials won't let you enter with live plants, animals and any fresh fruits or vegetables.

• There are lots of restrictions on taking fruits, plants and animals out of Hawaii, too. All baggage bound from Hawaii to the US mainland is subject to pre-flight inspection by the US Department of Agriculture. You can bring only pre-packed and pre-inspected fruits home.

Money and Currency Exchange – Currency can be exchanged at most banks. Currency-exchange services are also available at Honolulu International Airport, but not at the other island airports. Some major stores on Oahu will accept Japanese yen.

For cash transfers, **Western Union** *(800-325-6000; www.westernunion.com)* has agents throughout the Hawaiian Islands. Banks, stores, restaurants and hotels accept travelers' checks with picture identification. To report a lost or stolen credit card: **American Express** *(800-528-4800)*; **Diners Club** *(800-234-6377)*; **MasterCard** *(800-307-7309)*; **Visa** *(800-336-8472)*.

Driving in the US – Visitors bearing valid driver's licenses issued by their country of residence are not required to obtain an International Driver's License. Drivers must carry vehicle registration and/or rental contract, and proof of automobile insurance at all times. Gasoline is sold by the gallon (1 gal=3.78 liters). Vehicles in the US are driven on the right-hand side of the road.

Electricity – Voltage in the US is 120 volts AC, 60 Hz. Foreign-made appliances may need AC adapters (available at specialty travel and electronics stores) and North American flat-blade plugs.

Taxes and Tipping – Prices displayed in Hawaii do not include the state sales tax of 4%, which is not reimbursable (1% sales-tax discount is given to citizens age 85 and older), or the hotel tax of 7.25%. It is customary to give a small gift of money—a tip—for services rendered, to waiters (15-20% of bill), porters ($1 per bag), hotel housekeeping staff ($1 per day) and cab drivers (15% of fare).

Measurement Equivalents

Degrees Fahrenheit	95°	86°	77°	68°	59°	50°	41°	32°	23°	14°
Degrees Celsius	35°	30°	25°	20°	15°	10°	5°	0°	-5°	-10°

1 inch = 2.5 centimeters   1 foot = 30.48 centimeters
1 mile = 1.6 kilometers   1 pound = 0.45 kilograms
1 quart = 0.9 liters   1 gallon = 3.78 liters

Time Zone – Since it sits so far out in the Pacific, east of the International Date Line, the state of Hawaii has its own time zone, **Hawaiian Standard Time (HST)**. Hawaiian Standard Time is two hours behind Pacific Standard Time (in California) on the mainland, and five hours behind Eastern Standard Time (in New York). Hawaii is 10 hours behind Greenwich Mean Time.

Unlike the US mainland, Hawaii does not observe daylight-saving time. From late April to late October, when the rest of the US is on daylight-saving time, add another hour to the time difference (i.e., Hawaii will be three hours behind California, and six hours behind New York).

Learning the Lingo

Aloha, and shaka!
You just noticed someone giving you a sign: pinkie and thumb of the right hand is up, while the other fingers curl under, shaken side to side. No, it's not a bad thing; it's shaka, a greeting that can mean "way-to-go," "nice-to-see-you" or "be cool." Here are some other useful Hawaiian words:

Aloha (ah-LOH-ha): Used for nearly everything good—hello, goodbye, love
Hale (ha-leh): House or building
Haole (how-leh): Foreigner, or Caucasian
Kane (KAH-nay): Man
Keiki (kay-kee): Children
Mahalo (muh-HA-low): Thank you
Makai (muh-kaee): Towards the sea
Mauka (mau-kuh): Toward the mountains
Nani (nah-nee): Beautiful
Ohana (oh-HA-nah): Family
Ono (oh-noh): Delicious
Pupu (poo-poo): Appetizer
Wahine (wah-HE-nay): Woman

ACCOMMODATIONS

For a list of suggested accommodations, see Must Stay.

Hotel Reservation Services

RSVP Hawaii – 800-663-1118; www.rsvphawaii.com.

Hawaiian Bed & Breakfast Association – 866-323-2248; www.stayhawaii.com.

Pleasant Hawaiian Holidays – 800-448-3333; www.2hawaii.com.

Hostels – A no-frills, inexpensive alternative to hotels, hostels are a great choice for budget travelers and students. Amenities vary from hostel to hostel, ranging from private oceanfront rooms and suites to dorm-style lodgings, on-site restaurants and guest kitchens, TV and Internet access, equipment rentals and tours. *For listings of hostels throughout Hawaii, check out the Web sites: www.hostelz.com or www.hostels.com.*

GETTING HITCHED IN HAWAII

Hawaii's swaying palms, fragrant blooms and ocean vistas make the perfect backdrop for a wedding. You've done the hard part—finding someone you can't wait to live "happily ever after" with—here's the rest of the story.

Get a Marriage License – To get a license, you must appear together, in person. In Oahu, go to Room 101 of the Health Building at 1250 Punchbowl Street. For other islands, check online at *www.hawaii.gov/doh.* You can download a marriage license application from this site. After that, you've got 30 days to use it. You can use it on whichever island you choose, but only in Hawaii. Next, you need a licensed marriage performer to tie the know *(for information, call 808-924-0255).* There are no residency requirements or length-of-stay provisions.

Choose a Venue – This is the fun part! There are several wedding and event planners on the islands; also, many hotels have wedding creators on staff to make things easy for starry-eyed couples *(for a sampling of these, visit www.gohawaii and click on weddings).* Of course, the barefoot-with-leis beach-front wedding has major appeal; other locales include the **Byodo-In Temple**, a beautiful Buddhist temple on Oahu; botanical gardens with open-air chapels, even the Big Island's **Parker Ranch★** *(see Big Island/Historic Sites),* where you can make a smashing arrival—or getaway—in a white carriage pulled by a Belgian horse. On Maui, favorite wedding venues include the summit of a volcano, a rain forest, or alongside a waterfall, where the mist creates a permanent rainbow.

Ask for Details – *For more information about wedding planning on the islands, visit www.gohawaii.com.* The free pamphlet, *Getting Married,* is available by sending a self-addressed, stamped envelope to: State Department of Health, Marriage License Office, P.O. Box 3378, Honolulu, HI 96801 *(808-586-4545; www.hawaii.gov/doh).* Many resort hotels offer honeymoon and wedding packages; ask about them when you make your reservations.

The Hawaiian Islands

Pearls of the Pacific: The Hawaiian Islands

Tossed like a lei into the blue Pacific, the Hawaiian Islands are farther from any other landmass than anyplace else on the planet. Their closest neighbors (though each is more than 2,000 miles away) are California and Tahiti; you might notice a bit of both as you travel this chain of 132 volcanic islands, many no more than rocky bird sanctuaries, that stretches 1,600 miles across the North Pacific Ocean. There's a dash of California's laid-back neo-hippie ambience here, and a touch of Tahiti's floral-scented exoticism, but there's also something uniquely Hawaiian about this place. The eight principal islands—Oahu, Hawaii, Kauai, Maui, Lanai, Molokai, Kahoolawe and Niihau—are clustered at the southeastern end of the archipelago, scattered over a little more than 500 miles.

The islands of Hawaii are actually the tops of a huge mountain range that rises from the floor of the Pacific Ocean. Created ever so slowly by raging fires and spewing magma within a rift on the ocean floor, the islands grew layer by layer until they soared above the waves. Mother Nature sculpted the impossibly green landscape into dramatic peaks and valleys, encircled with a necklace of beaches in hues of black, white, red, green and gold.

Revealed in ancient chants, dances and stories passed on through the centuries, Hawaii's history is rich with tales of kings, queens and powerful gods ruling an isolated island paradise. Native Polynesians, who spread across the ocean and became Hawaiians over time, were attuned to the powers, and bounty, of the earth and the sea. When they sailed from the Marquesas and Tahiti—the first arrivals stepped ashore sometime after AD 400—they brought pigs, yams, taro, bananas and breadfruit. They called their new world *'aina* (the land), as opposed to *kai* (the sea).

Getting Bigger All The Time

Surprisingly, this island chain is still growing. More than 80 volcanoes have bubbled from this Pacific hotspot over the last 44 million years. Since it began its present round of eruptions in 1983, Kilauea Volcano has added more than 500 new acres to the Big Island. Today, 20 miles off the coast of Hawaii, a new island is being born. Called **Loihi,** this infant islet is erupting in a red-hot flow beneath the sea.

When British captain James Cook, the first European to sight the islands, stepped ashore in 1778 with his crew, he renamed the archipelago the Sandwich Islands—after his sponsor, the Earl of Sandwich. After Cook was killed by Hawaiians in 1779 *(see p 46)*, no Western ships called in Hawaii for several years.

The island of Hawaii was the home of **King Kamehameha I** (c.1758–1819), who united the islands as he conquered other rival chiefs. Yet the monarchy lasted less than a century before pressure from Protestant missionaries, traders, whalers and sugar planters led to political change. Briefly a republic (1893–1898), Hawaii was annexed as a US territory in 1898 during the Spanish-American War.

In 1941 the Japanese bombing of Pearl Harbor propelled the US directly into World War II. When the war ended, tourism on Waikiki Beach exploded; later other islands, notably Maui and the Big Island, joined in the boom. With sugar and pineapple dominating its economy, Hawaii became the 50th US state in 1959.

Today each island seems to have its own vibe. For example, Oahu—home of Honolulu, the only large city in the state—has a cosmopolitan feel, while Kauai boasts a riot of blooms, with each garden more gorgeous than the last. Maui is a funky place where artists and surfers merge in happy harmony, and the Big Island exhibits a rugged, rocky landscape that has a bit of an edge, thanks to its hissing volcanoes and roaring surf. Most visitors can't resist taking in more than one island on a visit. The only hard part is choosing among them!

Fast Facts

- Seven of Hawaii's eight principal islands—with a total land area of 6,422 square miles—are inhabited.

- The largest and geologically youngest is the Island of Hawaii, more popularly known as "The Big Island."

- Kahoolawe is an uninhabited former bombing range; Niihau is a private island occupied by a couple of hundred native Hawaiians.

- Oahu, home of Pearl Harbor and the state capital of Honolulu, is by far the most heavily populated island, home to more than 876,156 of the state's 1.2 million people.

- The Hawaiian greeting *aloha* can mean hello, goodbye, love or welcome.

Hawaii, The Big Island★★

Visitor information: 808-961-5797 or www.bigisland.org.

The least explored among the Hawaiian Islands, the Big Island is not for everybody. It's an island of contrasts, from the raw, primal beauty of **Hawaii Volcanoes National Park**★★★ in the south to the glitzy resorts and manicured golf courses of the **Kohala Coast**★. Hawaii defies the notion of "palmy paradise" with a landscape that includes 11 out of 13 climate ecosystems, from subarctic mountain summits to eerie, lava-black deserts. To spend all your time here lazing on the beach would be missing the point. Not that the beaches aren't wonderful. In fact, you could visit a different Big Island beach every day for a month and still not see them all. Even beach sand offers variety on this island; you can hop from black sand to gold to white to green.

Fast Facts

The Big Island is just that . . . big!

- Hawaii, the island, measures 4,028 square miles—nearly twice as large as all the rest of the Hawaiian Islands combined, and three times the size of Rhode Island.

- Because volcanic eruptions regularly add more lava to the shoreline, the Big Island is actually getting bigger!

- For all its bulk, however, the Big Island is sparsely populated, with about 148,670 residents; there are more cattle than people here.

- The island of Hawaii boasts 266 miles of coastline, not to mention the world's most active volcano, **Kilauea**★★★.

Two volcanic mountains dominate the landscape. In the north, **Mauna Kea**★★ (13,796 feet), long dormant, is home to several astronomical observatories. In the south, **Mauna Loa**★ (13,677 feet) is considered active but is usually sleeping. Meanwhile, **Kilauea**★★★, the world's most active volcano, continues to spew lava from the lower slopes of Mauna Loa. On the north coast, the spectacular one-mile-wide **Waipio Valley**★★ *(accessible only by foot or four-wheel-drive vehicle)* wedges itself between 2,000-foot cliffs that funnel ribbon-like waterfalls onto a sandy ocean beach far below.

It's the adventurous traveler who discovers the Big Island's magic. Divers and snorkelers are drawn to the underwater world on the leeward side of Hawaii, where a watery landscape of caves, cliffs and tunnels reveals colorful tropical fish and other marine life. Kayakers explore the island's 266-mile coastline, where pristine coves and inlets await. This is a place where you can hike (or ride horseback) in a crater, hunt for petroglyphs, hook a blue marlin, or catch sight of a rare bird or a migrating whale. This is a place where you can ski and golf in the same day. And it's the only place on Earth where you can drive up to a volcano *(see Kilauea, p 30)*!

The Big Island has its historic side, too. The great monarch, **Kamehameha I** (1758–1819), was born on the Kohala Coast, and these shores were his base for conquest and unification. Temples and ruins tuck into the hillsides, sometimes where you'd least expect to find them.

Hilo★★

Move over, Seattle. Hilo, Hawaii, holds the record as America's wettest town, with 128 inches of wet stuff each year. Nobody seems to mind, there's so much to do here. Tsunamis (aka tidal waves) are another story—this town has been ravaged twice (in 1946 and 1960) by towering walls of water. Many of the abandoned downtown buildings remain today, brightly painted Victorians dripping with funky charm; some are listed on the National Register of Historic Places.

Hawaii Volcanoes National Park is just a half-hour's drive away, making Hilo a dandy spot to stay. Lovers of exotic flora are in heaven here; known for its orchids, the Hilo area is home to Liliuokalani Gardens, Hawaii Tropical Botanical Garden, Nani Mau Gardens and more *(see Gardens)*. The classic Hilo sight, though, is **Rainbow Falls★** *(see Parks and Natural Sites)*. Catch this 80-foot cascade in early morning or late afternoon, when the sun glints through the mango trees and creates prisms of color on the falls.

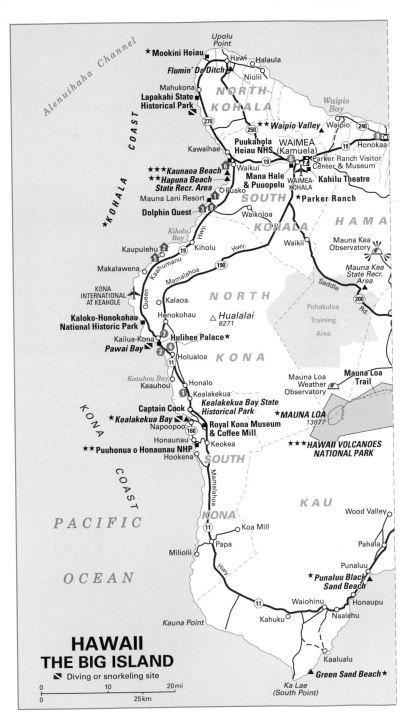

HAWAII
THE BIG ISLAND

◥ Diving or snorkeling site

| 0 | 10 | 20mi |
| 0 | 25km | |

Hotels

1. Fairmont Orchid
2. Four Seasons Hualalai
3. Hilton Waikoloa Village
4. Kilauea Lodge
5. Kona Village Resort
6. Mauna Kea Beach Hotel
7. Namakani Paio Cabins
8. Waikoloa Beach Mariott Resort

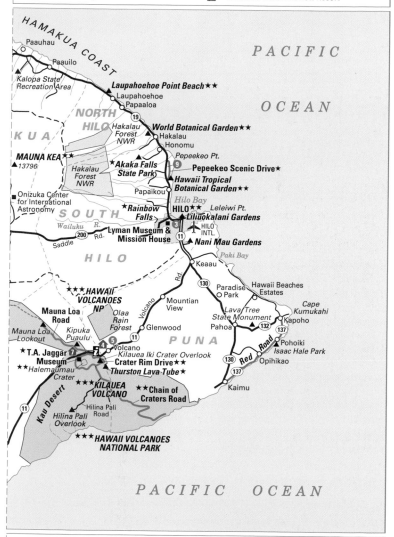

Restaurants

1. Aloha Angel Café
Donatoni's 3
2. Huggo's
3. Ken's House of Pancakes
Kilauea Lodge Restaurant 4
4. Kimo's Family Buffet
5. Lava Rock Café
6. Merriman's
7. Oodles of Noodles
8. Tex Drive In
9. What's Shakin'

Must-See Beaches

Kaunaoa Beach (Mauna Kea Beach)★★★

Hwy. 19, behind the Mauna Kea Beach Hotel, Kohala Coast.

Despite the fact that beach authority Stephen P. Leatherman *(see sidebar)*, named it "America's Best Beach" in 2000, Kaunaoa is still less crowded than nearby Hapuna Beach—go figure! All of Hawaii's beaches are public, so no worries about pulling out a beach blanket here. This quarter-mile crescent of white sand contrasts nicely with its lava headlands; beyond the beach rises a grassy slope and the manicured grounds of the Mauna Kea Beach Hotel. Thanks to the hotel, the beach is clean and well-maintained. Rough water makes it a better beach for boogie-boarding and bodysurfing than swimming. Stick around to watch the sunset; this sultry spot is a wonderful destination for watching the sun melt, sherbet-hued, into the aqua water.

> **Dr. Beach**
>
> Director of the Laboratory for Coastal Research at Florida International University, Stephen P. Leatherman, aka "Dr. Beach," is America's most-quoted authority on beaches. In 1991 the Ph.D. in Coastal Sciences premiered his list of America's Best Beaches, which has become an annual event ever since. Leatherman's annual beachy accolades have become to tourism officials what the Oscars are to the movie industry.

Hapuna Beach State Recreation Area★★

Hwy. 19, 12mi north of Waikoloa. 808-974-6200. Open year-round daily, sunrise to sunset.

Hapuna, like most of the Big Island's white-sand beaches, is found on the Kohala Coast. (Look for black- and green-sand beaches on the south coast.) The best beach on the west coast (the dry side) of the island, Hapuna's half-mile stretch of sparkling sand leads to cerulean water and the occasional lava-rock outcropping. Facilities include a picnic pavilion, a snack bar and a fairly icky set of restrooms. Bring your own beach toys; there are no vendors here.

Laupahoehoe Point Beach★★

Hwy. 19, Laupahoehoe, 25mi north of Hilo. Follow signs from Hwy. 19. Open year-round daily, sunrise to sunset.

As long as you don't expect a wide, sandy beach, you'll love this spot. A grassy area opens up to a wonderfully craggy stretch of lava-rock coastline, with pounding surf and dazzling ocean views. Camping is allowed here and the big picnic pavilion makes this a popular place with locals on Sunday afternoons. You'll get some wonderful photos on this beach and a pleasant dose of serenity, off the tourist track. *Purchase camping permits directly from the Department of Parks and Recreation (25 Aupuni St., Hilo) or online (www.ehawaiigov.org/HawaiiCounty/camping).*

Green Sand Beach★

3mi east of South Point (Ka Lae), Kau District. A 2.5mi drive by four-wheel-drive vehicle or an hour or so by foot. Check with your rental-car company to see if you're allowed to drive here; even with a four-wheel-drive, some companies forbid it.

You'll walk straight into the wind to get here, and once you do, the surf is fierce and dangerous, but how often do you get a chance to see a green-sand beach? The olive-green-colored "sand" is actually made up of a mineral called olivine. Olivine is created when basaltic lava cools. This semiprecious stone is also found in Iceland (the site of much geothermic activity) and on the moon. Nearby Ka Lae is the southernmost tip of the United States, and is also believed to be the first landfall of arriving Polynesians.

Touring Tip

The trailhead to Green Sand Beach is located at the base of Puuo Mahana cinder cone. Walk for 2.5 miles to the top of the cliff, and then climb down the cliff to the beach. The unmarked trail begins at the rocky overhang here. Going over the edge of the cinder cone is the easiest way down; even this is a difficult and treacherous walk. Allow about an hour to reach the beach.

Punaluu Black Sand Beach★

Hwy. 11, 5mi west of Pahala.

Lava from the Kilauea Volcano obliterated the world-famous Kalapana Black Sand beach in the 1990s, but there are others to explore in Puna and Kau (KAH-oo), near Hawaii Volcanoes National Park. Fringed with coconut palms, Punaluu offers the choicest setting for a swim in impossibly blue water. This picturesque stretch of shoreline is also a popular nesting spot for Hawaii's green sea turtles.

Color Me Sandy

Two cool things about Hawaii's beaches: they're all public—even the most exclusive resorts must provide access to the public—and they come in many colors. The classic white-sand beaches are composed of coral, pounded into a powder by powerful waves. Hawaii's black-sand beaches are, of course, made of lava rock—fairly coarse stuff that's hot to walk on and sticks like crazy to skin that's slathered with sticky sunblock. Still, you've gotta go, if only to see the pale bodies against dark sand; it looks like a photographic negative.

The reddish-hued stuff at Red Sand Beach at Hana, on Maui, comes from the caldera of a cinder cone and is made up of finely ground red cinders. Green Sand Beach *(see p 27)* on the Big Island is a hidden gem with a gem-like color—an olive green, which contrasts nicely with the azure sea and foamy white surf that abuts it!

Must-See Parks and Natural Sites

Hawaii Volcanoes National Park★★★

*Mamalahoa Hwy. (Hwy. 11), in Volcano, 28mi southwest of Hilo. 808-985-6000.
www.nps.gov/havo. Open year-round daily. $10 per vehicle; pass good for 7 days.*

This is the only National Park—not to mention one of the few places in the world—where casual travelers can visit a live volcano. At this 377-square-mile park, the major attraction is the erupting Kilauea Volcano, and its simmering-but-sleepy neighbor, Mauna Loa. The park encompasses the summit calderas of both of these, along with a rain forest, a desert, ancient petroglyphs, and the unique landscapes created by the force and drama of past eruptions.

> **Touring Tip**
>
> Most people drive through the park and feel they've done it all—indeed, you can see a lot by driving the park's Crater Rim Drive and pulling off at key spots along the way. But the best way to really visit the park is to spend a couple of days hiking the weird lava landscapes or paths that snake through deserts, rain forests, and beaches (the park has 150 miles of trails). You can even camp within the park *(tent camping is free; for details, call 808-967-7321 or visit www.nps.gove/havo).*

Unlike such deadly volcanoes as Mount St. Helens and Mount Pinatubo, Hawaii's shield volcanoes produce slow, quiet eruptions, not violent explosions. Rather than fleeing Kilauea's spectacular fireworks, people show up and bring a picnic! The show is really something at night, when red-hot sparks splatter against a backdrop of inky sky. Of course, lava flow has the potential to be dangerous, and park rangers continually change hiking-trail routes as the lava changes its course.

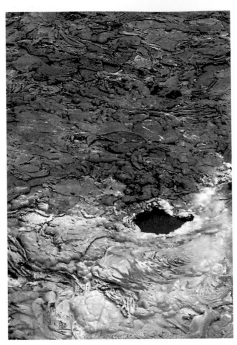

Park Highlights

Kilauea Visitor Center★★
– *On Crater Rim Dr., .25mi from the park entrance off Hwy. 11. Open year-round daily 7:45am–5pm. 808-985-6000.* Here you'll learn the secrets of volcanoes and how to view the craters safely. You can still stay at **Volcano House** *(808-967-7321; www.volcanohousehotel.com)*, a rambling wooden hotel first built in 1877, which sits on the brink of Kilauea Volcano, at 4,000 feet elevation.

Kilauea Volcano★★★ –
Although Kilauea has been erupting continually since January 3, 1983, it is generally unseen. Magma moves through 7 miles of lava tubes under the surface, and only where it breaks out above the island's southern shore is it visible. The 2,000°F molten rock oozes into the water, creating a boiling sea and sending steam high into the sky—a plume seen from the end of the 20-mile **Chain of Craters Road★★**, extending off Crater Rim Drive four miles southeast of Volcano House. Park rangers can advise you which path, if any, is cool enough to approach the lava. The road itself is often slick with red-hot lava—think of it as Mother Nature's blacktop!

Crater Rim Drive★★ – *See Scenic Drives.*
The 11-mile Crater Rim Drive circles the great pit of **Halemaumau Crater★★**, which erupted most recently in 1982 and likely will do so again, and offers the chance to see (and smell!) steam and sulfur fumes emanating from the ground. The drive crosses the moonlike Kau Desert, where the **Thomas A. Jaggar Museum★** *(see Museums)* displays geological exhibits and readings from inside the volcano.

The Road Not Taken

The **Kau Desert** within Hawaii Volcanoes National Park is so similar to the moon's surface, NASA astronauts have trained for lunar landings here. To get a peek at this eerie moonscape yourself, take the 9-mile Hilina Pali Road, off Chain of Craters Road at the 2.2-mile marker. Few tourists take this route, so you'll enjoy grand vistas of cliff, sea and sky in solitude when the road ends at the Hilina Pali Overlook.

Remember, this isn't Disneyland. Whether you see a real show or visit during the volcano's "downtime" is up to Mother Nature—or, rather, the goddess Pele *(see p 32)*! For updates on volcanic activity, visit the Hawaiian Volcano Observatory Web site (www.hvo.wr.usgs.gov), or call the park's hot line (808-985-6000).

Mauna Loa★

Mauna Loa Road starts 2mi west of the entrance to Hawaii Volcanoes National Park, off Hwy. 11. The road climbs 3,000ft to the Mauna Loa Lookout, 13.5mi from Hwy. 11. Mauna Loa Trail begins where Mauna Loa Rd. ends, 14mi north of Hwy. 11. Call 808-965-6000 for maps and details.

At a mere 13,677 feet, Mauna Loa comes up short compared to Mauna Kea, the highest peak in the Pacific. It is, however, the most massive mountain on earth, 100 times the size of Mount Rainier. Rising 18,000 feet from the floor of the Pacific Ocean, this perfectly shaped shield volcano is considered active, but last erupted in 1984. Given all that, and the fact that you've come this far, you really must see it! There are two ways to do this: by car or by foot.

Mauna Loa Road – The road climbs up 6,662 feet from Highway 11 to give you a good sense of the mountain. You'll drive through a curtain of rain forest to reach the **Mauna Loa Lookout**, taking a turn-off to see the lava trees. The phantom forest was created when lava flows engulfed trees and fossilized them. You'll also see Kipuka Puaulu, a forest grove that has escaped Mauna Loa's 37 eruptions unscathed. This is a quiet beauty of a spot, teeming with native plants, birds and insects, surrounded by fields of lava.

> **Touring Tip**
>
> Look for plumed Kalij pheasants, natives of Nepal that were brought to the island in 1962. Once you reach Mauna Loa Lookout, you'll appreciate the enormity of the mountain and, chances are, you'll feel very small! At the end of the road, the hiking trail begins.

Mauna Loa Trail — This is 7.5 miles of perhaps the toughest hiking in Hawaii. It ascends from the Mauna Loa Lookout to a cabin at Red Hill, then 12 miles up to the Mauna Loa summit cabin at 13,250 feet. It's a 7,000-foot-high, steep route up, through a moonscape of lava flow. This is a serious trip, for those in excellent condition—only experienced hikers need apply! Expect to spend four days doing the mountain, along with some advance planning (pre-registration is required). The climate is subarctic up here, with whiteouts and overnight temperatures below freezing year-round. Snow in July is not uncommon. Altitude sickness is another issue. Most hikers spend the night at the cabin at Red Hill to acclimatize themselves. Talk to the rangers at the park visitor center for more details. Hikers can also access Mauna Loa in less-daunting fashion, by starting at the Mauna Loa Weather Observatory, via Saddle Road.

Pele

The goddess of fire and volcanoes, Pele arrived in Hawaii by canoe, looking for a fiery dwelling place. As the legend goes, Pele moved south along the island chain, quickly fleeing the islands as her sister Namakaokahal, the goddess of the sea, attempted to destroy them. Ultimately, Pele found the perfect digs in the Halemaumau Crater of the Kilauea Volcano, where she resides to this day. Pele's love affairs and rivalries are the stuff of legend and literature here.

Locals say Pele appears to this day as a lovely woman dressed in red, or as a wizened crone who hitchhikes along the roadway. If you pass her by, you'll be cursed with car trouble. If you pick her up, she will vanish when you turn around to gaze at her.

Mauna Kea★★

*It's a one-hour drive from Hilo
or Waimea to the Onizuka
Center for International
Astronomy (808-961-2180;
www.ifa.hawaii.ed/info/vis;
open daily 9am–10pm). The
drive to the summit takes 30–
45 minutes. Take Saddle Rd.
(Hwy. 200) from Hwy. 190,*
*19mi to Mauna Kea State Recreation Area. Go 9mi to the Summit Rd. turnoff at mile
marker 28. A four-wheel-drive vehicle is necessary to get to Observatory Hill.*

You'll feel like you're at the top of the world here. Certainly, you're close—when
measured from its base on the ocean floor, Mauna Kea reaches an amazing 13,796
feet! Set out into the Pacific, with clear skies and no light pollution, Mauna Kea is
the best place on earth, they say, to stargaze *(see Musts for Outdoor Fun)*. No
wonder that 11 nations have set up infrared telescopes here, to peer into space.

Touring Tip

On Saturday and Sunday, free summit
tours depart from the visitor center
(1pm–5pm). Participants must be 17 and
older, in good health, and have a four-
wheel-drive vehicle. Stargazing is offered
at the visitor center nightly *(6pm–10pm)*
following an astronomy lecture. Dress
warmly. Families are welcome.

Prepare for a serious drive, in low
gear. The 6-mile road climbs from
9,000 feet to nearly 14,000 feet.
Once you arrive, you'll see the Keck
Telescope—the world's largest—and
360-degree **views**★★★ that defy
description. You'll also see Lake
Waiau, a glacial lake that's one of the
highest lakes in the world.

Polynesian Powder: Skiing on Mauna Kea

Want to ski and swim on the same day? You can do it on the Big Island, if you're a hard-
core skier! For four months of the year *(Dec–Mar)*, the heights of Mauna Kea are covered with snow. The volcano has no lifts, no ski shops, no grooming—but, then again,
there are no lines and no lift tickets to buy. If you're in good shape (altitude sickness
applies at the lofty summit), the thrill of skiing on a volcano is a once-in-a-lifetime
experience. *For details, contact Ski Guides Hawaii: 808-885-4188 or www.skihawaii.com.*

Akaka Falls State Park★

*Hwy. 220, 3.6mi southwest of Honomu. 808-974-6200.
Open year-round daily 24 hours.*

An easy-going, one-mile loop trail will get you to
some of Hawaii's prettiest **waterfalls**★. Hike through
a rain forest, along bamboo- and ginger-lined trails,
and past banks of wild impatiens and orchids to get
to the observation point of 442-foot Akaka Falls and
its little sister, 100-foot Kahuna Falls. Be sure to
watch for rainbows!

Kohala Coast★

On the northwest tip of the Big Island, along Hwy. 270.

Kamehameha the Great was born here on the Kohala Coast, which is as impressive as it gets in these parts! Add some of the oldest temples in Hawaii and a sprinkling of prehistoric petroglyphs, and you'll get a sense of why this region exudes such a special power.

Luxury resorts have been chiseled out of lava rock on the dry, sunny coast, and some boast amenities even more alluring than gorgeous swimming pools or lavish lobbies: ancient rock paintings. The **Kona Village Resort** *(Queen Kaahumanu Hwy.; see Must Stay)* boasts images that date back 900 years. These can be viewed from a boardwalk at the resort, which is set up in the style of an old fishing village with thatched huts. At **Mauna Lani Resort** *(68-1400 Mauna Lani Dr.; 808-885-6622; www.maunalani.com)*, interpretive signage guides visitors through restored fishponds and nearly 30 acres of archaeological preserve. From the resort's parking lot, you can take a 1.4-mile hike along the **Malama Trail** to view a series of more than 3,000 petroglyphs.

Hotel Highlights

While you're hotel-hopping along the Kohala Coast, take in a couple of other properties—simply because they *must* be seen. The **Mauna Kea Beach Hotel** *(see Must Stay)* has such an extensive collection of Asian and Pacific art, they offer tours to showcase it all *(62-100 Mauna Kea Beach Dr.; 808-882-7222; www.maunakeabeachhotel.com)*. Meanwhile, the **Hilton Waikoloa Village** *(425 Waikoloa Beach Dr.; see Must Stay)* is set on an immense 62 acres of oceanfront, laced with canals and dreamy lagoons. Guests here may be whisked to their rooms by boat!

Rainbow Falls★

Waianuenue Ave., Hilo (next to the hospital.) Open year-round daily 24 hours.

Nestled amidst a riot of colorful blooms, this waterfall tumbles 80 feet into a round natural pool surrounded by wild ginger. Behind the waterfall is a cave, said to be the home of Hina, the mother of the god Maui. Rainbow Falls gets its name from the play of early-morning sunshine on the waterspray, which creates thousands of tiny rainbows.

Must-See Scenic Drives

See map pp 24-25.

Crater Rim Drive★★

Off Hwy. 11, in Hawaii Volcanoes National Park (28mi southwest of Hilo). $10 /vehicle; pass good for 7 days. For individual sight descriptions, see Parks and Natural Sites.

Yes, it will take the better part of a day to see everything along this 11-mile road, but how often do you get to peer into craters, walk on glossy black lava, and see the steaming vents of active volcanoes? Even if you don't have a whole day, at least do a drive-by, to take in the amazing lunarlike landscape of lava-rock hillsides plunging to the sea.

Start at the Kilauea Visitor Center (on Crater Rim Dr., .25mi from the park entrance off Hwy. 11) and continue southwest on Crater Rim Drive.

You can see the steam vents from the car, but the small **Thomas A. Jaggar Museum**★ *(3mi west of Volcano House;*

> ### Touring Tip
>
> Plan on one to three hours to cover the entire Crater Rim Drive, depending on where and how long you stop. Start early in the day (**Kilauea Visitor Center**★★ opens at 7:45 am) if you plan to hike Devastation Trail, walk through the lava tube, and do the longer (but well worthwhile) 4-mile hike at **Kilauea Iki**. Add another 90 minutes to drive **Chain of Craters Road**★★ *(a 38mi round-trip; see p 37)*, longer if you plan to hike the end of Chain of Craters Road to see the recent lava flow. Be sure to wear hiking boots or other closed-toe shoes when walking around the lava.

see Museums) is worth a stop to get a sense of the science of volcanology. Next up: **Halemaumau Crater**★★, the site of the most eruption action over time (you can park and walk to the crater, except on days when the fumes are so toxic, it's closed). A ten-minute walk gets you to this mammoth hole-in-the-ground, punctuated by smoking fissures. The crater is cordoned off, and is designated as a sacred site.

Back on Crater Rim Road, you'll see blacker lava from a September 1982 eruption that looks like a torn-up road, with chunks of rock an inch thick. As you drive along, note the signs marking when lava flows occurred. You'll want to pop out of the car to stroll the **Devastation Trail**, a half-mile path through a forest that was devastated by the eruption of Kilauea Iki in 1959. This boardwalk trail looks fresher and greener than its name implies; back in 1959, lava, ash and hot gases roared into the sky from this tranquil spot, gushing some 1,900 feet into the air and turning the forest to cinders. Now, vegetation has sprouted up and softened the bleak landscape here.

> **Touring Tip**
>
> At Devastation Trail, you can connect with **Chain of Craters Road**★★ *(see opposite)* and follow it down to the current lava flows, or continue the loop of Crater Rim Drive.

If you continue along Crater Rim Drive, don't miss a stop at **Thurston Lava Tube**★ *(2mi east of Volcano House; see Musts for Kids)*. Across the street is the **Kilauea Iki Crater Overlook**, where you can peer into an enormous "frozen" lava lake, still steaming from the 1959 eruption. Want to get closer? There's a terrific hike that descends 400 feet through native rain forest into the crater, where you can wander across the lava lake. The park says it's a two-hour loop, but it can take a bit longer, so allow yourself plenty of daylight to do this. Even if you don't go all the way down to the lake, it's worth hiking the beginning of this trail; it's a pretty rain-forest romp, with lovely views—a cool respite on a hot day.

Chain of Craters Road★★

Connects with Crater Rim Drive at Devastation Trail, Hawaii Volcanoes National Park. Allow at least 3 hours round-trip. For current lava conditions, call 808-985-6000 or check at the Kilauea Visitor Center.

This 38-mile road is one of the most spectacular drives in the world. The two-lane blacktop curves through a vast landscape of lava fields, descending 3,700 feet to the coast and ending where lava crossed the road in 2003. At times, the hillsides are rust-colored, where orangey lava and spiky vegetation slope toward the sea. In other places, fields of ropy pahoehoe lava are glossy and black, like chocolate syrup poured over a hot-fudge sundae.

Take a Hike – Park the car along the road, grab a bottle of water, put on a hat and sturdy shoes (lava can be cracked, uneven and slippery) and follow the path.

Here, lava flows from several hundred years ago meet recent flows, and petrogyphs (images etched in lava) are numerous; look for the buried highway sign. Lava flow is always changing, so you never know what you'll see. You might see flumes on the hillside, or steam clouds over the ocean, or, after dark, flowing lava and an eerie red glow in the distance.

Hiking Hawaii

Be flexible and be prepared. Those instructions are key when you're hiking in Hawaii. Weather and conditions can change abruptly—one minute, it's fine to swim in the pools along the waterfall; the next minute, rangers are advising people not to do it! Count on a sudden cloudburst, and bring a rain shell and a waterproof pack for your camera, even if it's totally sunny when you leave. Fog is common, especially in the rain forest. Pack snacks, and bring more water than you think you'll need. Stay on the trail, even if it's muddy; loose soil off-trail can send you sliding down a ravine. The forest service is good about closing trails if conditions are dangerous, so be flexible with your itinerary. There's always another lovely trail to explore!

Pepeekeo Scenic Drive★

Off Hwy. 19, 4mi north of Hilo.

This little jog is worth a trip if you're heading from Hilo to Volcano Village or vice-versa. The 4-mile detour features wonderful views of lava-rock coastline, waterfalls and fragrant jungle.

Stop for a fruit smoothie at **What's Shakin'** *(27-999 Old Mamalahoa Hwy.; 808-964-3080)*, then follow the narrow road that winds alongside rain forest and ocean. Twisty vines fall like fringe from the road-sides, bridges are barely one lane—and traffic is two-way, so beware! Dense vegetation even-tually falls away to a backdrop of sapphire blue. Stops along the way include **Hawaii Tropical**
Botanical Garden★★ *(27-717 Old Mamalahoa Hwy.; see Gardens)*, and, just beyond, the spectacular **Onomea Overlook**, where you can pull over to park and peek through a tangle of foliage for gorgeous views of too-blue-to-be-true Onomea Bay. A short walk from the overlook leads to the **Onomea Foot Trail**, where you can walk along the shoreline and stretch your legs (they won't let you sneak into the botanical gardens, though).

Mauna Loa Road

Off Hwy. 11, 4mi west of Volcano Village.

At nearly 14,000 feet, Mauna Loa is the most massive mountain on Earth—not the highest, but the biggest. Its summit caldera is three-miles long; Mauna Loa last erupted in 1984.

While the trip to the top is a rigorous, four-day hike, the drive up (to 6,662 feet) provides a sense of the grandeur of this volcano. Stands of stately koa trees line the roadway, where, if you're lucky, you might catch a glimpse of the Kalij pheasant. One of the highlights is **Kipuka Puaulu**, or Bird Park, where an eruption 400 years ago resulted in pockets of untouched forest set within a sea of lava. A 1.2-mile loop meanders through this enchanted environ-ment, where the air is full of birdsong.

> **Touring Tip**
>
> Bring a picnic; there are tables at the base of the trail to Mauna Loa's summit.

Red Road

Hwy. 137, 27mi south of Hilo.

You'll feel like a local when you take a jaunt down this 14.6-mile-long old coastal road, originally paved with red lava. The stretch from Kalapana to Paradise Park features natural pools fed by volcanic springs, basalt cliffs, co-conut groves and black-sand beaches. A string of beach parks line the shore; a local favorite is **Isaac Hale Park** at Pohoiki, where everyone goes on Sunday afternoons to fish, swim and picnic. Nearby, check out **Lava Tree State Monument**, off Highway 132, with its lava-wrapped koa trees *(808-974-6200; www.hawaii.gov; open year-round daily dawn–dusk).*

Say What?

One of the coolest things about driving around Hawaii is trying to pronounce the words on the highway signs. You're on your own with that (and good luck to you!), but here's what some of the place names mean on the Big Island:

Hilo – To twist or braid; also, the name of a famous Polynesian navigator

Kaupulehu – Roasting oven of the gods.

Kawaihea – Water of wrath

Kealakekua – Pathway of the gods; also, the area in South Kona where Captain James Cook was killed

Kona – Whispering sea

Laupahoehoe – Smooth, flat lava

Pahoa – Daggers

Mauna Kea – White mountain (snow-covered)

Mauna Loa – Long mountain

Waikoloa – Strong wind

Waimea – Red water

Must-See Gardens

Hawaii Tropical Botanical Garden★★

Off Hwy. 19 on Pepeekeo Scenic Drive, Onomea Bay (8mi north of Hilo). 808-964-5233. www.htbg.com. Open year-round daily 9am–4pm. Closed Jan 1, Thanksgiving Day & Dec 25. $15.

Getting here is half the fun. The 4-mile **Pepeekeo Scenic Drive**★ *(see Scenic Drives)* is a rain-forest-lined twist of roadway, skirting cliffs that tumble to the sea. You'll cross one-lane wooden bridges and get tantalizing glimpses of aqua waters as you follow the serpentine drive that leads, 1.5 miles in, to this tropical paradise set on Onomea Bay. *Onomea* means "good feeling," and you'll certainly pick up that vibe here. Set in a valley that slopes to the sea, this tamed jungle displays a variety of orchids, palms (some as tall as 100 feet), heliconias, gingers, bromeliads and other plants—more than 2,000 species at present, some rare and exotic. A three-tiered waterfall and natural streams add to the serenity of the setting.

Wander through a torch-ginger forest, where some gingers stand sentry-like on 12-foot stalks, and meander through a banana grove. The golden bamboo grove positively thrums when breezes whistle through it. In addition to serving as a sanctuary for plants (including some endangered species), this garden serves as a living seed bank and study center for tropical trees and plants.

> **Touring Tip**
>
> Mosquitoes thrive at Hawaii Tropical Botanical Garden, too. Happily, the garden staff provides bug repellent for visitors. Allow about two hours for a leisurely visit.

World Botanical Garden★★

Off Hwy. 19 near mile marker 16 in Umauma, Honomu. 808-963-5427. www.wbgi.com. Open year-round Mon–Sat 9am–5:30pm. Closed Sun & major holidays. $8.50.

Hawaii's largest botanical garden features some 5,000 species and other pleasant diversions, such as a children's hedge maze. Tykes who successfully navigate the hedge-lined pathway are rewarded with a go at the grassy playing field. Among the other nice touches here: free samples of juices from garden fruits in season, and a rain-forest nature walk that's wheelchair-accessible.

The treat at the end of the bloom-edged trail is views of 300-foot Umauma Falls. Check out the Hawaii wellness garden, displaying medicinal endemic plants, and a garden planted with trees and plants arranged according to when they first appeared on earth. They're currently pumping up the educational aspects here, and hope to ultimately showcase 30,000 species of plants.

> **Touring Tip**
>
> Look for two-for-one admission coupons for many gardens and other island attractions in local tourist brochures like *101 Things to Do on the Big Island*, which is widely available in island visitor centers, hotels and many shops.

Liliuokalani Gardens

Banyan Dr., Hilo. 808-826-1053. www.123hawaii.net. Grounds open daily 24 hours.

Named after Hawaii's last queen, Liliuokalani, this 30-acre park is the largest formal Japanese garden east of the Orient. Features are exactly as you'd expect them: koi ponds, pagodas, and a moon bridge that makes an excellent photo opportunity. Cross the bridge to Coconut Island for views of Hilo Bay with a backdrop of mountains. The garden is located on Banyan Drive on the Waiakea Peninsula, where the towering trees have their own stories: many were planted in the 1930s by famous folk such as Babe Ruth and Amelia Earhart.

Nani Mau Gardens

421 Makalika St., Hilo. 808-959-3500. www.nanimau.com. Open year-round daily 8:30am–5pm. $10.

Nani Mau means "forever beautiful" in Hawaiian, and it's an apt moniker here. This 20-acre property—once a papaya plantation—is filled to bursting with eye-popping blooms. Wide walkways are accessible to wheelchairs; take a self-guided tour or a 20-minute narrated **tram ride** *($8)*. Every flowering plant in Hawaii is represented here, they say. Highlights include the perfectly manicured Japanese gardens and the dazzling collection in the orchid house. Other features include an art gallery, an all-you-can-eat restaurant, and, oddly enough, a hair salon.

Must-See Historic Sites

Puuhonua o Honaunau National Historical Park★★

Hwy. 160, Honaunau, 22mi south of Kailua-Kona. 808-328-2288. www.nps.gov/puho. Open year-round Mon–Thu 6am–8pm, Fri–Sun 6am–11pm. Visitor center open year-round daily 8am–4:30pm. Closed state holidays. $5 (pass good for 7 days).

During the 16C, defeated warriors and *kapu* (religious taboo) violators found refuge at this lava-black place by the sea. Places of refuge *(pu'uhonua)* were found on every island in ancient times. A lawbreaker who reached one of these sacred sites was purified by a priest; at that point, he could not be harmed by his pursuers, even after he left. Puuhonua o Honaunau is especially important because it holds the bones of 23 high chiefs.

Great Wall – An impressive, 1,000-foot-long rock wall marks the location of Puuhonua o Honaunau. Look for its reflection in the fishpond—this is also a wonderful place to frame a photo of a sherbet-hued Hawaiian sunset.

Self-guided Tour – Take a 30-minute walk around the 180-acre property and see the thatched huts, burial sites, temple, ancient idols and ruins, and canoes made in the old way—lashed together with coconut fiber. Along the way, you may see local canoe builders, wood carvers and other traditional craftspeople at work.

Touring Tip

A great time to visit the historical park is the first weekend in July, when a cultural festival called **Establishment Day** is celebrated here, featuring crafts, music, hula and community net fishing. This is one of the best places on the island to get a sense of traditional Hawaiian ways.

Whenever you visit, bring picnic supplies and camp out at one of the on-site picnic tables set near the beach under the shade of coconut palms. After lunch, you can walk the mile-long hiking trail that leads along the coast past several archaeological sites where temples and homes once stood.

Hulihee Palace★

75-5719 Alii Dr., Kailua-Kona. 808-329-1877. www.daughtersofhawaii.org/hulihee. Visit by guided tour only, year-round daily 9am–4pm (last tour at 3pm). Closed major holidays. $5.

Once the most elegant residence on the Big Island, Hulihee Palace was built in 1838 by the island's governor, John Adams Kuakini. Made of lava rock and coral mortar, the house served as the summer home of Hawaii's *ali'i* (royal family). You'll see beautiful koa furniture and 19C artifacts on the guided tour. Try to plan your visit during one of their frequent concerts of Hawaiian music and hula, typically held at the palace the last Sunday of the month *(call for schedule)*.

Mookini Heiau★

Hwy. 270, N. Kohala. 808-591-1170. www.kohala.net/historic/mookini.

Accessible by four-wheel-drive vehicle only, this three-story stone temple is dedicated to Ku, the Hawaiian god of war. A *heiau* is a living spiritual temple, or sacred site, and this one—built in AD 480—numbers among Hawaii's oldest and most sacred. Approximately the size of a football field, this temple was built out of lava stones, without mortar, and is said to have been created in a single night!

Parker Ranch★

Kawaihae Rd. (Hwy. 19) & Mamalahoa Hwy. (Hwy. 190), Waimea-Kamuela. 808-885-7655. www.parkerranch.com. House open year-round Mon–Sat 10am–5pm. Closed Sun. Museum open year-round Mon–Sat 9am–5pm. Closed Sun, Jan 1, Thanksgiving Day & Dec 25. $6.50.

Experience the life of a Hawaiian *paniolo* (cowboy) at Parker Ranch. With about 350 square miles and more than 55,000 head of cattle, these pasturelands make up one of the largest ranches in the US. Exhibits and a short film at the **Parker Ranch Visitor Center and John Palmer Parker Museum** *(Rte. 19, Waimea)* tell the history of the ranch, which began as a land grant from Kamehameha I to John Parker, a sailor from Massachusetts who married a Hawaiian princess and stayed to build his own cattle kingdom on Hawaii.

Wagon Rides

If time permits, treat the kids—and yourself—to a 45-minute excursion in a horse-drawn wagon. Rides leave from the Parker Ranch Visitor Center on the hour *(Tue–Sat 10am–2pm; $15 adults, $12 children ages 12 and under)*, and feature narrated tales about life on the range.

Mana Hale – *On Hwy. 190, just outside Waimea-Kamuela. 808-885-5433. Visit by guided tour only Mon–Sat 10am–5pm. Closed Sun. $8.50 (includes tour of Puuopelu).* The Parker family's original 1840s ranch house, whose name means "house of the spirit" in Hawaiian, once formed the centerpiece of the Parker lands. Today you can tour its handsome koa-wood interior, which includes handmade furnishings and Hawaiian quilts.

Puuopelu – *On Hwy. 190, just outside Waimea/Kamuela. 808-885-5433. Visit by guided tour only Mon–Sat 10am–5pm. Closed Sun. $8.50 (includes tour of Mana Hale).* Named for the pretty knoll on which it sits, Puuopelu ("meeting place" in Hawaiian) now showcases former owner Richard Smart's fine collection of French Impressionist paintings and Chinese art.

Kaloko-Honokohau National Historic Park

Hwy. 19 (Queen Kaahumanu Hwy.), 3mi south of Kona International Airport, Keahole. 808-329-6881. www.nps.gov/kaho. Open year-round daily 8am–3:30pm. Closed state holidays.

Set at the base of the Hualalai Volcano on the Kona Coast, this 1,160-acre site marks an ancient Hawaiian settlement, stretching from mountain to sea. Wander past fishponds, *kahua* (house site platforms), *ki'I pohaku* (petroglyphs), *holua* (stone slides), and *heiau* (religious sites). On the recreational side, there are hiking trails and good birding, along with fishing and boating (bring your own boat).

Lapakahi State Historical Park

Akoni Pule Hwy., N. Kohala. 808-882-6207. www.hawaiimuseums.org. Open year-round daily 8am–4pm. Closed state holidays.

In its heyday from the 14C through the 19C, this site was a fishing village. Self-guided walking paths feature interpretive signs, providing a sense of what it was like to fish the traditional way, with salt-making pans, nets, and fishing gear from days gone by. You'll also stroll past thatched huts and fishing shrines, and visit an overlook where fishermen played a game similar to checkers while they waited for schools of fish to show up.

> **Touring Tip**
>
> They allow snorkeling just off the coral beach at Lapakahi State Historical Park. Throw some clothes on over your swimsuit if you decide to come back and visit the site, though; they frown on visitors wearing bathing attire at the park facilities.

Lyman Museum & Mission House

276 Haili St., Hilo. 808-935-5021. www.lymanmuseum.org. Open year-round Mon–Sat 9:30am-4:30pm. Closed Sun & major holidays. $7/person, $15/family.

Mark Twain slept here. That's one of the claims to fame of the Lyman House, built in the 1830s by missionaries David and Sarah Lyman. Located in Hilo, the mission house is the oldest wooden structure on the Big Island, and one of the oldest in the state. The house served as a boarding school for young Hawaiian men, the Lyman family home, and as guest quarters for several notables, including Twain and many members of the Hawaiian *ali'i* (royal family). Exhibits feature furniture, tools and household items used by the Lymans and other missionary families, plus collections of seashells, minerals, ancient Chinese art, Hawaiian art and temporary exhibits.

Puukohola Heiau National Historic Site

2mi north of the intersection of Hwys. 19 & 270, Kawaihae. 808-882-7218. www.nps.gov/puhe. Open year-round daily 7:30am–4pm. Closed state holidays. $2.

Ancient archaeological sites mark the windswept coastline of north Kohala. Puukohola Heiau was built as a temple around 1550 and reconstructed in 1791 by Kamehameha I, who treacherously murdered his last Big Island rival here to dedicate the temple and make himself supreme chief. As British sailor John Young looked on, the king built the temple himself, along with his chiefs and commoners—men, women and children. A rival was sacrificed, so the war god Ku would be pleased.

- **Interpretive programs for children** are a highlight here; kids can take a hike, play ancient Hawaiian games, and become a Junior Ranger.

Aloha Festivals

This 50-year-old traditional celebration is Hawaii's largest, featuring more than 300 events on six islands. Aloha Festivals *(800-852-7690; www.alohafestivals.com)* showcase Hawaii's traditions and history with a host of special ceremonies, parades, carnivals, contests and arts and crafts, as well as music and dance. More than a million people attend the two-month-long festival, which begins in September.

Captain Cook

On Mamalahoa Hwy. (Hwy. 11), 14mi south of Kailua-Kona.

No name is more synonymous with exploration in the Pacific Ocean than that of Captain James Cook. He made three voyages between 1767 and 1779, and is credited with discovering nearly all there was to be found in the vast Pacific. Naturally, there's a town named after Captain Cook, located on the west coast of the island.

While you're in Captain Cook village, stop by **Royal Kona Museum & Coffee Mill** *(83-5427 Mamalahoa Hwy.; see Museums)* for a free sample of Kona coffee. From there, the road slopes downhill to **Kealakekua Bay★**, the site of Cook's death in 1779; a white obelisk marks the spot where the navigator is believed to have fallen.

The road ends near Hikiau Heiau. A *heiau* is a stone platform used by ancient Hawaiians for religious purposes, a sort of open-air temple. Cook conducted a Christian burial service at the spot. The bay is now a marine reserve, popular for snorkeling.

Captain Cook, The Man

Born in Yorkshire, England, in 1728, Cook escaped a humdrum life by joining the British navy. He gained acclaim as a navigator and cartographer, and at age 40, was commissioned to lead an expedition to Tahiti to observe the transit of Venus across the sun. During this voyage, which extended from 1767 to 1771, Cook discovered several islands and mapped the coasts of Australia and New Zealand.

On his second voyage (1772–75), Cook circumnavigated the earth while searching vainly for the fabled "great southern continent," a theory popular in Europe at the time. Along the way, he discovered Tonga, New Caledonia and Easter Island.

Cook failed in his third voyage (1776–79) to find a northern passage from the Pacific to the Atlantic, though he traced the west coast of North America from Oregon to the Arctic Ocean. When he discovered Hawaii, the natives welcomed him warmly, perhaps mistaking him for the peripatetic god Lono. But Cook and several of his men were later killed by Hawaiians in a skirmish over a stolen boat at Kealakekua Bay.

Must-See Museums

Thomas A. Jaggar Museum★

At Hawaii Volcanoes National Park, on Hwy. 11 (28mi southwest of Hilo). 808-985-6000. Open year-round daily 8:30am–5pm. $10 (park entrance fee). See Parks and Natural Sites.

Amateur volcanologists can't resist this place, named for the professor who founded the Hawaiian Volcano Observatory next door *(closed to the public)*. Get awesome views of the **Halemaumau Crater★★**, a half-mile across and 1,000 feet deep; look west to see **Mauna Loa★** in the distance. The museum is filled with seismometers and other gee-whiz stuff, so you can "see" every tiny earthquake on the island—there are several hundred tremors a day here! Videotapes show footage of days when the volcanoes spew fountains of fire and ash into the sky, and spill red-hot rivers of lava down their slopes.

Royal Kona Museum & Coffee Mill

83-5427 Mamalahoa Hwy. 808-328-2511. www.royalkonacoffee.com. Open year-round daily 9am–5pm.

Forget Seattle! Kona is America's premier coffee town, where some of the best coffee in the world is grown. Located at a coffee mill surrounded by a coffee plantation, this museum— more of a factory tour, really—shows how your morning cuppa joe goes from beans to brew. Exhibits and videos reveal the evolution of old-time coffee production to modern techniques. Of course, there are samples and a gift shop, so you can go home with an ample supply of Kona coffee.

Make Mine a Cuppa Kona

What is it about Kona coffee? Grown only on a narrow, 20-mile-long strip of land on the mountain slopes above Kailua-Kona on the Big Island, Kona coffee is beloved by coffee connoisseurs all over the world. The first trees, a variety of Arabica from Ethiopa, were planted here about 175 years ago. The combination of rich, volcanic soil and the region's distinctive weather worked like magic; now Kona is the only place in the US—besides Puerto Rico—where coffee beans are grown commercially.

• About 4,000 beans are required to produce a pound of coffee.

• Each tree yields only enough coffee cherries (one bright-red coffee cherry contains two beans) to produce only about one pound of roasted beans each year.

If you want to know more, take the self-guided **Coffee Country Driving Tour**, which is promoted by the Big Island Visitors Bureau *(250 Waikola Beach Dr., Waikola; 808-886-1652; www.bigisland.com)*, and leads you through coffee country, plantation by plantation.

Musts For Outdoor Fun

Stargaze on Mauna Kea★★

Getting to the 13,796-foot summit of Mauna Kea isn't easy. You can drive, but you'll need a four-wheel-drive vehicle to navigate narrow, winding Saddle Road (Hwy. 200), which is steep, unpaved and dangerous once you pass the visitor information station at Onizuka Center for International Astronomy *(located part-way up the mountain, at 9,300ft elevation)*.

Happily, the folks at **Hawaii Forest & Trail** offer guided trips to the world's tallest volcano at sunset *(74-50358 Queen Kaahumanu Hwy., Kailua-Kona; 808-331-8505 or 800-464-1993; www.hawaii-forest.com; $155)*. As darkness falls, you'll stand in the midst of the largest collection of telescopes anywhere, at Mauna Kea Observatory. The stargazing here is unparalleled; the air above the mountain is exceptionally dry, cloud-free and unpolluted, creating a high number of clear nights.

At a lower elevation, a naturalist/guide will share some of the specifics of Hawaii's natural wonders and ultra-clear night skies. The 7- to 8-hour trip (including pick-up from Waikoloa hotels) includes a picnic at a historic ranch. This guided hike is for adults only; no one under 16, please. It's not a difficult hike, but pregnant women and those prone to altitude sickness should skip it.

Nails for Breakfast: The Ironman Triathlon

Think you're buff and tough enough to compete with the best all-around male and female athletes in the world? Each October, laid-back Hawaii—or more precisely, Kailua-Kona on the Big Island—is home to the toughest multisport event around, the Ironman Triathlon World Championship. About 1,500 elite athletes, from all 50 states and some 50 countries, compete in a 26-mile marathon, a 2.5-mile ocean swim, and a 112-mile bike ride. The top finisher in the most recent Kona Ironman had a time of 8:33:29. Spectators line up along the seawall on Alii Drive to see the 7am start; the course closes at midnight. *For information, call 808-329-0063 or check online at www.ironmanlive.com.*

Swim with Rays★

Rays can be found, most days, from as far north as Keahole Point down to Keauhou Bay. Most dive companies offer trips to dive and snorkel with the rays. For more information, call one of these Kona-based companies: Jack's Diving Locker (808-329-7585 or 800-345-4807; www.jacksdivinglocker.com) or Hawaii Scuba Divers and Whale Watching Tours (808-324-4668; konahonudivers.com).

The Big Island's Kona Coast is the perfect place to swim with the Darth Vader of the undersea world, the manta ray. Related to sharks, these awesome creatures have no teeth and no tail stingers. They rely on their speed and aerodynamic design to outwit predators. The first thing you'll notice is, they're huge! The shy, harmless fish have triangular wings with spans that reach up to 20 feet across. Local divers have given these gentle giants names like Lefty and Nita Ray, distinguishing them by the spot patterns on their undersides.

The best way to find rays is to join a diving trip (participants must be certified divers); dive-boat captains know where these intriguing fish are known to gather. They also arrange night dives to see the manta rays, one of the coolest things imaginable. Divers must keep their distance, though, so these flying fish have plenty of room to maneuver. Manta rays are underwater acrobats, gliding, pivoting and somersaulting as they funnel plankton into their huge mouths.

Rundown on Rays

- Manta rays *(Manta hamiltoni)* are the largest type of rays; they can weigh up to 3,000 pounds.

- In Hawaiian, rays are called *hahalua*; the name manta is Spanish for "cloak."

- Rays eat small fish, tiny shellfish and microscopic plankton. Since they feed on the bottom of the sea, a ray's mouth is located on the underside of its body.

- Females give birth to one to two babies at a time; each infant ray can weigh up to 25 pounds when it's born.

- Manta rays have been reported to jump 15 feet out of the water.

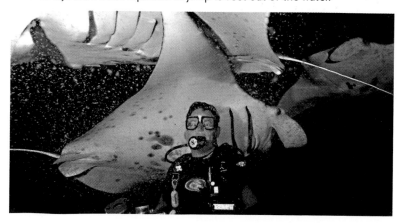

Flumin' Da Ditch

3-hour trip begins and ends at Hawi, where a van will take you to the Ditch at an entry point of 1,000ft elevation. Flumin' Da Ditch Outfitters are also based in North Kohala. 808-889-6922 or 877-449-6922. www.flumindaditch.com. Morning and afternoon cruises available. $98.96. Ages 5 and up only.

Kayaking an irrigation ditch? It's no joke. "Flumin" grew out of the days when North Kohala was home to sugar plantations, irrigated by a 22.5-mile ditch. Local kids used inner tubes (or anything else that floated) to navigate through the ditches, tunnels and flumes that make up the irrigation system. Now, an outdoor outfitter re-creates the thrill of the ride along a

3.5-mile portion of the ditch. Local guides navigate the kayak and chat about native culture and Big Island lore as you ride along—no white-water or rapids, but you'll definitely get wet! This is pure Big Island—not to mention, a total blast.

Hike Kilauea Iki

Once you get a look at the sunken lava lake at the Kilauea Iki Crater Overlook at **Hawaii Volcanoes National Park★★★** *(Hwy. 11, in Volcano; see Parks and Natural Sites)*, you'll want to get a closer look. It's possible—and so worth it!— if you're willing to hike for about three hours. The 4-mile loop begins at the parking area for Kilauea Iki Crater Overlook *(across the street from Thurston Lava Tube, about 1.5mi from the Kilauea Visitor Center off Hwy. 11)*. Bring water and a windbreaker on this challenging hike; it's cool in the crater.

You'll start out with a breathtaking view of what's ahead, and then descend about 400 feet through dense rain forest. The trail is pretty easy to follow, if somewhat steep at the beginning. As you get to the crater floor, look for *ahu* (rock piles) that mark the way. You'll pass the Puu Puai cinder cone and return along the crater's rim.

Play with Dolphins

Dolphin Quest at the Hilton Waikoloa Village, 425 Waikoloa Beach Dr., Waikoloa. 808-885-1234. www.hiltonwaikaloavilllage.com. $150.

Oh, you know you want to! The dolphins here seem pretty happy, frolicking as they do in the Dolphin Lagoon (no tiny cement pool for these critters). Trainers work with Atlantic bottlenose dolphins, and participants join right in, donning snorkel masks to watch the sleek creatures zoom through the water, learning trainer's commands, and, of course, getting that all-important dolphin "kiss."

What a Way to Fly

Talk about an overview! For a great aerial aspect of the islands, and a look at places you otherwise wouldn't be able to see, a helicopter tour is your best bet. You'll peer into craters and see hidden valleys dripping with waterfalls. **Sunshine Helicopters** operates flights on Maui, Lanai and the Big Island *(for information, call 808-871-0722; www. sunshinehelicopters.com). For helicopter tours on Kauai, see p 95.*

Snorkel at Kealakekua Bay State Historical Park

Located on the west coast of the Big Island, at the end of Beach Road in Napoopoo *(off Lower Government Rd. from Hwy. 11 at Captain Cook or Keei Junction)*, this underwater marine preserve makes a great snorkeling destination. Its warm, clear, usually calm water is great for kids and first-timers. There are two ways to do it: on large catamarans and on small rubber rafts. The former are great for families, since the powerboats offer onboard restrooms, food, a snorkeling lesson, and amenities such as flotation rings and jumping platforms.

- **Fair Wind Cruises** – Catamaran snorkel cruises depart from Keauhou *(808-322-2788; www.fair-wind.com; $65–$93).*

- **Captain Zodiac Raft Expeditions** – Raft trips to **Kealakekua Bay★** depart from Honokohau Harbor *(2.5mi north of Kailua on Hwy. 19; 808-329-3199; www.captainzodiac.com; $80).*

Pawai Bay

Here's another snorkeling fave on the west coast. Set between Honokohau Harbor and Kailua Bay, Pawai Bay is accessible only by boat, and is a great spot to see dolphins, manta rays, and, if you're lucky, sea turtles. Boats that offer trips to Pawai Bay include **Honu Divers** *(808-324-4668; www.konahonudivers.com; $59.95)* and **Kamanu Charters** *(808-329-2021; www.kamunu.com; $75)*, who specialize in non-swimmers and first-time snorkelers. Both companies depart from the marina at Honokohau Harbor *(2.5mi north of Kailua on Hwy. 19).*

Musts For Kids

Thurston Lava Tube★

At Hawaii Volcanoes National Park, on Hwy. 11. 808-985-6000. www.nps.gov/havo. Park open year-round daily 24 hours. $10/ vehicle (park admission). See Parks and Natural Sites.

Call it a theme-park ride, designed by Mother Nature! You'll hike through a fern-bedecked rain forest, with sound effects provided by native birds, then you reach this giant hole-in-the-ground. The lava tube is all dark, drippy and cobwebby, with gnarly tree roots hanging down like bizarre chandeliers. Bring a flashlight and poke around.

Must Go: Performing Arts

Kahilu Theatre

67-1186 Lindsey Rd., Waimea-Kamuela (behind Parker Ranch Center). Box Office: 808-885-6868. www.kahilutheatre.org. Box Office opens 1 hour prior to each performance. Performance times and ticket prices vary. Arrive one hour early for best seating.

Hula, Hawaiian music groups and international stars take center stage here, at the "cultural heart" of the Big Island. Recently on the bill: George Winston, Ladysmith Black Mambazo, the Flying Karamazov Brothers, and the Harlem Gospel Choir—how's that for cultural variety? They also offer a film series and youth concerts.

Touring Tip

For pre-concert dining, try Merriman's restaurant, featuring innovative Hawaiian regional cuisine *(see Must Eat)*. As for post-concert dining, forget about it! As they'll tell you at the theater, this is *paniolo* (cowboy) country. Cowboys go to bed early and wake up with the cows. None of that late-night stuff for them!

Merrie Monarch Hula Festival

Various locations in Hilo. 808-935-9168. www.merriemonarchfestival.org.

The Granddaddy (or Big Kahuna) of all of Hawaii's annual events is the Merrie Monarch Hula Festival, which takes place the week following Easter Sunday. A parade kicks off the festivities leading up to Hawaii's most prestigious hula competition, held at Edith Kanakaole Stadium in Hilo. Craft fairs and other cultural happenings add to the pageantry and fun. Events sell out early, so act fast.

Web Site for the Arts

Visit *www.gohawaii.com/arts* for a listing of what's happening while you're in the islands.

Must Shop

Cook's Discoveries

64-1066 Mamalahoa Hwy. (Hwy. 11), Waimea-Kamuela. 808-885-3633.

Crafts, quilts and collectibles—it's all here, along with little must-haves you didn't know you needed, like shell necklaces, coconut-fiber purses, and owner Patti Cook's chocolate-chunk cookies.

Hilo Farmers' Market

Kamehameha Ave. at Mamo St., Hilo. 808-933-1000. Open Wed & Sat, sunrise to 4pm. www.hilofarmersmarket.com.

Fish sausage, soursop, and puka-shell ankle bracelets—now that's one-stop shopping! More than 100 vendors set up shop here, offering fresh flowers, vibrant produce (including some exotic stuff you've never seen before), handicrafts and warm baked goods, "from dawn 'til it's gone," as they say. Many consider this to be Hawaii's best farmers' market. There's no place better to stock up for a picnic, or to get some tasty road food for your trip to the volcano!

Kailua Candy Company

74-5563 Kaiwi St., at Kuakini St., Kailua-Kona. 808-329-2522. www.kailua-candy.com.

Named one of the ten-best chocolate shops in the US by *Bon Appetit* magazine, this shop/factory specializes in chocolate *honus* (turtles) and Kona coffee swirls. Pick up some for the folks back home, but don't trust yourself not to rip into these irresistible treats on the way.

Volcano Art Center

In Hawaii Volcanoes National Park, next to Kilauea Visitor Center. Mamalahoa Hwy. (Hwy. 11), Volcano (28mi southwest of Hilo). 808-967-8222.

Does living near an active volcano inspire some primal creative spirit? Decide for yourself at Volcano Art Center, where changing exhibits feature the works of nearly 300 artists, mostly from the Big Island. Paintings, woodcrafts, jewelry, mixed media, photography and more are represented, housed in the 1877 Volcano House, the original hotel in Hawaii Volcanoes National Park.

Waimea General Store

Parker Square, Hwy. 19, Waimea-Kamuela. 808-885-4479. www.waimeageneralstore.com.

Call it Gift-buying Central. Browsing is a blast at this general store, which is chock-full of enchanting small stuff, like soaps, lotions, local edibles, cookbooks and Hawaii-themed books. Want a "Learn How to Hula" video? This is the place to get it!

Must Be Seen: Nightlife

Kona Village Luau★

At Kona Village Resort, Queen Kaahumanu Hwy., Kaupulehu. 808-325-5555. www.konavillage.com. Held Fri at 6:30pm.

Ask anyone on-island "What's doing after dark?" and they'll mention this, the longest continually running luau on the Big Island, and one of the best. The evening begins with a ceremony, when the pig is unearthed from an underground oven; then the feasting begins. It's a traditional Polynesian buffet that includes ahi poke, lomi salmon, taro chips, fresh limpets, coconut pudding and the delectable shredded kalua pig. The musical revue that follows is an intriguing pastiche of South Pacific cultures, and decidedly un-cheesy.

Blue Dolphin

61-3616 Kawaihae Rd., Kawaihae. 808-882-7771.

This is the Big Island's best venue for live jazz. On Friday night *(7pm–9:30pm)* local musicians jam with visiting jazz stars, and the result is always a heady mix. The Blue Dolphin is small, fun, funky, and a pleasant change from the one-size-fits-all hotel bars around town.

Huggo's on the Rocks

75-5828 Kahakai Rd., next to Royal Kona Resort, Kailua-Kona. 808-329-1493. www.huggos.com.

Now this is a beach bar! Perched on the sandy edge of Kailua Bay, Huggo's is as close to the ocean as you can get without getting wet. Listen to the waves crash and order the Kiluaea, a concoction for two that arrives in a bowl spouting a pool of fire (get it?) and sip—with caution—from two-foot-long straws. Come for live jazz and blues on Sunday and Wednesday nights.

Palace Theater

38 Haili St., Hilo. 808-934-7010. www.hilopalace.com. This restored, neoclassical gem shows first-run movies and art films, and is also the scene for concerts and live theater performances.

Shooters

121 Banyan Dr., Hilo. 808-969-7069.

Looking for a rowdy scene? The weekend live music draws crowds here to down cheap drafts during Happy Hour *(3pm–8pm daily)*, and take in Hawaiian Country acts as the night goes on *(Shooters is open until 3am on Sat, and until 2am every other night)*.

Must Be Pampered: Spas

Hualalai Sports Club and Spa

Four Seasons Resort Hualalai, 100 Kaaupulehu Dr., Kaaupulehu-Kona. 808-325-8440 or 800-983-3880. www.fourseasons.com.

The only danger here is that you'll never want to leave! Fitness has never been so much fun, with choices ranging from a lava-rock snorkeling pond to an open-air gym. Water-related fitness activities are so numerous at this luxe resort, they offer guides (*alaka' i nalu,* or "leaders of the waves") to direct you. After your workout, report to the spa. Few can resist the body treatments here, each sounding more delicious than the last. Perhaps a South Seas sugar scrub, with Hawaiian cane sugar, coconut and honey, or maybe the Hualalai herbal wrap, featuring hibiscus and Hawaiian red clay?

Willow Stream Spa

The Fairmont Orchid, 1 N. Kaniku Dr., Kohala. 808-885-2000. www.fairmont.com.

Imagine enjoying the long, rhythmic strokes of a lomilomi massage in an open-air cabana, surrounded by waterfalls, bright orchids and coconut palms. Fantasy becomes reality here, where massage *hale* (houses) are set along the waterfront, or nestled within tropical flora. Bamboo blinds ensure privacy. The spa's signature treatment is the Big Island Vanilla Coffee Exfoliation, an aromatic scrub that mixes organic Kona coffee beans with an orange-crème lotion.

Spa Terms—A Cheat Sheet

Here's a quick glossary of some you'll encounter in Hawaii:

Ayurveda – An ancient Indian holistic system of healing, based on the concept of balance between mind and body, and achieved with herbs and essential oils.

Haipi – *Haipi* (Hawaiian for "pregnant") refers to a massage for expectant mothers.

Japanese furo bath – Uses gently bubbling water to relax and rejuvenate the body.

Lomilomi – A traditional Hawaiian massage technique employing a light, rolling motion. Lomilomi is said to restore the free flow of *mana,* or life force.

Noni/Nonu – This plant that grows in Hawaii's volcanic soil was used by ancient Polynesians to treat illnesses (noni and nonu are both names for the same plant). Mineral-rich, it's now employed as a healing agent in facials and other treatments.

Pohaku massage – *Pohaku* is Hawaiian for "stone." This is the local version of hot-stone therapy.

Maui★★

Visitor information: 808-244-3530 or www.visitmaui.com.

Maui no ka oi! This is the local motto, meaning "Maui is the best!" The T-shirts that read "Eat, Drink, and Be Maui," seem to sum up this island's attitude. There's a young, vibrant ambience here, where locals seem to feel outrageously blessed by their good fortune of living on Maui, and visitors tap into that feeling of goodwill. Of course, one has to make a living, even in paradise, and there's nothing low-key about tourism here. Local entrepreneurs have found a million and one ways to provide Island fun, from zip-lining through the trees on the slopes of Haleakala, to tunneling through a lava tube at Kaeleku Caverns. Not enough of a workout for you? How about a tour that combines kayaking, snorkeling and hiking? Well-heeled tourists find more than enough ways to spend their money on Maui, and also play a major role in supporting the burgeoning arts community that draws inspiration from the island's glorious scenery.

Fast Facts

- With an area of 727 square miles, Maui is the second-largest island in the Hawaiian chain. The island measures 48 miles long and 26 miles wide at its widest point.

- Although 120,780 people live on Maui, less than 20 percent of the island is inhabited.

- Maui claims 120 miles of shoreline and 81 accessible beaches—that's more swimmable beaches than any of the other Hawaiian Islands.

- You'll find the world's largest dormant volcano, Haleakala, on Maui. Hawaii's coldest temperature—11°F—was recorded on this summit in 1961.

- For 10 consecutive years, Maui has been voted a top travel destination and the best island in the world by *Condé Nast Traveler*.

Fun Fact

Two million years ago, Maui, Lanai, Molokai and Kahoolawe all formed part of one big landmass known as Maui Nui, or Big Maui. Six different volcanoes created this body; over the eons, rising sea levels separated the islands.

What attracts more than 2.4 million visitors to Maui each year? Certainly, the island's four marine preserves and spectacular coastline are strong draws, as is **Haleakala**, the island's mammoth volcano. Now dormant, Haleakala has left its mark on Maui's landscape. Haleakala ("House of the Sun") rises 10,023 feet, and boasts a moon-like crater surrounded by towering forests, waterfalls and jagged sea cliffs. What else would you expect but powerful beauty from an island named for the Polynesian demigod Maui, who managed to capture the sun as it rose from Haleakala's crater?

Beautiful though it is, Maui is about more than good looks. Whether you're a surfer or a socialite, there's something about the place that dictates simple pleasures—the sheer bliss of running barefoot on a beach, or admiring the countryside on horseback. Maybe Maui is simply blessed by the gods.

The Allure of Lahaina

There's nothing ordinary about the town of **Lahaina**★★, the hub of Maui's visitor scene: Lahaina is home to the biggest **banyan tree** in the US, shading almost an acre; it also boasts the biggest Buddha outside of Asia. Celebrated in James Michener's novel *Hawaii*, Lahaina exudes an atmosphere reminiscent of the 19C, when pious missionaries and rowdy whalers vied for the attentions—and affections—of native Hawaiians. The whalers are long gone, but the whales remain an attraction. From November to June, the giant cetaceans play, mate and give birth offshore here before migrating to northern waters for the summer.

Other highlights: loads of outdoor expeditions, great eats … everything but parking. Since two million people visit Lahaina each year, and there seem to be about 15 parking spots, finding a parking space here may well be the most demanding activity on the island!

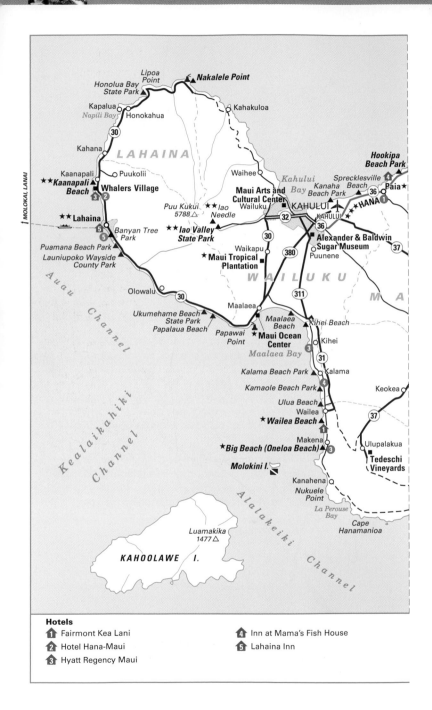

Hotels

1. Fairmont Kea Lani
2. Hotel Hana-Maui
3. Hyatt Regency Maui
4. Inn at Mama's Fish House
5. Lahaina Inn

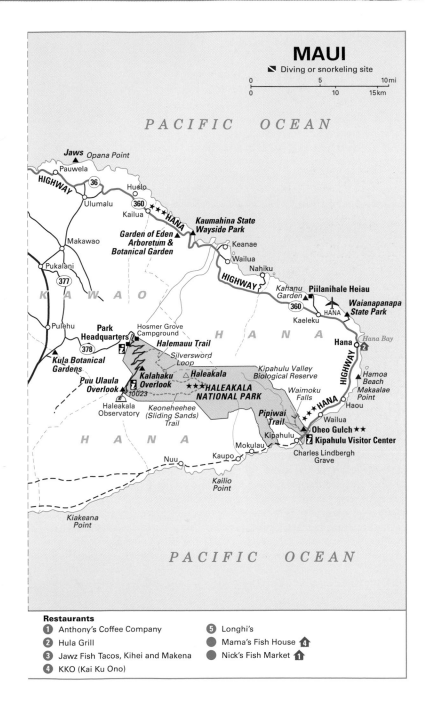

MAUI

◥ Diving or snorkeling site

0   5   10mi
0   10   15km

PACIFIC OCEAN

Jaws Opana Point
Pauwela
HIGHWAY 36
Huelo
Ulumalu
360
Kailua HANA ★★★
Kaumahina State Wayside Park
Garden of Eden Arboretum & Botanical Garden
Keanae
Makawao
Wailua
Nahiku
Pukalani
HIGHWAY
Kahanu Garden **Piilanihale Heiau**
K A W A O
377
360 HANA **Waianapanapa State Park**
Pulehu
Kaeleku
Park Headquarters
Hosmer Grove Campground
H A N A
Hana Hana Bay
378
Halemauu Trail
Silversword Loop
HIGHWAY
Kula Botanical Gardens
△ **Haleakala**
Kipahulu Valley Biological Reserve
Hamoa Beach
Puu Ulaula Overlook
Kalahaku Overlook ★★★
HALEAKALA NATIONAL PARK
Waimoku Falls
HANA
Makaalae Point
10023
Haleakala Observatory
Keoneheehee (Sliding Sands) Trail
Pipiwai Trail ★★★
Haou
Wailua
Oheo Gulch ★★
H A N A
Kipahulu
Kipahulu Visitor Center
Mokulau
Kaupo
Charles Lindbergh Grave
Nuu
Kailio Point
Kiakeana Point

PACIFIC OCEAN

Restaurants

① Anthony's Coffee Company
② Hula Grill
③ Jawz Fish Tacos, Kihei and Makena
④ KKO (Kai Ku Ono)
⑤ Longhi's
● Mama's Fish House
● Nick's Fish Market

Must-See Beaches

Kaanapali Beach★★

Hwy. 30, 2mi north of Lahaina, in Kaanapali.

Dubbed "Dig Me Beach," this is a see-and-be-seen place, where the tans are dark, the bikinis are tiny, and myriad beachside vendors are eager to take you para-sailing. The beach backs up to a strand of resort hotels, linked by a sidewalk, as well as Whalers Village, home to waterfront restaurants like the Hula Grill *(see Must Eat)*. Three miles long, Kaanapali is great for walking, and the tumbling surf makes it good for bodysurfing, too. It's a fun scene after dark, when you might luck into an empty lounge chair where you can get cozy and watch the stars.

Big Beach★

Off Hwy. 31, Shoreline Rd., Makena.

Set in Southwest Maui, Big Beach (aka Oneloa Beach) is the largest undeveloped white-sand beach on the island. To find the beach, a good landmark is Jawz taco stand, across the street *(see Must Eat)*; to the right you'll find a parking lot. The surf can be rough, but the views are great. Locals set up tent villages here on Sundays and make a day of it. Had enough of that sticky swimsuit? Follow the beach west until you reach a path that climbs up lava rocks to Little Beach, where clothing-optional sunbathing is illegal but fairly common, nonetheless.

Surfer Strip

Surfing in Hawaii began, they say, about AD 400, and the scene on Maui is still as live-ly as ever. During the winter months, waves can range in size from 4- to 20-foot faces at beaches like Hookipa, Honalua Bay and Hamoa Bay. Then there's **Jaws**, the huge, rideable waves located in Peahi Bay, east of Paia. These awesome waves rarely break, and faces can be big enough to fit a bus in, so a ride on Jaws is recommended for expert surfers only. Less-menacing waves await you along Maui's south shores, at Maalaea Harbor, Big Beach, and the string of beaches between Lahaina and Maalaea, including Papalaua Beach, Ukumehame Beach, and Launiupoko Wayside County Park. There's parking at these beaches, so even if you're not a long-boarder, you can drive up and take in the scene. Around sunset, it's really gorgeous, when the sea turns to sil-ver and the riders appear in silhouette. This is one of those only-in-Maui moments!

Wailea Beach★

Off Hwy. 31, just south of the Shops at Wailea, in Wailea.

Named America's Best Beach in 1999 by Stephen Leatherman (aka Dr. Beach; *see Big Island/ Beaches*), Wailea is located in South Maui, behind the Grand Wailea and Four Seasons hotels. Long and wide, this white-sand strip features high dunes, a sandy ocean bottom, and a shallow drop-off into deeper water. Calm waters make snorkeling popular here.

Hookipa Beach Park

Hwy. 36, 6mi east of the intersection of Haleakala & Hana Hwys., about 2mi east of Paia.

North Maui's Hookipa Beach (Hookipa means "hospitality" in Hawaiian) is Windsurfer Central. Thanks to strong trade winds and consistent surf, Maui is nirvana for windsurfers, and Hookipa is the real deal. It's the most-photographed windsurfing site on the planet. Powerful rip currents, exposed reefs and snaggletoothed lava rock make this one the perfect match for more experienced sailors (get the hang of it at Kanaha Beach Park or Sprecklesville Beach first). There are numerous places on the island to rent equipment. If you'd rather just soak up the scene, this is a peachy spot. Windsurfers show up at 11am or so; beyond the reef, the northern swells churn up big, surfable waves. The beach borders a coral reef, creating a shallow area that's great for kids.

Whale of a Time

Whales have the right idea. Come November, when northern climes get chilly, more than 1,500 humpbacks arrive in the Hawaiian Islands to mate. They birth their two-ton babies in the warm waters, then head north again in April, to their Arctic feeding grounds. Large numbers of humpbacks congregate in the channel between Maui and Molokai, and you'll find no lack of boat captains eager to take you out to watch the whales breach, spy hop, and swim alongside their young. Maui has the largest whale-watching fleet in the islands *(for details, check online at www.visitmaui.com or contact the Pacific Whale Foundation, which sponsors cruises out of Lahaina Harbor, Dec–mid-May; 808-249-8811; www.pacificwhale.org).*

Besides humpbacks, Hawaiian waters host other wintering whales, including false killer whales, melon-headed whales and sperm whales. Don't count on seeing a sperm whale, though, since these gentle giants frequent the deepest waters. Black pilot whales may be seen off the Kona Coast of the Big Island.

- **Here's a tip**: During whale season, you can often see migrating cetaceans from Papawai Point, a scenic overlook off Route 30, just west of Maalaea.

Must-See Parks and Natural Sites

Haleakala National Park★★★

36mi southeast of Kahului via Haleakala Hwy. (Rte. 37) to Rte. 377 to Rte. 378. 808-572-4400. www.nps.gov/hale. Park open year-round daily 24 hours. Visitor Center open year-round daily 8am–4pm. $10 per vehicle (pass is good for 7 days).

Tripping off the tongue as it does, the word Haleakala (ha-lay-AH-ka-la) means "house of the sun" in Hawaiian. According to myth, the god Maui climbed to the top of the Haleakala Volcano and lassoed the sun to force it to move more slowly across the Hawaiian sky. In turn, La, the sun god, agreed to slow his pace for half of the year so that people could enjoy longer days in summertime.

Haleakala, now a dormant volcano, completely dominates the landscape in east Maui. The spectacular desolation of its enormous crater valley—7.5 miles long, 2.5 miles wide and 3,000-feet deep—has been compared to the mountains of the moon. Pastel hues of red, yellow and orange, as well as gray, purple, brown, black and pink, accent cliffsides and cinder cones.

It's worth waking up in the dark of early morning to drive from your beach-front resort and watch the sunrise over the Halekala's 10,023-foot summit. Along Haleakala Highway, you'll see the surroundings change from lush vegetation at the base to lurid lavascape at the top—all this in a span of 40 miles.

Nene Bird

The endangered nene (pronounced nay-nay), also known as the Hawaiian goose, is Hawaii's state bird. They look like Canada geese, with black faces and caps, cream-colored cheeks, and black-and-white-striped necks. Once hunted to near extinction, nene have been successfully bred in captivity and released back into the wild. You'll find wild nene populations in Maui's Haleakala National Park, in Hawaii Volcanoes National Park, Mauna Loa, and Puu Waawaa on the Big Island; and at the Kilauea National Wildlife Refuge and along the Na Pali Coast on Kauai.

Park Highlights

Kalahaku Overlook – This is a good place to spy sprouts of silversword *(see sidebar below)*. Silverswords bloom just one time per human generation, and then the plant promptly dies.

Stalking the Elusive Silversword

Also known as *ahinahina*, or gray-gray, silversword is among the rarest of plants. So rare is this relative of the common sunflower that it only grows at an elevation of 7,000 feet on the Haleakala Volcano on Maui. Another variety grows on the high slopes of Mauna Kea and Mauna Loa on the Big Island. Bursting from the ashy cinders of the volano, the silversword erupts into bloom between June and October, sprouting a stalk from 3 to 9 feet tall. Pinecone shaped, the plant is covered with purple blossoms that emerge from the center of silvery, swordlike leaves. Look, but don't touch; these plants are a threatened species.

Puu Ulaula Overlook – Get to this overlook at sunrise to take in the sweeping views. It's located near the visitor center.

Visitor Centers – You'll find maps and other information at the park's three visitor centers:

• **Park Headquarters** – *Near park entrance on Rte. 378. 808-572-4400. Open year-round daily 8am–4pm.*

• **Haleakala Visitor Center** – *11mi south of the park headquarters at Puu Ulaula summit. Open summer daily 6am–3pm, winter daily 6:30am–3pm.*

• **Kipahulu Visitor Center** – *10mi south of Hana on Hana Hwy., at the east end of the park. 808-248-7375. Open year-round daily 9am–5pm.*

Hiking and Camping in the Park

Thirty-six miles of trails crisscross the crater floor. Only experienced hikers should attempt these, and it takes twice as long to get out as it does to go in. The park service leads guided hikes daily *(check at the visitor centers for information)*, and an outfitter runs horseback rides to the floor of the caldera *(Pony Express Tours; 808-667-2200; www.ponyexpresstours.com)*.

If you're prepared for changeable conditions—rain, cold and wind—you're the type of camper that will enjoy sleeping near a volcano! **Hosmer Grove Campground** *(no permit required)* is located at 6,800 feet elevation, and connects with **Hosmer Grove Nature Loop**, a pretty, half-mile nature trail that meanders though a cloud forest. Campsites have grills, picnic tables, water and accessibility to toilets. The park also offers primitive campsites *(available by permit, issued at park headquarters)* and wilderness cabins.

Iao Valley State Park★★

Iao Valley Rd. (Hwy. 32), 5mi west of Wailuku. 808-984-8109. www.hawaii.web. Open year-round daily 7am–7pm. www.hawaiiweb.com/maui.

Iao is the reason Maui was nicknamed the "Valley Island." Ancient Hawaiians carried their royal dead into the valley for secret ceremonial burials. Now, the bright green cliffs and gurgling stream at the eroded core of an age-old volcano have made it a popular picnic and hiking venue. The 6.2-acre park is laced with hiking trails, including a short loop that crosses a stream and offers beautiful vistas of a velvet-green valley. The highlight here is **Iao Needle★★**, a basaltic spire that rises 1,200 feet above the 2,250-foot-high valley floor. A 1.5-mile trail meanders beneath cliffs that spout spectacular waterfalls after heavy rains.

Oheo Gulch★★

On Pulaui Hwy., 10mi south of Hana. 808-248-7375.

One of the highlights along the famed **Hana Highway★★★** *(see Scenic Drives)* is Oheo Gulch, set in the Kipahulu District of **Haleakala National Park★★★** *(see p 62)*. At this picturesque spot, a series of small waterfalls tumbles from the southeast flank of Haleakala, feeding from one pool to another. These are often referred to as the Seven Sacred Pools—although there are two dozen of them, and the ancient Hawaiians apparently never regarded them as sacred!

• The simple marble grave of celebrated aviator **Charles Lindbergh** (1902–1974) rests on a promontory in the churchyard of the 1850 Palapala Hoomau Hawaiian Church, located 1.2 miles past Oheo Gulch.

Nakalele Point

Follow Hwy. 30 (Hana-Honoapiilani Hwy.) 7mi north of Kapalua.

Set on Maui's western coast, Nakalele Point is an otherworldly scene of twisted lava and hissing ocean. Standing out in stark contrast to its lush, green surroundings, the point is marked by a US Coast Guard lighthouse. Hike down the hill to the awesome blowhole below the beacon. The blowhole resulted when the sea wore away the shore below the lava shelf. Water now erupts from the hole like a geyser. When the tide is high and the surf is strong, the scene is at its most dramatic.

Must-See Scenic Drives

See map p 58-59.

Hana Highway★★★

The road begins as Rte. 36 at Kahului Airport; it then becomes Rte. 360. 65mi.

Got nerves of steel? Then you can probably handle this hairy-but-gorgeous day-long journey. If you can't, there are several car services that will be more than happy to handle the task, while you sit and ogle *(for information, contact the Maui Visitors Bureau; see p 56)*. Beyond-skinny curves and narrow bridges snake past rain-forested tangles of countryside that will make you feel like you're driving through a botanical garden. You'll cruise at about 10mph around 500 curves, they say, flanked by great walls of bushy, Dr. Suess-like trees in some spots, skinny bamboo and drippy waterfalls at others.

The (barely) two-lane road is in good condition; paved in 1984, it was truly a slice of Old Hawaii before it was modernized. Don't go too slow, or you'll annoy the locals who use this as a commuting road, and be sure to honk your horn at the hairpin turns to warn oncoming traffic; whoever gets to the stop sign first has the right-of-way!

Touring Tip

They warn you to gas up and pack snacks before you attempt the Hana Highway, and the gas part is true. There are no gas stations past **Paia**★ *(see Must Shop)* until you reach Hana town. There are several fruit stands along the way; try some cold coconut and homemade smoothies. Start out early in the morning, as the highway tends to get more trafficked as the day goes on. Keep in mind that you must yield to  oncoming traffic on the one-lane bridges. It's best to have two drivers on this exhausting route; you'll want to switch so each of you can enjoy the views. And finally, plan your trip so you're not driving the Hana Highway after dark.

Along the Hana Highway

Garden of Eden Arboretum & Botanical Garden – *Mile marker 10 1/2. 808-572-9899. www.mauigardenofeden.com. Open year-round daily 8am–3pm. $8.*
If this garden looks familiar, it's because scenes from *Jurassic Park* were filmed here. Walk the trails, have a picnic, and enjoy views of jungly hillsides and rocky coast.

Kaumahina State Wayside Park – *Mile marker 12.*

Alas, the access to Puohokamoa Falls has been closed due to accidents, but you'll want to get out and explore Kaumahina Wayside, where gardens burst with torch and shell gingers, and you can walk an unmarked trail through a eucalyptus forest and admire sweeping views of the ocean.

Waianapanapa State Park – *Mile marker 32. 808-248-4843. Open year-round daily dawn–dusk.* Attractions at this state park include a black-sand beach, caves, and cave pools for swimming. You'll probably see tour vans here, but it's still a nice place to stop for a picnic.

Hana – *At the end of Rte. 360.* Hana is home to the Hana Ranch Hotel, the terrific Hana Coast Gallery, a general store and a gas station. Keep going, and you'll find yourself out of the rain forest. Fog-shrouded hillsides greet you on one side of the car; look out the other side for expansive ocean views. The road south of Hana is quite lovely, and it's not as hair-raising as the northerly stretches. You'll encounter a series of seriously beautiful waterfalls, and eventually, the southern entrance to **Haleakala National Park**★★★ at Kipahulu *(see p 62)*.

Must-See Museums

Alexander & Baldwin Sugar Museum

Puunene Ave & Hansen Rd., Puunene. 808-871-8058. www.sugarmuseum.com. Open year-round Mon–Sat 9:30am–4:30pm. Closed Sun & major holidays. $5.

Smelling pleasantly of molasses, this museum is housed in the former residence of the manager of Hawaii's largest sugar company. Next door is a working sugar mill. Photographs, murals and artifacts chronicle the sweeter side of Maui's history, and the interplay of geography, water and people in growing sugarcane and producing sugar. Immigrant workers from China, Japan, the Philippines and Portugal formed the heart of the business in the mid-1800s; their presence helped make Hawaii the melting pot it is today.

Must-See Gardens

Kula Botanical Gardens

Hwy. 377 (Kekaulike Ave.), 1mi from junction of Hwys. 377 & 37. 808-878-1715. www.123hawaii.net/ attractions. Open year-round Mon–Sat 9am–4pm. Closed Sun & major holidays. $5.

Touring Tip

Kula Botanical Gardens makes a great place for a picnic. Skip the vending machines and bring your own goodies.

For a sense of what Hawaii might have looked like before the Polynesians arrived at the islands (bringing their own plants and animals by canoe), take a look at the collection of native plants here. This five-acre site, perched at an elevation of 3,300 feet, features orchids, proteas, bromeliads, poisonous plants, native fauna, even the mighty koa tree, a broadleaf ever-green that can reach heights of 100 feet. Also look for kukui trees, bearing oil-filled nuts; ancient Hawai-ians burned the oil from kukui nuts to light their homes. This picture-pretty garden spot, located in upcountry Maui, also features an aviary, unusual rock formations, waterfalls, and expansive views of the West Maui Mountains.

Must-See Historic Sites

Piilanihale Heiau

On Hana Hwy., at the Kahanu Garden. 808-248-8912. Open year-round daily 10am–2pm. Closed major holidays. $10.

Overlooking the Hana coastline, just north of town, Piilanihale is the largest temple in Hawaii, with walls rising to 90 feet high. The temple was built by King Piilani during the late 14C, and is still maintained by his descendents. So powerful is the temple's energy force that pilots approaching Hana Airport refuse to fly over it!

Musts For Fun

Maui Tropical Plantation★

1670 Honoapiilani Hwy., Waikapu. 800-451-6805. www.mauitropicalplantation.com.
Open year-round daily 9am–5pm. Fee charged for tram tour.

It's touristy alright, but it's fun—and a great way to get all of your souvenir shopping done in one swoop! This 60-acre working plantation offers narrated tours past fields of papaya, guava, mango, avocado, macadamia nuts, coconuts, coffee, bananas, sugarcane, orchids and ginger. The gift shop sells them all, and then some. Free samples will help you decide what's good.

Bike Down a Volcano

Several companies rent mountain bikes and offer van trips and guided bike tours to Haleakala. Some companies specify a height requirement; others have a minimum age requirement (call to check before you go). Rental prices start at around $25 per day; tour prices range from about $60–$80.

Imagine biking down the summit of a 10,000-foot volcano with a backdrop of fiery sunrise. Biking down Haleakala ("House of the Sun" in Hawaiian) is an only-in-Maui adventure, and it involves getting up at the crack of dawn. You won't mind sacrificing a few hours of sleep, though, when you experience the thrill of cruising nearly 40 miles down a volcano! Average speed is 15–20mph, slowing down for turns and curves. Guided tours will take you by van to the summit of the volcano, provide gear, and ride with you as you glide down the mountain. Rather not do the group thing? If you do it yourself, your outfitter will rent you gear and transport you to the park. Expect some wild belly-flips as you careen down the mountain; you'll drop about 3,000 feet in 10 miles, and curve around 30 switchbacks.

The following **outfitters** will get you rolling:

- **Haleakala Bike Company** – *808-575-9575 or 888-922-2453. www.bikemaui.com.*

- **Maui Sunrise Bike Company** – *866-500-2453. www.mauibikeride.com.*

- **Upcountry Cycles** – *808-573-2888 or 800-373-1678. www.bikemauihawaii.com.*

- **Maui Downhill Volcano Rides** – *808-871-2155 or 800-535-2453. www.mauidownhill.com. For experienced riders only.*

Tedeschi Vineyards

Tedeschi Vineyards, Rte. 37 (Haleakala Hwy.), Ulupalakua. 808-878-6058. www.mauiwine.com. Free tours daily, 10:30am & 1:30pm.

Located in upcountry Maui, on the slopes of Haleakala, these vineyards sit on Ulupalakua Ranch, where cowboys still herd cattle. The pasturelands are beautiful, as are the views of the golden-sand-laced Kihei coastline below. Stroll the grounds, and sample some of the wines they make from grapes, pineapples and raspberries. The tasting room is housed in a renovated cottage; note the cool bar, cut from the trunk of a mango tree. Maui Blanc, made from pineapples, is a pleasant, and popular, wine. Maui Blush is sweetened by passionfruit. Most wines cost around $10 per bottle and up—bring back a bottle for your friends!

Free Hula for You-la

You might luck into a free Hawaiian dance performance in Lahaina's **Banyan Tree Park** *(off Front St. in downtown Lahaina; www.hawaiiweb.com/maui)* if you visit during one of the many annual festivals *(see Calendar of Events)*, but there are free hula demonstrations going on all the time, if you know where to look. You'll discover that hula isn't the hip-shaking extravaganza as depicted by Hollywood—and Elvis, in *Blue Hawaii*; it's a serious art form.

Generally, there are two categories of hula: kahiko (ancient) and anuana (contemporary). Hula Kahiko is performed mainly with percussion instruments, while Hula Auana typically features ukuleles, acoustic and steel guitars and bass. Look for free performances in Lahaina at the **Kaanapali Beach Hotel** *(2525 Kaanapali Pkwy.)* nightly at 6pm, at the **Kapalua Shops** *(adjacent to the Kapalua Bay Hotel)* daily at 10am, and at the **Lahaina Cannery Mall** *(on Hohoapiilani Hwy./Rte. 30, near Front St.).* The Cannery offers Polynesian Hula on Tuesday and Thursday at 7pm, and *keiki* (children's) hula on Saturday and Sunday at 1pm.

Musts For Outdoor Fun

Hike the Pipiwai Trail

Follow the Hana Hwy. south to Haleakala National Park entrance at Kipahulu (10mi south of Hana). $10/park admission. Trail is located and across the street from the parking lot.

Rather poorly marked, but well worth the effort, is this wonderfully scenic 3.7-mile trail, with an 800-foot elevation gain. Signage doesn't tell you how long the trail is, but plan about three hours round-trip; there's lots to see and you won't want to rush this.

You'll pass a 184-foot waterfall and then meander through a guava forest, where ripe fruit makes this one of the best-smelling hikes ever! You'll step over rocks and roots, and enter a lovely, but eerie, bamboo forest. It's rather dark amidst the bamboo, and when the wind blows through the forest, it sounds like maracas! After crossing a couple of streams (this is where those sensible shoes really come in handy), you'll reach 400-foot **Waimoku Falls**, a truly breathtaking waterfall. Return by the same route; it's so pretty, you won't mind retracing your steps!

More Great Hikes on Maui

Halemauu Trail to **Valley Rim** is an easy two-mile-plus walk featuring spectacular views of the Hana coastline *(in Haleakala National Park; trailhead is located on the road that leads from the park headquarters to Puu Ulaula Overlook)*. Or choose to do the entire 10-mile trail—a challenging all-day hike with a 2,000-foot elevation change—which takes in **Silversword Loop**, where you can see these unique, only-in-Hawaii plants *(see p 63)*.

If you're in good shape, try the strenuous **Keoneheehee Trail**, also called **Sliding Sands Trail** in Haleakala National Park *(trailhead is located near the entrance to Haleakala Visitor Center parking lot)*. It's a difficult half-day hike to the first cinder cone—an elevation change of 2,800 feet in 4 miles—but it's a once-in-a-lifetime experience of the breathtaking Mars-like landscape of red, orange, silver and blue cinder cones within the crater.

One of the best ways to explore **rain forests and waterfalls** is to take a guided hike. **Hike Maui**, the islands' oldest outfitter, leads hikes on lush private lands that you won't otherwise be able to access. *For more information, contact Hike Maui at 808-879-5270 or www.hikemaui.com.*

Learn to Surf

Nancy Emerson's school has three locations: 505 Front St., in Lahaina; and 2mi south of Lahaina at Launiupoko and Puamana beach parks. 808-244-7873. www.surfclinics.com. $75 for a 2-hour lesson.

"If a dog can surf, so can you!" boasts Nancy Emerson of the Nancy Emerson School of Surfing. Well, when you put it that way, why not give it a try? Emerson claims she can get beginners going in only one lesson on a soft surfboard (only experienced surfers use the hard, fiberglass boards). Along with form and technique, you'll learn water safety and surfing etiquette—you'll be a surfer dude or surfer chick in no time!

As far as surfing on Maui goes, the south shore boasts some gentle breaks that are great for beginners, including the "fastest right in the world" at Maalaea Harbor, north of Kihei on the west coast. Honolua Bay, on the northwest tip of the island, is famous for its winter waves, which can range in size from 4- to 20-foot faces (gulp!). Then there's **Jaws** *(see Beaches)*, the mother of all waves, in Peahi Bay, where the humongous swells are truly jaw-dropping and (need you ask?) for experts only.

Snorkel off Molokini Island

Excursions cited below depart from Maalaea Harbor, off Hwy. 30.

Three miles off Makena on Maui's west coast lies an enchanting crescent of crater rim known as Molokini Island. Eighteen-acre Molokini rises 160 feet above waters filled with coral heads and a dazzling array of tropical fishes. This protected area, a Marine Conservation District, is irresistible to snorkelers and divers. Molokini is also a seabird sanctuary, and a great place to see migrating whales in season *(Dec–May)*. Don't miss it!

Boats run year-round from Maalaea and Lahaina. Companies who run trips to the island include **Trilogy Excursions** *(808-661-4743 or 800-809-0892; www.sailtrilogy.com)* and **Pride of Maui** *(808-242-0955 or 886-867-7433; www.prideofmaui.com)*. With four locations on Maui, **Snorkel Bob's Maui** will point you in the right direction, depending on your individual interests *(808-661-4421; www.snorkelbob.com)*.

Windsurfing on Maui

People move to Maui just for the windsurfing—that's how awesome it is! Expert board sailors go airborne at **Hookipa Beach Park**, taking advantage of the strong trade winds that blow in from the north *(Hwy. 36, 6mi east of the intersection of Haleakala & Hana Hwys.; see Beaches)*. Everyone else heads to the gentler waters at **Sprecklesville** and **Kanaha** *(west of Hookipa Beach on the north coast)*, as well as **Kihei Beach** *(on the west coast at the junction of Hwys. 311 & 31)* for lessons and practice. No need to plan ahead for lessons; windsurfing schools often set up shop on the beach. You can rent gear at one of the many sports shops in Paia, Wailuku and Kahului.

Then there's **kiteboarding** (aka kite sailing or kite surfing), yet another way to get an adrenalin rush, and a growing sport on the island. This one involves standing on a surfboard of sorts, with a kite hoisted on your head—fun to watch, until newbie kiteboarders come screaming toward you on the beach! Hot spots include the west end of Kanaha Beach Park, Kihei beaches and the westside beaches, north of Lahaina.

See? Turtles.

If you're lucky enough, you'll go flipper-to-flipper with a *honu* while you're snorkeling or diving in Hawaii. A honu is a green sea turtle *(Chelonia mydas)*, an endangered species that feeds in coastal waters around the Hawaiian Islands. Adults can weigh up to 400 pounds, with a carapace (upper shell) around three-and-a-half-feet long. Why are green sea turtles green? They eat a lot of algae.

Musts For Kids

Maui Ocean Center★

192 Maalaea Rd., Maalaea. 808-270-7000. www.mauioceancenter.com. Open Sept–Jun daily 9am–5pm. July & Aug daily 9am–6pm. $20 adults, $13 children (ages 3-12).

If your kids agree with Sebastian the Crab (from the Disney hit *The Little Mermaid*) that "everything's bettah down where it's wettah," they'll love this place. The state-of-the-art aquarium puts little ones in the center of a giant fishbowl, where tiger sharks glide past and spotted eagle rays swoop through a 750,000-gallon tank. The **Living Reef** houses live corals and teems with moray eels, reef fish, sharks, octopi and more. Outdoor pools are home to sea turtles, tide-pool creatures and stingrays, while the **Whale Discovery Center** lures kids with the eerie song of the humpback, calling from the deep. Here, you can follow a pod of humpback whales from their feeding grounds near the Arctic Circle to their breeding and birthing waters in Hawaii.

Whale-Watching

Few things are more thrilling to kids—and adults—than seeing a whale in the wild. Whale season in Hawaii runs roughly from December through April, before the massive cetaceans head north.

There's no lack of whale-watching excursions in Maui—the most serious of these is operated by the **Pacific Whale Foundation** *(808-879-2615; www.pacificwhale.org)*. This nonprofit group, a marine research and conservation organization, runs trips led by certified naturalists. They report a 99-percent success rate in seeing whales; trips run from December to mid-May. And kids will love listening to whale song on underwater hydrophones. Trips depart from Lahaina *($19.95 adults, $15 children ages 7-12, free for kids 6 and under)* and from Maalaea Harbor *($26.95 adults, $15 children ages 7-12, free for kids 6 and under)*. Look for discount coupons on their Web site.

Whales on the Cheap

You can see whales without spending a dime at McGregor Point *(mile marker 9 on Hwy. 30)* in Lahaina, in the shallow waters directly offshore. Look for the beasts as they migrate past the island's west coast. Want to learn more about these gentle giants? Take a peek at the **Whalers Village Museum** in Kaanapali to see whaling artifacts, weapons, ship models, scrimshaw, and a way-cool sperm whale skeleton *(2435 Kaanapalai Pkwy., in Whalers Village; 808-661-5992; www.whalersvillage.com/museum; open year-round daily 9:30am–10pm)*.

Must Go: Performing Arts

Maui Arts and Cultural Center

1 Cameron Way, off Kahului Beach Rd., Kahului. Box Office: 808-242-7469.
www.mauiarts.org. Box office open Mon–Sat, 10am–6pm. Performance times and ticket
prices vary.

Ziggy Marley and Tony Bennett
number among the luminaries
who have appeared at this
state-of-the-art performance
space/visual-arts gallery, which
opened in 1994. It's best known
as a showcase for world music

and arts. And if you want to discover the hottest local theater groups and
dance companies, this is the place.

Must Shop

Lahaina★★

Front Street, the main drag in
downtown Lahaina, is chock-a-
block with shops, restaurants and
the like. Need a pair of rubber
slippahs (local lingo for flip-flops),
a plumeria-scented candle, or
surfer gear? It's all here, and then
some. Yes, there's a huge amount
of cheesy stuff—loads of T-shirts,
and lots of questionable craft
items made elsewhere—but if
you're willing to put in some

effort, you'll turn up some gems here. And how bad can a shopping street be
when it's across the road from the ocean?

- Check out **The Village Galleries** *(120 Dickinson St.)* for crafts from all over
  the world, ranging from $5 to $3,000. The Russian-made, ultra-delicate
  blown-glass animals are wonderful; so are the jewelry and quilts.

- **Maui Hands** *(612 Front St.; also at 3620 Baldwin Ave., Makawao)* boasts a
  collection created solely by Maui-based artists. Items range from Christmas
  ornaments, at $6.50 each, to tables carved from koa wood for a cool
  $10,000. Earrings made from junk hardware are almost too hip, and make a
  great gift for your eco-friendly gal pals.

- Also on Front Street, visit the shop at the **Pacific Whale Foundation**, where
  you'll find cute, whale-related stuff for *keiki* (kids), surf wear, and information on their trips to Molokini Island *(see p 71)* and sunset sailing cruises.

Paia★

Located 7mi east of the Kahului Airport on the Hana Hwy.

A former plantation town, Paia, (say pah-EE-ah) has evolved into a bohemian beach hangout, a place with small boutiques and natural-food shops. Where else on the islands can you find **Hemp House**, a shop specializing in hemp goods *(16 Baldwin Ave.)* with a T-shirt whose graphics read "good bush" (a marijuana plant) and "bad bush" (George W.)?

The town makes a fun place to wander, even if the shops keep irregular hours. ("When the wind is right at Hookipa, everybody takes off," is how one local explained it.) Try **Paia Mercantile** *(corner of Hana Hwy. & Baldwin Ave.)* for pottery and art glass; **Nuage Bleu** *(76 Hana Hwy.)* for trendy girlie duds from Trina Turk, Blue Cult, Miss Sixty; **Necessories Boutique** *(21 Baldwin Ave.)* for "Hawaiian Bohemian Funk" (translation: fabulous handmade gifts); and **Maui Girl Beachwear** *(12 Baldwin Ave.)*, for the tiniest bikinis imaginable. Follow your nose to **Cakewalk Paia Bakery** *(corner of Hana Hwy. & Baldwin Ave.)* for their famous sinful cinnamon rolls—positively *ono* (delicious)!

Island Soap & Candle Works

Maalaea Harbor Shopping Village (next to Maui Ocean Center). 808-986-8383 or 877-610-7627. www.mauisoapworks.com.

Botanical products are absolutely huge on Maui—not surprising, considering the agricultural bounty of the island, and the local emphasis on health and wellness. You'll find body lotions and potions made with local herbs and flowers in nearly every shop, but you *know* it's locally made when you watch them do it here! Master soap and candle-makers mix up batches of natural soaps, candles and bath salts. Most enticing, perhaps, are the super-gentle soaps, made with kukui- and macadamia-nut oils and cured for 21 days or more; the pineapple-scented bar will give you a wonderful whiff of Hawaii when you're back in the bath at home.

Surf Shops

You'll find surf shops all over Maui. A couple of the best-known are **Maui Tropix** *(90 Hana Hwy., Kahului; 808-871-8726)*, the exclusive dealer of Maui Built gear (boards, tees, sunglasses, etc.); and **Neil Pryde Maui** *(400 Hana Hwy., Kahului; 808-321-7443; www.neilprydemaui.com)*. Once a windsurfer shop, Neil Pryde has expanded into a watersports superstore, catering to surfers and kiteboarders as well as the windsurfing crowd.

Maui Swap Meet

Puunene Ave., next to Kahului Post Office, Kahului. Open Sat 7am–noon. 808-877-3100.

Forget the strip malls that proliferate on Maui, and do your shopping here, where you can find all sorts of trash and treasures, from local produce to ancient muumuus and handmade jewelry.

Maui's Gallery Scene

Everybody knows about the island's wet-and-wild outdoor scene, but Maui isn't all surfer dudes and babes in bikinis. Surprise: the island has a high concentration of art galleries, more than 50 in all, and an active, thriving community of artists. Their work turns up in some surprising places, too, like outdoor fairs, upscale resort shopping villages, and artists' cooperatives in towns like Paia and Makawao.

The Shops at Wailea

3750 Wailea Alanui Dr., Wailea. 808-891-6770. www.shopsatwailea.com. Free shuttles run from Wailea resort hotels to the Shops at Wailea every 30 minutes.

Maui's newest, most glamorous shopping address features more than 65 shops and restaurants, plus gallery receptions and live entertainment (on Wednesday). The list of galleries in the mix is truly impressive—ten, at last count—ranging from **Celebrites** (where you can find artwork created by David Bowie, John Lennon and the like) to **Elizabeth Doyle**, where you can see work by renowned glass artist Dale Chihuly, among others, amidst one of the largest collections of studio art glass in Hawaii. **Martin & MacArthur** is the place to go for that ultimate Maui souvenir, a koa wood box or bowl. Here, the **Gap** coexists happily with **Dolce & Gabbana**, and you can even find an outpost of Hawaii's answer to a general store, **ABC Stores**, which stocks everything from Hawaiian jewelry to hula dolls for your dashboard *(www.abcstores.com).*

Whalers Village

2435 Kaanapali Pkwy., Kaanapali. 808-661-4567. www.whalersvillage.com. Free shuttle to Whalers Village operates daily throughout the Kaanapali Beach resort area.

You can browse **Gianni Versace** with sand between your toes— that's the beauty of Whalers Village, a real shopping destination set on Maui's most famous beach. There's a whaling museum here, too, with a giant whale skeleton as a centerpiece but, really, it's all about the shopping. Some of these names, like **Tiffany & Co**. and **Louis Vuitton**, you can certainly find elsewhere, but, hey, you can't beat the ambience! For more unique goods, check out the batik designs at **Blue Ginger** and **Blue Ginger Kids**, the dancing dolphin pendants (accented with Tahitian black pearls) at **Jessica's Gems**, the too-cute hula-girl tote bags at **Sand People**, and all the latest Hawaiian music at **Island Music & More**.

Special Events – Whalers Village is also the place to go for fun free events, like lei-making, hula lessons and dance performances. Events calendars are posted throughout Whalers Village as well as on their Web site *(above)*.

Always in Style: The Aloha Shirt

Eye-popping shirts adorned with hula girls and pineapples aren't just for tacky tourists in Hawaii, nosirree Bob! Every guy in Hawaii has a closet full, with a few favorites, and he wears them most every day. Even the stuffiest of offices observes "Aloha Friday" (Hawaii's answer to business casual), when the colorful shirts come out to play. Vintage models from the 1930s and 40s, with real coconut buttons, are collectibles, worth thousands of dollars.

Hollywood hotties like Woody Harrelson wear Aloha shirts with just the right amount of panache. A laundry list of Aloha-shirt fans would include such names as Elvis Presley, Harry Truman, Montgomery Clift, Frank Sinatra, John Wayne, Bing Crosby (he wore his with a porkpie hat), and, of course, Tom Selleck in the TV series *Magnum, P.I.*, which was filmed on the islands.

The earliest Hawaiian shirts were made for plantation workers, evolving in the 1920s into wild floral designs. With the birth of rayon, the dazzlingly hued, tropical-themed garments became a must-have souvenir for the cruise-ship crowd. Now, thanks to laser technology, those old designs are new again, and hotter than ever.

Must Be Seen: Nightlife

Hapa's Nightclub

41 E. Lipoa St., Kihei. 808-879-9001. $5–$10 cover charge.

Most of Maui's nightlife happens in Kihei, and Hapa's is the epicenter of the action. Live music or DJs, drink specials, and good local bands make this place a party every night. It's open until 1:30am nightly.

Jacques Northshore

130 Hana Hwy., Paia. 808-579-8844.

Impossibly young and buff, the local wind-surfing crowd hangs here, under a canopy of colorful umbrellas. The place serves dinner, and a host of tasty appetizers (including a good, spicy ahi roll), but it's really all about the music—and the beer.

> **Who's Playing Where?**
> Want to know who's playing where? Pick up a free copy of *Maui Time Weekly*, which provides loads of entertainment listings *(www.mauitime.com)*.

Rusty Harpoon Restaurant & Tavern

Whalers Village, Kaanapali. 808-661-3123. www.rustyharpoon.com.

Kaanapali's bar scene is pretty dead, but scores of happy, shiny (OK, sun-burned!) people show up on the beach after dark—or earlier—to sample the frozen concoctions that give the Rusty Harpoon bragging rights as "the daiquiri capital of the world."

Tsunami Nightclub

3850 Wailea Alanui Dr., at Grand Wailea Resort, Kihei. 808-875-1234. www.grandwailea.com. $10 cover charge. No beach clothing, flip-flops, tank tops, or torn clothing.

Feel like dressing up for a night on the town? See and be seen here, where the hottest DJs set the scene for a lively night *(until 2am on weekends)* on the dance floor. No one under age 21 need apply.

Hawaiian Music

The first musical instruments on the islands were simple wooden drums, covered with sharkskin. Dancers held small stones between their fingers and clicked them, and they tied coconut shells to their arms and legs and tapped them with sticks to create percussion. The earliest wind instruments were bamboo flutes and conch shells! Storytellers chanted poems and myths while the music played. When Portuguese immigrants arrived in the 1880s, they brought with them a small, four-stringed instrument that has become Hawaii's signature sound, the ukelele. In Hawaiian, ukelele translates to "jumping flea," referring to nimble fingers jumping over those strings.

Must Be Pampered: Spas

Spa Grande

Grand Wailea Resort, 3850 Wailea Alanui Dr., Wailea. 808-875-1234 or 800-772-1933. www.grandwailea.com.

From its $50 million art collection to its 50,000-square-foot spa, the Grand Wailea resort simply dazzles. A typical spa experience here begins with a one-hour termé Wailea hydrotherapy session—meaning, you choose a pool, perhaps an aromatic bath, a coconut milk soak or a bubbly Japanese *furo* bath in healing waters. Next comes the *really* hard part, choosing among the lavish list of body treatments, including Eastern or Ayurvedic therapies, plus only-in-Hawaii options like the coco-java body scrub. The latter features a medley of regional ingredients that smell good enough to eat: freshly ground coffee beans and Hawaiian honey, followed by a mango-coconut-latté moisturizer. The best massage here, among 12 options, is the deep shiatsu barefoot massage, wherein a barefoot therapist walks on your back. Say ahhh!

Spa Kea Lani

Fairmont Kea Lani Maui, 4100 Wailea Alanui Dr., Wailea. 808-875-4100 or 800-257-7544. www.fairmont.com.

Suffering from the effects of too much sun? They know just what to do at this wonderfully calming spa: a gentle application of aloe and native ti leaves. Facials are absolutely irresistible here, especially the Awapuhi-chai treatment that uses organic mud scented with gingered chai, sure to leave you happily atingle and aglow. Opt for a coconut-milk-and-honey wrap, and you'll be massaged with this fragrant mixture, and then wrapped in a linen cocoon as the concoction rehydrates your skin. After that, you soak in a fizzy bath, feeling like the twist in a tropical cocktail! Aiming for total, pull-out-all-the-stops decadence? Try the kokoleka massage, featuring chocolate body syrup!

Kauai★★

Visitor information: 808-245-3971 or w ww.kauaivisitorsbureau.com.

Grand and diverse, Kauai is the big sister of the Hawaiian Islands, the oldest and fourth-largest of the main islands. Lush fields of greenery and thick rain forests spill down from Mt. Waialeale, the island's central peak, earning Kauai the nickname, "The Garden Isle."

The rain that falls on the 5,148-foot peak of **Mt. Waialeale** feeds seven rivers, including the state's only navigable river, and produces an on-going show of gushing waterfalls. A deep cleft runs across the western end of the island, creating the impressive **Waimea Canyon★★**, nicknamed the "Grand Canyon of the Pacific" *(see Parks and Natural Sites)*. The stunning **Na Pali Coast★★★**, with its plunging 2,700-foot sea cliffs, lies on Kauai's northwest coast. Backpackers flock here to hike the strenuous, 11-mile **Kalalau Trail★★**, considered one of the finest short hiking trails in the world *(see Musts for Outdoor Fun)*. Indeed, Kauai claims more hiking trails than any other island.

Fast Facts

- Kauai is home to some 58,000 people.

- The 533-square-mile island measures 33 miles long and 25 miles wide at its widest point.

- Most of Kauai's land—97 percent—has been set aside as a nature preserve.

- Mt. Waialeale, located roughly in the middle of the island, is one of the wettest spots on earth, with an average annual rainfall of 444 inches.

- No building on Kauai is permitted to be more than four stories high, roughly the height of a palm tree.

Island Ferry Service

Daily ferry service between Hawaii's four major islands is scheduled to begin in 2006. Think mini cruise. New, four-story, 900-passenger ships will have play areas for the *keiki* (children), live TV, high-speed Internet, movies, snacks, full-service bars, and a restaurant. The ships will run daily from Honolulu to Kahului on Maui, Nawiliwili on Kauai, and Kawaihae on the Big Island. *For updates, check online at www.hawaiisuperferry.com.*

If your idea of Hawaiian paradise is lounging on tropical beaches, don't despair. Kauai's southern and western sides are sunny and dry, and ringed with pretty stretches of warm, white sand. In fact, of all the Hawaiian islands, Kauai boasts the most miles of beach per coastline.

The first settlers came to Kauai around AD 500, some 500 years before the rest of the islands were settled. Throughout a succession of kings, the island prospered. Kauai is distinguished as being the only island that was not conquered by King Kamehameha during his quest to unify the islands under one sovereign. Kauai's King Kaumuali'I finally conceded that upon his death, the island would fall under Kamehameha's rule; Kauai remained an independent kingdom until 1810.

Most of Kauai's residents now live along the Coconut Coast on the east shoreline, including **Lihue**, Kauai's main town, **Wailua**, and **Kapaa**. Tourist services cluster around three island resort areas: Lihue, sunny **Poipu**★ on the south shore, and the **Princeville** and **Hanalei Bay**★★ areas on the north shore.

KAUAI

◼ Diving or snorkeling site

0 — 5 — 10mi
0 — 15km

Hotels

1 Hanalei Bay Resort
2 Hyatt Regency Kauai
3 Kauai Marriott Resort
4 Kiahuna Plantation and Beach Bungalows
5 Princeville Resort
6 Radisson Kauai
7 Sheraton Kauai Resort
8 Waimea Plantation Cottages

Restaurants

1 Beach House
● Café Hanalei 5
2 Gaylords
3 Kintaro's
4 Ono Family Restaurant
5 Pacific Café
6 Roy's Poipu Bar and Grill
● Tidepools 2

Must-See Beaches

Hanalei Bay Beach★★

North shore, off Hwy. 560. Any road off Hwy. 560 will take you to the water.

This large, classically beautiful half-moon-shape beach is one of the most popular on Kauai's north shore. The curving crescent of white sand sits at the base of picturesque mountains—some call it the most scenic beach in Hawaii. It's tough to argue the point.

Hanalei, featuring a series of three beaches strung along a too-blue-to-be-true bay, offers a bit of everything. The western end features the calmest waters. The center of the bay boasts the highest surf, luring the island's top wave riders. You can walk the entire stretch; there are picnic areas, rest rooms, and showers along the way.

For a special treat, visit Hanalei Bay in the early morning, when the flat shimmering waters mirror the surrounding mountains. Hanalei Beach Park, near the east end, is a good spot for sunset viewing.

Want to Know a Secret?

Want to get away from it all and discover your own private slice of sand under the swaying palm trees? Head to aptly named **Secret Beach** on Kauai's north shore. It's a 10-minute walk through tropical woods to the beach (all part of the fun!). You'll share this golden stretch of sand and frothy surf with a handful of locals on a busy day; walk down the beach toward the Kilauea Lighthouse, and you'll have even more privacy. Public nudity is against the law in Hawaii, but you may find some flaunting it here. To get there, take Kalihiwai Road, off Highway 56, a half-mile west of Kilauea. Turn right onto the first dirt road and follow it to the parking lot at the end. The trail to the beach is easy to spot and follow.

Poipu Beach Park★★

South shore, off Poipu Rd.

Located on the sunny, dry side of Kauai, this hard-to-resist beach is consistently ranked as one of the top in the nation. In fact, the Travel Channel ranked Poipu Beach number-one in America in its 2004 survey. It has everything going for it: fine, white sands, tropical trade winds, and a range of water conditions to keep swimmers, snorkelers and surfers all blissfully content.

The beach actually consists of a string of three white crescents of sand, running from the Sheraton Kauai Resort east to Poipu Beach Park. Surfers and boogie boarders head to the rocky outcroppings to ride offshore breaks (rentals and lessons are available from small beachside concessions). Families and bathers stick to the east side of the rock jetty, where the relative absence of surf makes for calm waters. It's easy to make a day of it here; popular Poipu Beach Park has showers, lifeguards and picnic areas.

Spouting Horn★ – If you're in the Poipu Beach area on the southern tip of Kauai, stop to see the Spouting Horn, Kauai's answer to western geysers. The frothy surf gushes under a lava tube, and then bursts through a small opening at the surface. Sprays can reach up to 50 feet in the air, especially on windy days. At dusk, the warm-colored rays of the setting sun paint the spray in a rainbow of colors.

Monk Seals

What a sight! If you're lucky, you may walk out on the beach one morning to find the cute, whiskered face of a Hawaiian monk seal basking in the warm sand. The seals come ashore to rest on beaches throughout the islands. Of course, you'll be tempted to get a closer look—but don't! The Hawaiian monk seal remains one of the most endangered species on earth; approaching them might cause stress and harm. (There are less than 30 Hawaiian monk seals that call the waters and beaches of Kauai home.) Stay at least 100 feet away; when taking pictures, leave the flash off; and never shout or throw things at the seals in order to make them move. *For more information about monk seals, visit www.kauaimonkseal.com.*

Kee Beach★

North shore, at the end of Hwy. 560.

The backdrop at Kee Beach—sea cliffs and tropical, jungle-like woods—is hard to beat. Add a perfect place to swim, complete with a sandy bottom and gentle waters, and you've found a beachgoer's paradise. It's especially popular with families.

Nestled at the end of the road on Kauai's picturesque north shore, Kee sits near the start of the famed Kalalau Trail *(see Musts for Outdoor Fun)* along the Na Pali Coast *(opposite)*. Looming to your left, as you approach the shoreline, is the impressive 1,280-foot-tall sea cliff dubbed Bali Hai, as it was known in the movie *South Pacific*.

Bring your snorkeling gear; you'll spot neon-colored tropical fish as they dart around the reef toward the right side of the cove. Rest rooms and showers are located near the parking lot.

Polihale Beach★

West shore, off Hwy. 50. Take Hwy. 50 west from Waimea, all the way to the end of the paved road. Continue straight on the dirt road to Polihale. The state park is at the north end of the beach. Queen's Pond, with calmer waters for swimming, is located at the south end.

Stand on the sweeping dunes of this vast, expansive beach, looking out into the wild surf, and you'll think you've been transported back in time. It's hard to imagine that beaches like this still exist in America: miles of golden sand, rugged dunes—and you won't have to fight the crowds! The isolated, golden beach, stretching 17 miles, is the state's longest and one of its most serene and picturesque. Granted, Polihale Beach is a bit difficult to get to, resting on the westernmost point on the island down a long, dirt road, but it's well worth the trek to experience this place.

According to ancient Hawaiian mythology, Polihale was the gateway to the afterworld, drawing spirits and ghosts to its shores. After resting, the spirits would climb the towering sea cliffs and leap off to get to Po, the offshore afterworld. *Polihale* means "House of Po."

Today you'll find solitude, surf (often high and dangerous) and sun here. Polihale State Park sits at the northern end of the beach, equipped with rest rooms, showers and picnic areas.

Must-See Parks and Natural Sites

Na Pali Coast★★★

Begins at the end of the road at Kee Beach, on Kauai's northwest coast.

The 22-mile stretch of rugged and remote coastline along Kauai's northwest shores is arguably one of the most beautiful natural spots on earth. Known the world over, the Na Pali Coast, stretching from Kee Beach in the north to Polihale State Park in the west, has inspired poets, artists and photographers for thousands of years. It's also been the backdrop for several movies *(see sidebar below)*.

Some historians believe that this area was the first to be settled in Kauai by the early Hawaiians. Today, it is only accessible by the strenuous **Kalalau Trail★★** *(see Musts for Outdoor Fun)*, guided boat or kayak trips (several outfitters offer Na Pali Coast excursions), or viewed from a helicopter *(see Musts for Fun)*.

No matter how you see the dramatic coastline—with its soaring sea cliffs, hanging valleys, gushing waterfalls, sea caves, lava tubes and pristine beaches— you won't be disappointed. Make sure you have plenty of film or an extra battery pack for this excursion!

Pretty as a Picture

It's no surprise that many people get an eerie sense of déjà vu when they land in Kauai; after all, the island has been a favorite of filmmakers and Hollywood location scouts for decades. Who can forget the classic movie scene in *Blue Hawaii* of Elvis Presley and Joan Blackman crossing the hotel lagoon to be married, to the tune "On this our wedding day . . . " ? Or, the beachy, island scenes in the 1958 musical *South Pacific*, including Mitzi Gaynor in front of the Bali Hai mountain, trying to "wash that man right outta my hair . . ." The waterfall you see at the beginning of *Jurassic Park* is Manawaiopuna Falls in Hanapepe Valley; the jungle scenes from *Outbreak* were filmed in the ancient Kamokila Village along the Wailua River. In all, Kauai has served as the backdrop for more than 70 movies—and counting.

Kokee State Park★★

Off Hwy. 550, 15mi north of Waimea. 808-274-3444. Open year-round daily dawn–dusk.

Had enough of hot, dry weather? Head to this cool, mountainous park on the far west end of Kauai. On your way there, you'll have several great views of Waimea Canyon *(opposite)*. Once in the park, there are not-to-be-missed lookouts across the deep Kalalau Valley, plunging to the remote Na Pali Coast *(see p 85)*. The 4,345-acre park features forests of koa and red-blossoming ohia lehua trees, and a spider web of rippling streams. On clear days, you may have views of rainy Mt. Waialeale, and below to Alakai Swamp.

Kokee Natural History Museum – *Located at mile marker 15. 808-335-9975. www.kokee.org. Open year-round daily 10am–4pm.* Stop by this tiny museum, located at the park headquarters, to check out the displays of ancient artifacts and local plants.

Hiking in the Park – There are 45 miles of trails to explore in Kokee State Park, from easy nature walks to strenuous day hikes. Most offer fabulous views across the rugged Kauai interior. Pick up trail maps at the Kokee Natural History Museum.

- The short **Nature Trail** near the museum offers a quick stretch of the legs and a look at native plants.

- One of the most popular hikes in the park, the **Pihea Trail** *(3.5mi; allow 2 hours; trailhead located about 4mi past museum)* traverses a high ridge between the Kalalau Valley and the Alakai Swamp, with sweeping views of valley cliffs dropping to the ocean.

- If you're up for a challenge (and don't mind getting muddy and wet!), try the **Alakai Swamp Trail**. The mossy 3.5-mile path cuts through thick rain forests and swampy bogs before reaching Kilohana Lookout.

Cabins for Rent

If you're looking for an economical place to stay, close to hiking trails and fabulous mountain scenery, check into the cabins for rent at Kokee State Park. The Lodge at Kokee operates 12 cabins, each sleeping up to six people. The older cabins feature one room with bunk beds, kitchen and bath. Newer cabins have two bedrooms, a living area, kitchen and bath. All come equipped with bed linens and cooking utensils. You can rent the cabins year-round, but make sure you reserve months in advance *(contact the Lodge at Kokee, P.O. Box 367, Waimea, HI 96796; 808-335-6061; http://kokee-lodge.com)*.

Waimea Canyon State Park★★

11mi north of Kekaha on Hwy. 550 (Kokee Rd.). 808-274-3444 (information) or 808-245-6001 (weather conditions). Open year-round daily dawn–dusk.

Mark Twain called it the "Grand Canyon of the Pacific." Although it measures some 10 miles long, one mile wide, and more than 3,500 feet deep, it's not only the size that's impressive about Waimea Canyon (the largest in the Pacific)—it's also the colors! The deeply scarred canyon walls, carved from rivers that pour down from Mt. Waialeale's wet summit, shimmer and shine in the sunlight like a palette of deep-hued jewels. Emerald-green folds and rugged dark cliffs plunge into the rust-colored rivers below. On clear days (mornings are the best times), you may see waterfalls and rainbows against the eons-old volcanic rock.

There are several lookout points along the **Waimea Canyon Drive**★★ *(see Scenic Drives),* and the canyon is accessible for hiking, camping and fishing. Check in with the staff at Kokee State Park headquarters *(opposite),* which also administers Waimea Canyon State Park, for more information on recreational activities in and around the canyon.

Touring Tip

Don't waste your time driving around the perimeter of Kauai to find "Barking Sands," even though playful locals might urge you to go see them! Barking Sands is not a natural wonder, but the name of a military installation and missile range. Perhaps the sands really do bark, but you'll have to get past security in order to investigate!

Don't Feed the Birds

If you're hungry, the lodge next door to the Kokee Natural History Museum *(opposite)* serves breakfast and lunch. Just don't feed the local jungle fowl that often congregate in the area. They may look like chickens but they're actually moa, brought over to the islands by early Polynesians. Today, moa live only on Kauai, the only island free of the mongoose, which loves to eat moa eggs for breakfast!

Fern Grotto★

Boat rentals and guided excursions to the grotto are available at the Marina Section off Kuhio Hwy. (Hwy. 56).

It's too bad you can't have this pretty place to yourself: a lava-rock cave heavily draped in tropical ferns, set along the historic Wailua River. Alas, misty Fern Grotto is one of Kauai's most popular attractions and, some say, a bit too commercialized. Rental boats, kayaks, pleasure boats and guided pontoons ply the Wailua River on their way to the grotto. It's a popular spot for weddings, too. Why miss it? Join the crowds on a guided trip up the river (the only navigable river in the state), where you'll see historic sites, tropical gardens and waterfalls along the way.

Kayak and Boat Tours:

- **Rainbow Kayak** – *808-826-9983 or 866-826-2525. www.rainbowkayak.com.*

- **Kayak Wailua** – *808-822-3388. www.kayakwailua.com.*

- **Smith's Tropical Paradise** – *808-821-6892. www.smithskauai.com.* Smith's offers guided boat tours to the grotto, along with nightly luaus.

A Place for the Birds

Birders flock to the **Kilauea Point National Wildlife Refuge**, off Kuhio Highway (Hwy. 56) on the north shore of Kauai *(see Musts for Kids)*. The refuge, overlooking rugged sea cliffs and Kilauea Bay, is home to nesting red-footed boobies *(Feb–Aug)*, laysan albatrosses *(Nov–Jun)*, wedge-tailed shearwaters *(Apr–Oct)* and red-tailed tropicbirds *(Mar–Sept)*. Look for great frigate birds that come here to feed, and for the endangered nene *(see p 62)*. You'll also have fine views of the northern coastline from the refuge.

Must-See Scenic Drives

See map p 81.

Waimea Canyon Drive★★

Begin in Waimea, on Hwy. 50, on the southwest coast of Kauai. See Parks and Natural Sites.

Waimea Canyon is one of Hawaii's most dramatic sites. The 10-mile-long, one-mile-wide, 3,500-foot-deep canyon, the largest in the Pacific, offers majestic views akin to Arizona's Grand Canyon. Schedule a half-day for this excursion, more if you plan on doing one of the hikes in **Kokee State Park★★** *(see p 86)*.

Head west on Highway 50 to the town of **Waimea**, a good place to stop for picnic makings to take with you on the drive through the canyon. You'll pass the small Captain Cook Monument (the British explorer landed in Waimea Bay in 1778), before reaching Kokee Road (Hwy. 550) heading up to the canyon. As the narrow road climbs through wild sugarcane fields, look back toward the southeast for glimpses of the blue ocean streaked with frothy white surf.

Lookouts – Stop at **Waimea Canyon Lookout** for sweeping views of the plunging 3,500-foot-high walls and a kaleidoscope of multihued ridges. Below, the Waimea River shimmers, snaking through the lush valley, and waterfalls tumble down the canyon like shiny silver ribbons.

Continue on to **Puu Hinahina Lookout**, where, on clear days, you can look out to the ocean and the island of Niihau, 17 miles southwest of Kauai. There's also another fine view of the canyon from here.

Follow Highway 550 to the **Kokee Natural History Museum** and park head-quarters *(see p 87)*, and stop to pick up information about the canyon, local flora and fauna, and hiking trails in Kokee State Park.

You'll be tempted to turn around here, but don't. Continue to the end of the road and you'll discover two more fine views of the rugged sea cliffs of the **Na Pali Coast**★★★ *(see Parks and Natural Sites)* along the way at the **Kalalau** and **Pulu o Kila lookouts**.

Shrimp Shacks and Plate Lunches

A favorite stop along Highway 50 on Kauai's western shore is the tiny **Shrimp Shack** in Waimea *(south side of Hwy. 50, in the town center)*. Order up a heaping plate of fresh coconut-battered Kauai shrimp, with hand-cut spicy fries and cold lemonade to go. Or, stop by the **West Kauai Craft Fair** *(south side of Hwy. 50, in the center of Waimea)*, where a local vendor serves classic Hawaiian-style **plate lunches**, platters of barbecue chicken, marinated pork or salmon, with sides of rice and cabbage. He's there every Saturday and Sunday from about noon to 5pm. Then, browse the open-air stands of locally made crafts, including jewelry, art and wood products.

North Shore★★

Begin in the town of Kapaa on Kauai's east coast and take the Kuhio Hwy. (Hwy. 56) north.

Verdant taro fields, cloud-shrouded mountains, tumbling waterfalls, postcard-perfect tropical beaches, rain forests, rivers and rugged sea cliffs await visitors who travel the narrow, winding roads and one-lane bridges of Kauai's pristine north shore.

Take the Kuhio Highway north from the town of Kapaa to your first stop, the **Kilauea Point National Wildlife Refuge** *(see Musts for Kids)*. Located on the northernmost point of the Hawaiian Islands, the oceanside preserve features a 1913 lighthouse, overlooking the crashing surf. This is a favorite spot for birdwatchers. Back on the highway, you'll pass the ultra-luxe **Princeville Resort** *(see Must Stay)*, before reaching the beautiful **Hanalei Lookout**. Be sure to stop here for views of the luxuriant, ancient taro fields that spread across the valley. As you continue west, you'll have views of flat pasturelands (and a few grazing horses), bumping up against the folded mountain range.

Java Stop

The friendly town of **Hanalei** is a good place to stop for replenishment. There's a small shopping center with a cluster of craft and souvenir shops, and a handful of good restaurants. **Java Kai** *(5-5183C Kuhio Hwy.; 808-826-6717)* serves up breakfast and a great cup of coffee. Hit the **Aloha Juice Bar** for fresh smoothies *(this mobile juice bar is parked in the lot of Old Ching Young Center, 5-5190 Kuhio Hwy.)*, and the **Polynesian Café** *(5-5190 Kuhio Hwy., in the Old Ching Young Center; 808-826-1999)* for pork sandwiches, stir-frys, and fresh fish-and-chip baskets.

Heading west out of town, there are pretty views of **Hanalei Bay**★★ and its crescent-shape beaches *(see Beaches),* as the road slices through mountains laced with waterfalls on one side and the turquoise-hued ocean on the other. There are a number of pullouts and overlooks along the way, including **Lumahai Beach**★, made famous by Mitzi Gaynor in *South Pacific.*

You'll pass **Tunnels Beach** and **Haena Beach Park**, popular with locals and campers, before reaching pretty **Kee Beach**★ *(see Beaches)* and the start of the **Na Pali Coast**★★★ *(see Parks and Natural Sites)* at the end of the road. Hopefully, you've saved time for a refreshing swim in the balmy, gentle waters here.

Stop the Car! Now!

Keep your eyes peeled for the yellow and red **Lappert's Ice Cream** sign, and pull over fast when you see it *(1-3555 Kaumualii Hwy., Hanapepe; 808-335-6121).* Lappert's super-rich Kauai-made ice cream (it contains 16- to 18-percent butterfat) is flavored with fresh island ingredients. Try Kauai pie, a decadent mixture of Kona coffee ice cream, chunky macadamia nuts, coconut and chocolate fudge, piled into a large waffle cone; or go for guava cheesecake, mango, Poha berry, banana fudge . . . so many flavors, so little time.

Must-See Gardens

Limahuli Garden★★

Next to the entrance of Haena State Park, off Hwy. 560, Haena. 808-826-1053. www.ntbg.org. Open year-round Tue–Fri & Sun 9:30am–4pm. Closed Mon, Sat & major holidays. $10 self-guided tour, $15 guided tour. Children under 12 free.

Located on the dramatic north shore of Kauai, Limahuli is considered one of the top botanical gardens in the US. A short loop takes you along ancient taro terraces and aside pretty Limahuli Stream, to a stunning overlook of rugged cliffs and open ocean views. The garden specializes in native Hawaiian culture and plants, encompassing more than 1,000 acres. The public gardens spill over 17 acres; the surrounding 988 acres is a nature preserve.

McBryde and Allerton Botanical Gardens★★

On Lawaii Beach Rd., across from the Spouting Horn, Poipu. 808-742-2623. www.ntbg.org. Open year-round daily 9am–4pm. Closed major holidays. $15 McBryde; $30 Allerton guided tour.

These two side-by-side botanical gardens are popular stops for Kauai visitors and locals alike. Both places feature impressive displays of rare and endangered tropical plants.

McBryde Garden

This garden is a living laboratory where scientists are still discovering the secrets of rare tropical plants. Hop on the tram for a self-guided tour of McBryde Garden; the tour follows a meandering stream through the moist valley floor *(daily tram tours depart the visitor center every hour on the half-hour from 9:30am–2:30pm).*

Allerton Garden

Next door at the 100-acre Allerton Garden, you'll see the wavy roots of a Moreton Bay fig tree, featured in the movie *Jurassic Park*, and exotic plants from around the world, showcased against a backdrop of shimmering pools and garden sculpture. To learn more about the flora here, take the 2$^1/_2$ - hour guided walk through Allerton Garden *(tours run Mon–Sat at 9am, 10am, 1pm & 2pm, and Sunday at 10am & 1:30pm).*

Garden Luau

For a pleasant evening out, head to **Smith's Tropical Paradise** *(174 Wailua Rd., Kapaa; 808-821-6892; www.smithskauai.com)*, a pretty 30-acre site at the mouth of the Wailua River on Kauai. Tram rides take visitors around formal botanical gardens, featuring local and exotic plants and trees, a lily-studded lagoon, and Polynesian villages. Stay for the nightly luau, including a pageant and traditional food cooked in an underground oven. River boats also depart from here to **Fern Grotto**★ *(see Parks and Natural Sites).*

Must-See Historic Sites

Grove Farm Homestead★

Nawiliwili Rd., off Waapa Rd. near Lihue. 808-245-3202. Visit by 2-hour guided tour only, year-round Mon, Wed & Thu 10am & 1pm (reservations required). Closed major holidays. $5 adults, $2 children (ages 12 and under).

For a good look at life on an early sugar plantation, sign up for the two-hour tour of this historic homestead. Grove Farm, nestled in the pastures above Lihue, was founded in 1864 by George N. Wilcox, the son of Hanalei missionaries. The 80-acre farm preserves the lifestyle of the sugar plantation from the period 1864 to 1978, and includes the restored Wilcox family home, plantation office and workers' houses. On the extensive grounds, you'll discover gardens, orchards, poultry and livestock.

Must-See Museums

Kauai Museum

4428 Rice St., Lihue. 808-245-6931. www.kauaimuseum.org. Open year-round Mon–Fri 9am–4pm, Sat 10am–4pm. Closed Sun. $7.

You'll find all things Hawaiian at this small, but top-notch, museum in Lihue. The museum traces the island's history from its volcanic beginnings, through sugarcane farming and missionary work, and features an impressive collection of Hawaiian paintings and artifacts, including more than 1,000 stone implements, feather work, weapons, drums and more. There's a nice gift shop on-site, too *(see Must Shop)*.

Do You Believe in Menehunes?

Hawaii folklore tells of mischievous "little people" named menehunes, who roamed the forests at night. The shy creatures, it's said, were great engineers and master builders, capable of completing major construction projects in one night. The creation of **Menehune Fishpond** and **Waimea Ditch** on Kauai are credited to the menehunes. Not just workers, these jolly folks; according to legend the menehune also enjoyed singing and dancing, and have been known to use magic arrows to pierce hearts and ignite feelings of love. Some people believe that menehune still hide out in the forests of Kauai.

Musts For Fun

Take a Helicopter Ride★★

If you do only one thing on Kauai (besides sunbathe on the beach), make it a helicopter tour of the island. More than 90 percent of the island's diverse and spectacular landscape is inaccessible; the best way to see it is from the air.

Most tours fly out of **Lihue**, heading toward the sunny south shores of **Poipu★**, with its long stretches of sandy beaches and turquoise bays. You'll chopper over the dramatic **Waimea Canyon★★**, with its multi-hued gorges and cliffs *(see Parks and Natural Sites)*. If you're lucky, it will have just rained and you'll see countless, minutes-old waterfalls tumbling down the canyon walls.

Heading north, the spectacular **Na Pali Coast★★★** comes into view, with its lush cliffs, plunging 3,000 to 4,000 feet to the sea *(see Parks and Natural Sites)*. Inaccessible by roads, this remote coastline, with its rugged cliffs and verdant valleys, was once home to thousands of ancient Hawaiians. Its jungly, primeval landscape has been seen in several movies, including *Jurassic Park*.

The flight continues up the coast, passing sparkling **Hanalei Bay★★** *(see Beaches)* and a smattering of pretty beaches. If weather permits, the pilot may take you into the middle of the island's crater, once sacred burial grounds for kings, then over Mt. Waialeale, the center of the island and one of the rainiest spots on earth.

Have you counted the waterfalls along the way? One young passenger got to 100, then gave up the count.

Touring Tip

One of the oldest and most reputable helicopter tour operators is **Island Helicopters** *(808-245-8588 or 800-829-5999; www.islandhelicopters.com)*. For a complete list of operators, contact the **Kauai Visitors Bureau** *(808-245-3971 or 800-262-1400; www.kauaivisitorsbureau.com)*. You'll save up to 40 percent if you book helicopter tours online.

Join a Hawaii Movie Tour

Tours run about $100 per person and include lunch and pick-up and return from most resort properties. For more information, contact Hawaii Movie Tours: 800-628-8422; www.hawaiimovietour.com.

Even if you're not a movie buff, you'll enjoy the incredible scenery on this fun-filled tour of famous movie scenes and locations shot on Kauai. The island has long been a favorite of location scouts and filmmakers, who've shot more than six-dozen movies on the Garden Isle. On this guided tour, you'll see a variety of famous film scenes on the bus (shown on digital video with surround sound), as you tour the actual sites. Along the way, you'll be treated to in-depth commentary, behind-the-scenes gossip, and a good amount of hilarity.

The tour visits a number of well-known public sites, like the waterfall shown in the opening scene of the TV show *Fantasy Island*, and the beach where Mitzi Gaynor vowed to "wash that man right outta my hair" in the movie *South Pacific*. But you'll also visit private locales and hidden, off-the-tourist-track spots. Remember the scene in *Raiders of the Lost Ark* where Indiana Jones was chased by a band of South American warriors, then swung on a rope to escape on a waiting seaplane? You'll visit the private ranch where it was filmed. The rope is still hanging, and, if you like, you can take a swing on it, too, Indiana-style. (Don't tell anyone, but according to the tour guides, Harrison Ford had to have a stunt double step in to do that trick.)

Bali Hai Lookout

One of the finest views on the island of Kauai is from the opulent **Princeville Resort** on the north shore *(5520 Ka Haku Rd., Princeville; see Must Stay)*. But you don't have to fork out the princely sum to stay here in order to soak up the views. Reserve a table at the resort's **Café Hanalei** *(see Must Eat)* or simply pull up a chair at the poolside terrace bar. You'll have a stunning view of Hanalei Bay, the famous Bali Hai rock formation, and the cliffs of Na Molokama. Stick around as the sun slips into the water and the resort's twinkling lanterns alight.

Musts For Outdoor Fun

Hike the Na Pali Coast★★★

Kalalau trailhead begins at Kee Beach at the end of Hwy. 560. Permits are required on Kalalau Trail beyond Hanakapiai Beach. Camping along the Kalalau trail costs $10 per day. For more information, and to purchase permits, contact the Division of State Parks (1151 Punchbowl St., Room 131, Honolulu; 808-587-0300; www.hawaii.gov/dlnr/dsp/kauai.html).

If you're a hiker, or even a quasi outdoor adventurer, you've likely heard of the spectacular **Kalalau hiking trail★★** that hugs the remote and rugged Na Pali coastline. It's arguably one of the best short-distance hikes in the world.

> ### Touring Tip
>
> If you can't carve out time to do the entire trail, the first two miles to Hanakapiai Beach is worthwhile and will give you a good peek at the stunning Na Pali coastline. From here you can also make a four-mile round-trip to **Hanakapiai Falls**.

It's not easy. The 11-mile, one-way trek includes some 5,000 feet of elevation gain and loss, often across a narrow, steep, muddy and slippery ridgeline. But you'll be rewarded with spectacular views. On the first leg of the trip—the relatively easy one, though it gets slippery when wet—you'll walk through a tropical forest of dewy ferns, sweet-smelling papaya and mango trees, with sweeping ocean vistas, before descending onto sugar-white **Hanakapiai Beach**. Here, a freshwater stream bubbles into the ocean and wet and dry caves line the shoreline.

Back on the Kalalau trail, you'll climb up and down into **Hoolulu Valley**, then **Hanakoa Valley**, rich with tropical plants, mango and guava trees. The final leg takes you into breathtaking **Kalalau Valley★★**, rippled with streams and waterfalls. There's camping on the beach at Kalalau.

Camping on Kauai

You'll find some of the best camping in Hawaii on Kauai, including three state parks and several county beach parks. Cabins are available at **Kokee State Park**★★ *(15mi north of Kekaha on Hwy. 550)* and free backcountry permits are offered for sites in the **Waimea Canyon**★★ *(11mi north of Kekaha on Hwy. 550)* and adjoining Kokee State Park. For the best beach camping, consider **Polihale State Park** *(at the end of a 5mi-long dirt road from Mana Village, off Hwy. 50)*, with its lofty sand dunes, miles of secluded beach, picnic areas and fresh water. And you can pull your vehicle right up on the beach here!

Touring Tip

Camping fees on Kauai are $5 per campsite per night; $10 per person per night on the Na Pali Coast. To purchase permits, contact the Division of State Parks *(1151 Punchbowl St., Room 131, Honolulu; 808-587-0300; www.hawaii.gov/dlnr/dsp/kauai.html)*. For county park permits, contact the Kauai Dept. of Parks and Recreation *(4444 Rice St., Lihue; 808-241-6660; www.hawaii.gov/dlnr/dsp/kauai.html)*.

Sunset Viewing on Kauai

For a splurge, reserve a table for the sunset seating at upscale and oh-so-romantic **Beach House** restaurant on the south shore *(5022 Lawai Rd., Koloa; see Must Eat)*. You'll feast on award-winning Pacific Rim cuisine while you enjoy jaw-dropping views of the sun as it slips into the Pacific.

Of course, you don't have to bust your budget for dinner. The tiny beach alongside the restaurant is accessible to all, and boasts the same spectacular views. Or park your car anywhere along ocean-hugging Lawai Road for the nightly sky show.

Golf Kauai

Golfers can hardly go wrong on the island of Kauai, home to several dramatic, award-winning resort courses.

Kauai Lagoons Resort – *3351 Hoolaulea Way, Lihue. 808-241-6000 or 800-634-6400. www.kauailagoonsgolf.com.* Kauai Lagoons boasts two Jack Nicklaus-designed courses on the southeast corner of the island, including the top-ranked Kiele course that snakes through 40 acres of tropical lagoons.

Poipu Bay Resort – *At the Hyatt Regency Kauai, 2250 Ainako St., Koloa. 808-742-8711. www.kauai.hyatt.com.* A Robert Trent Jones Jr. design, the course at Poipu Bay features rolling terrain, sweeping ocean views, and a choice of four sets of tees at each hole. The PGA Grand Slam is held here every November.

Princeville Resort – *5520 Ka Haku Rd., Princeville. 800-826-1105. www.princeville.com.* Robert Trent Jones Jr. designed both of the resort's courses. Set against a backdrop of open ocean, the 45 holes of the **Prince Course** are named for Prince Albert, the only son of King Kamehameha IV; the **Makai Course**, considered among the top 100 resort courses in the country, features three sets of nines that skirt the ocean, wind around lakes, and meander through woodlands and tropical forest.

Best Golf Shop

If you're a golfer or you have duffers on your gift list, you'll want to check out **The Golf Shop at Poipu Bay Golf Course** *(above)*, rated as one of the finest in America. PGA Grand Slam and Kauai Resort logo wear fly off the shelves here.

Musts For Kids

Children's Garden

*Na Aina Kai Botanical Gardens, 4101 Wailapa Rd., Kilauea. 808-828-0575.
www.naainakai.com. Visit by guided tour only year-round, Tue, Wed & Thu at 9am,
9:30am & 1pm. $25/person for 1-hour tour (reservations recommended). Family tours
available by appointment: $25 adults, $15 children.*

The fun-filled Children's Garden is the newest space at the Na Aina Kai
Botanical Gardens, where kids can roam through a gecko-shaped maze of
bushes and plants, climb a treehouse, splash in the water, and learn about the
environment through a variety of exhibits and hands-on activities. Rising 16
feet in the middle of the Children's Garden is a bronze statue of Jack and the
Beanstalk; alas, it's not for climbing, but kids still love it nonetheless.

Other features of 240-acre Na Aina Kai include 12 theme gardens, a hardwood
plantation, a moss- and fern-draped canyon, and a sandy beach along the
ocean. More than 60 sculptures dot the landscape.

Go Snorkeling

A pair of rubber slippers and a snorkel mask (don't forget the sunscreen!) is all
you'll need to catch Kauai's amazing underwater show. The best family-friendly
snorkeling beaches on the island are **Poipu Beach Park★★**, Anini and Salt Pond
Beach on the south shore, and **Kee Beach★** on the north shore *(see Beaches).*

Check out **Lydgate Park Beach** *(off Hwy. 56 between Kapaa and Lihue; take
Leho Rd. past the Holiday Inn Sunspree),* too, for great swimming, tide pooling,
and snorkeling. Lydgate also has an awesome playground with a maze of caves,
slides and tunnels that will keep the little ones occupied for hours.

Kilauea Point National Wildlife Refuge

*On the north shore, off Hwy. 56; take Kilauea Rd. to the end. 808-828-1413.
www.pacificislands.fws.gov/wnwr/kkilaueanwr.html.*

Take a hike on the wild side. Red-
footed booby birds, soaring frig-
ates, spouting humpback whales,
basking monk seals and frolicking
spinner dolphins are just some of
the wildlife your family may see at
the Kilauea Point National Wildlife
Refuge, perched on a cliff overlooking the Pacific Ocean. Take a
walk out to the 1913 lighthouse,
stop by the visitor center for
information and maps, then join a

guided walk through the trails that crisscross the 203-acre preserve. Located on
the northernmost tip of the Hawaiian Islands, Kilauea Point is one of the few
Hawaiian refuges open to the public.

Must Shop

Coconut Marketplace

4-484 Kuhio Hwy. (Hwy. 56), Kapaa. 808-822-3641. www.coconutmarketplace.com. Open year-round Mon–Sat 9am–9pm, Sun 10am–6pm. Special holiday hours apply on Thanksgiving Day & Dec 25.

This open-air marketplace, with more than 70 shops and restaurants, is the largest on Kauai. If you're looking for one-stop shopping, this is it. Here, you'll find fine specialty stores next to inexpensive gift shops, tacky souvenirs cheek-to-jowl with pricey Tahitian pearls. When you've worked up an appetite, there are a handful of places to stop for picnic-style snacks or sit-down meals.

Kauai Museum Shop

4428 Rice St., Lihue. 808-245-6931. www.kauaimuseum.org. Open year-round Mon–Fri 9am–4pm, Sat 10am–4pm. Closed Sun, Thanksgiving Day & Dec 25.

This is where the locals go to shop for special gifts. It's also the best place for top-quality, one-of-a-kind, island-made arts and crafts. An impressive selection of items awaits you at this tiny museum shop, including fish-hook necklaces, Lauhala hats, wooden bowls, and authentic Niihau shell necklaces ranging from $75 to $15,000.

Sunshine Markets

You can't beat the fresh, locally grown produce offered at one of Kauai's farmers' markets. Sunshine Markets, as they're called by the locals, are set up Monday through Saturday at various locations on the island. Get there early for the best picks.

Here's the schedule:

Monday – noon at Koloa Ballpark *(Maluhia Rd., Koloa).*

Tuesday – 3:30pm at Kalaheo Neighborhood Center *(on Papalina Rd., off Kaumualii Rd., Kalaheo).*

Wednesday – 3pm at Kapaa New Town Park *(at the intersection of Kahau & Olehena Rds., Kapaa).*

Thursday – 4:30pm at Kilauea Neighbor-hood Center *(on Keneke Rd., off Lighthouse Rd., Kilauea);* and 3:30pm at Hanapepe Town Park *(behind the fire station in Hanapepe).*

Friday – 3pm at Vidinha Stadium in Lihue *(on Hoolako St., off Queen Kapuli Rd.).*

Saturday – 9am at Kekaha Neighborhood Center *(on Elepaio Rd., Kekaha).*

Red-Dirt Shirts

Looking for something unique to Kauai? Pick up a T-shirt that was hand-dyed using Kauai's famous red dirt. You'll see them in souvenir shops around the island, but some of the best-priced red-dirt shirts are found at the tiny Waimea Canyon Plaza on Highway 552 in Kehaha, on the island's west shore.

Must Be Seen: Nightlife

Keoki's Paradise

2360 Kiahuna Plantation Dr., at the Poipu Shopping Center, Koloa. 808-742-7534. www.keokisparadise.com.

This casual Polynesian-themed restaurant, decked out with waterfalls, thatched roofs and plenty of plants, is a hangout for young partyers on Friday and Saturday evenings when local bands perform in the bustling Bamboo Bar. Take your pick from the menu of tropical cocktails: Will it be a Blue Hawaiian (pineapple, lemon and lime juices blended with blue Curaçao and rum) or a Lava Flow (puréed pineapple and coconut erupting with strawberries and rum)? A bar menu of pupus (appetizers), salads and light fare is available until 11:30pm.

Stevenson's Library

1571 Poipu Rd., Koloa. 808-742-1234. www.kauai.hyatt.com.

Sip fine liquors, play a game of chess, enjoy a hand-crafted cigar . . . this opulent bar in the Hyatt Regency resort on Kauai's south shore feels like a big-city gentlemen's club. The upscale night spot is decorated in rich, dark woods and brass accents, and features a large, 27-foot-long koa-wood bar. Sink into the cushy sofas and chairs, order your favorite libation, then sit back and enjoy live jazz, offered nightly from 8pm to 11pm. On Fridays, Stevenson's hosts a popular sushi-and-martini night.

Moonbows

The best nightly performance on Kauai is often courtesy of Mother Nature. The Garden Isle is one of the few places in the world to see moonbows. Look for these ghostly light streaks when the moon is full, just after sunset. On the highway between Lihue and Waimea is a good place to spot them.

Must Be Pampered: Spas

Anara Spa

Hyatt Regency Kauai, 1571 Poipu Rd., Koloa. 808-240-6440. www.anaraspa.com.

This blissful and beautiful full-service spa, set on the lush grounds of the Hyatt Regency Kauai resort, is considered one of the top-ranked spas in the country. From the moment you walk through the doors, you'll feel pampered in the luxurious indoor and outdoor facilities and by the spa's unique, therapeutic treatments. Products are made on the island, exclusively for Anara customers. Popular treatments include the seaweed and mineral body masks, botanical baths, papaya pineapple polishes, and pohaku (hot stone) and lomilomi massages *(see sidebar below).* The outdoor shower, hidden in a private garden, is a special treat.

Massage in Paradise

"Touching with loving hands" is the literal translation of lomilomi massage. You'll think you've died and gone to heaven when you experience it. The massage technique has been passed down by Hawaiian elders and is now offered in spas throughout the islands. Therapists use both gentle and vigorous kneading strokes and incorporate elbow and forearm work for a deep, all-over body massage. It's firmer and faster than a Swedish massage, leaving you wet-noodle relaxed.

Spa Souvenirs

For a unique reminder of the islands, look for body products made with local ingredients (lavender essential oils, kukui nut cream) when you visit one of Hawaii's spas. And instead of bringing home yet another T-shirt, here are a few suggestions for other made-in-Hawaii souvenirs:
• Aloha shirts *(see p 77)*
• Surf shorts
• Lau hala placemats
• Woodcrafts (koa mirrors, picture frames, ukuleles)
• Music CDs recorded by popular island artists

Oahu★★

Visitor information: 877-525-6248 or
www.visit-oahu.com.

Aptly nicknamed "The Gathering Place," Oahu ranks as the most bustling and developed of all the islands. Tourists flood the area for its plethora of lodging, dining and shopping venues, and for its waterfront activities. Oahu is also home to the state's most popular tourist attraction, Pearl Harbor's **USS Arizona Memorial★★**, and to **Iolani Palace★★**, the only royal palace in the United States *(see Historic Sites)*.

Most of the island's activity is concentrated in the urban areas of **Honolulu★★** and **Waikiki★★**, resting on the south shore. But venture north along Oahu's 125 miles of coastline and you'll find impossibly blue bays, surf-slapped beaches (some of the finest in the islands) and verdant valleys. There are fertile farms, mountain rain forests, and green vistas of pineapple and sugarcane fields. Across the Koolau Range from Honolulu extends the lush windward coast of the island, with its suburban communities of Kailua and Kaneohe. West of Pearl Harbor is the drier Waianae coast and the big-wave beaches of Makaha. A route through the agricultural center of Oahu leads to the north shore, fabled for its country living and renowned surfing venues like Sunset Beach and Waimea Bay *(see Musts for Fun)*.

Oahu is the second-oldest of the islands. Populated before AD 1000, it was added to the island kingdom when King Kamehameha I, from the island of Hawaii, defeated Oahu's forces in 1795. It was to be the last battle fought between Hawaiian troops. By 1850, the Hawaiian Royal Court had moved permanently to Honolulu, making the harbor city the center of government and commerce for the islands.

Today, Oahu, with its 21C vibe and rich, cultural diversity, continues to beat as the heart of Hawaii.

Fast Facts
• At 608 square miles, Oahu is the third-largest of the Hawaiian Islands. The island measures 44 miles long and 30 miles wide at its widest point.
• Three-fourths of Hawaii's population of 1.2 million people live on Oahu.
• Oahu claims the state capital, Honolulu, which also ranks as the state's largest city and the financial center of the Pacific.
• Oahu is the most visited of the Hawaiian Islands.

Must-See Cities

Honolulu★★

Sprawling across the southeast quadrant of Oahu, the world's largest Polynesian city boasts a bustling modern **Downtown**★★ of skyscrapers and traffic, extending from Waikiki's surf-washed beaches to the 3,000-foot crest of the jungle-swathed Koolau Range *(from Honolulu Harbor to Vineyard Blvd., between Ward Ave. & River St.).* Here the first missionaries gathered their Hawaiian congregations and the only royal palace in the US was erected in 1882.

Accolades come easily to this sophisticated city; for decades, travelers have voted it the "Best City in the US." With its world-class destination status, though, comes congestion, noise, and a jungle of high-rise resorts and popular sites.

Honolulu Academy of Arts★★ – *900 S. Beretania St., at Ward Ave. See Museums.*

Iolani Palace★★ – *S. King & Richard Sts. See Historic Sites.*

Kawaiahao Church★★ – *957 Punchbowl St.* 808-522-1333. King Kamehameha IV married Queen Emma in this venerable house of worship, made from 14,000 blocks of coral cut from the offshore reefs. It took five years and more than a thousand men to complete the church, which was dedicated in 1842. Today Kawaiahao Church offers Sunday services in Hawaiian and English.

Mission Houses Museum★★ – *553 S. King St., at Kawaiahao St. See Museums.*

Hawaii State Capitol★ – *S. Beretania St., between Richards & Punchbowl Sts.* Completed in 1969 to replace the capitol at Iolani Palace, this modern structure rises out of a shallow pool, to represent volcanoes rising from the sea.

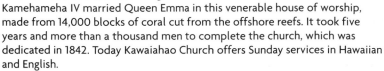

Aloha Tower★

Pier 9, downtown Honolulu. 808-528-5700. *www.alohatower.com. Observation deck open year-round daily 9am–5pm.* There's no missing this long-time beacon in downtown Honolulu. For nearly eight decades, the 10-story Aloha Tower—named for the greeting etched above its four clock faces (one on each side of the square column)—has greeted cruise-ship passengers and other visitors. Progress may have stripped the 1926 tower's claim to fame as Hawaii's tallest building, but it still offers some of the best views in town from its outdoor observation decks. Bring your credit cards; the **Aloha Tower Marketplace**, with its shops, galleries and restaurants, surrounds the base of the tower *(see Must Shop).*

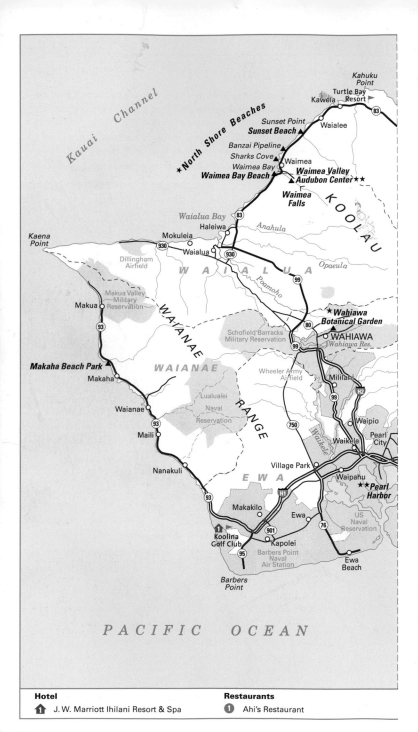

Hotel

🏠 J. W. Marriott Ihilani Resort & Spa

Restaurants

① Ahi's Restaurant

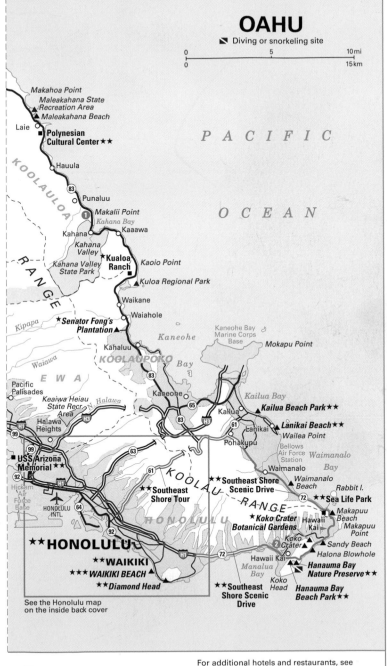

OAHU

⬙ Diving or snorkeling site

0   5   10mi
0   15km

P A C I F I C

O C E A N

Makahoa Point
Maleakahana State
Recreation Area
Maleakahana Beach
Laie
Polynesian Cultural Center★★
Hauula
83
Punaluu
Makalii Point
Kahana Bay
Kahana
Kaaawa
Kahana Valley
Kualoa Ranch
Kaoio Point
Kahana Valley State Park
Kuloa Regional Park
Waikane
Waiahole
Senator Fong's Plantation▲
Kahaluu
Kaneohe
Kaneohe Bay Marine Corps Base
Mokapu Point
Bay
Kipapa
Waiawa
KOOLAUPOKO
Kaneohe
65
Kailua Bay
Kailua Beach Park★★
Pacific Palisades
Keaiwa Heiau State Recr. Area
Halawa
Halawa Heights
83
83
H3
Kailua
Lanikai Beach★★
Lanikai
Wailea Point
61
Pohakupu
99
99
USS Arizona Memorial★★
Bellows Air Force Station
Waimanalo
92
Hickam Air Force Base
63
Waimanalo
Bay
61
KOOLAU
★★**Southeast Shore Scenic Drive**
Waimanalo Beach
Rabbit I.
HONOLULU INTL.
64
★★**Southeast Shore Tour**
RANGE
72
★★**Sea Life Park**
Koko Crater Botanical Gardens★
Hawaii Kai
Makapuu Beach
Makapuu Point
92
★★**HONOLULU**
11
★★**WAIKIKI**
72
Koko Crater
Sandy Beach
Halona Blowhole
★★★**WAIKIKI BEACH**▲
Hawaii Kai
Manalua Bay
Hanauma Bay Nature Preserve★★
★★*Diamond Head*
Koko Head
Hanauma Bay Beach Park★★
★★**Southeast Shore Scenic Drive**
See the Honolulu map on the inside back cover

② Roy's Restaurant

For additional hotels and restaurants, see the Honolulu map on the inside back cover.

Waikiki★★

If you want action, you'll find it here. Once a lounging place for Hawaiian royalty, the 2-mile-long suburb of Waikiki is recognized by the forest of towers created by its hotels, its carnival-like atmosphere, and its nonstop activities and diversions.

Waikiki Beach, stretching 1.5 miles from Ala Wai Canal to Diamond Head, remains one of the best places in the world to learn surfing, a sport invented here hundreds of years ago. At Waikiki Beach Center stands a statue of Duke Kahanamoku *(Kalakaua Ave. near Kaiulani Ave.)*, Hawaii's three-time Olympic swimming champion (1912–1920), who introduced surfing to California and Australia. Non-surfers may ride the waves in an outrigger canoe or take a cruise on a sailboat that casts off right from the shoreline.

Kapiolani Park – Located at the east end of Waikiki, 140-acre Kapiolani Park encompasses the **Honolulu Zoo★** *(see Musts for Kids)* and **Waikiki Shell**, a

venue for open-air concerts and the late-morning *Kodak Hula Show*. You can see denizens of the deep at the compact but well-designed **Waikiki Aquarium★**, also in the park *(see Musts for Kids)*.

International Market Place★

2330 Kalakaua Ave., next to Waikiki Town Center. 808-923-9871. www.internationalmarketplacewaikiki.com. Open year-round daily 10am–10:30pm. Opposite Waikiki Beach, visitors sort through the tacky souvenirs and arts and crafts in the small shops and stands that make up this outdoor marketplace, set under and around the same giant banyan tree for half a century.

Must-See Beaches

Waikiki Beach★★★

On Oahu's south shore, from the Outrigger Canoe Club at 2909 Kalakaua Ave. to Kahanamoku Lagoon at 2005 Kalia Rd.

This 1.5-mile stretch of sand, flanked by high-rise hotels and warm, turquoise waters, is one of the best big-city beaches in the world. It's also one of the most famous, drawing more than four million visitors a year to its high-energy, people-packed shoreline.

Running from the dramatic Diamond Head crater to the Ala Wai Yacht Harbor, the beach was once swampland, referred to by ancient Hawaiians as *Waikiki*, or "spouting water." Today it's a hotbed of activity; if you like to be in the center of the action, this is it. Waikiki Beach offers something for everyone: gentle waters for bathers; big, offshore breaks for surfers; and 80-degree waters for swimming. You can snag a warm patch of soft sand, slather your body with lotion, and spend the day relaxing in the sun. Or pick your pleasure: rent an outrigger canoe, take a surfing lesson (a variety of on-the-beach outfitters offer instruction for all ages), snorkel, play beach volleyball . . . the list is nearly endless. Stop for an ice-cold shave ice on busy **Kalakaua Avenue**, and take in the sights, sounds and smells of this infamous outdoor playground—it's sensory overload, for sure!

> **Touring Tip**
>
> Waikiki is actually a series of connecting beaches; each has its own name and each has something special to offer. For fabulous sunset viewing, head to the beach in front of the Outrigger Reef Hotel. For sea-turtle watching, look offshore near the breakwater in front of the Sheraton Moana Surfrider. Families will appreciate the calm waters in front of the Royal Hawaiian Hotel. For picnics, consider lovely Kapiolani Park *(opposite)* at the foot of Diamond Head.

> **Free For All**
>
> Looking for something fun for the entire family on Waikiki that won't bust the budget? Go to **Sunset on the Beach**, held every Saturday and Sunday evening at Queen's Surf Beach, across from the Honolulu Zoo *(151 Kapahulu Ave.; see Musts for Kids)*. Free open-air movies are shown on a 30-foot-wide screen, set up beachside. There's live music beginning at 4pm, and a variety of local food vendors are on hand, too. *For more information, visit www.sunsetonthebeach.net.*

Hanauma Bay Beach Park★★ – *Off Hwy. 72 in Hanauma Bay.*
See Parks and Natural Sites, and Musts for Outdoor Fun.

Kailua Beach Park★★

East shore, at the end of Kailua Rd.

You'll find this beachy gem on the windward side of the island, just around the corner from Lanikai Beach *(opposite)*. Wide, sloping sands and safe, calm waters make this a perfect place for sunbathing and swimming. There's also good parking, concessions, lifeguards, picnic areas, restrooms and showers on-site, adding to the overall comfort level. Kailua's fine, soft sand stretches for a mile, and the swaying palms and offshore islands in the distance make a post-card-pretty backdrop.

While the setting is serene, there's likely to be a lot of action on the water. Kailua Beach is a world-class windsurfing locale, drawing some of the best in the sport. Pull up your beach chair and take a front-row seat. Or get in on the action yourself; this is a great place to try your hand at the sport. Shops in the nearby town of Kailua offer gear and lessons.

Life's a Beach

Hawaii's beaches are gloriously open to the public, and that includes hotel beaches. Of course, you'll pay for using cabanas and ordering fruity beverages! At most hotel beaches, you'll find lifeguards and loads of facilities; at public beach parks, facilities vary, but restrooms tend to be unsavory. Don't count on lifeguards, either, but look for warning signs and flags to indicate unsafe swimming conditions: a yellow flag means there's a lifeguard on duty; blue means it's dangerous to swim; red means no swimming allowed. You probably won't pay an entrance fee, nor will you pay for parking.

Lanikai Beach★★

In Lanikai, on the east shore. Access via public walkways off Mokulua Dr.

It's no wonder this sun-drenched oasis on Oahu's east shore is a magnet for photographers—and ranks as one of the top beaches in the US. Picture paradise: a white, sandy beach fringed with palm trees and fragrant tropical plants, licked by crystal-clear, aqua-blue surf. That's Lanikai Beach. This nearly mile-long jewel has the added bonus of calm waters, making it perfect for swimming, too.

> **Touring Tip**
>
> A residential neighborhood development sits in front of Lanikai Beach, but you'll find several beach-access walkways off Mokulua Drive. Snag an on-street parking spot where you can.

If you're feeling energetic, you can kayak to the nearby islands of Mokumanu and Mokulua. Bring your binoculars; both islands are great for bird-watching. For a special treat, arrive at Lanikai at dawn for the best view of the rising sun you're likely to see anywhere.

North Shore Beaches★

During the winter months, the seven-mile string of beaches ringing Oahu's northern waters is most famous for its hugely popular surfing venues, including **Waimea Bay**, **Sunset Beach**, and the notorious **Banzai Pipeline**.

Sharks! – If you want the thrill of seeing sharks in the wild, head to **Sharks Cove** on Oahu's north shore. This natural reef is home to white-tipped reef sharks—see if you can spot their fins in the water, but don't try swimming here! The best time to go is between March and October when the seas are relatively calm. In winter, Sharks Cove is a wild place, with 40- to 50-foot swells crashing over the reef.

Giovanni's Shrimp

Beach boys, wave riders, hungry locals and savvy visitors know fresh shrimp (and a good deal!) when they taste it. That's why Giovanni's Shrimp is the favorite nosh on the north shore. You'll find this battered lunch truck parked along Highway 83, between Turtle Bay and Kahuku. Order up a heaping, half-pound plate of farm-raised, broiled Kauai shrimp, then top it with garlic or hot chile sauce. It doesn't get much better than this!

Diamond Head★★

Diamond Head Rd., Waikiki Beach. Open year-round daily 6am–6pm.

You can't miss it: this 760-foot-high natural landmark is a dominating feature in Oahu and, perhaps, one of the most famous craters in the world. Now a state monument, Diamond Head is located at the southern end of Waikiki Beach. The volcanic tuff cone and crater, once the site of an ancient Hawaiian temple, has been extinct for more than 150,000 years.

Early Hawaiians named the crater *leahi*, meaning "brow of the ahi" because they thought the silhouette looked like the brow of a tuna. Legend has it that ancient Hawaiian kings worshiped at the site and that some of the last human sacrifices were performed here.

In the 1800s, British sailors named the crater Diamond Head when they mistook calcite crystals for diamonds shining in the lava rock.

Hiking Diamond Head

Pack your sunscreen, sturdy boots and plenty of water before heading to the base of Diamond Head for the short hike to the summit. The hike is less than 2 miles round-trip but includes some steep sections, and more than 270 steps! About 15–20 minutes into the hike, you'll enter a dark, twisty tunnel (take along a flashlight for safety). You'll see light at the end of the tunnel and then your first set of stairs. Start climbing! There's another short tunnel and another set of stairs before you reach the top observation deck. It's worth every grunt and groan: you'll be rewarded with sweeping views of Oahu's stunning southeast coastline.

Remnants of Fort Ruger, built on the crater in the early 1900s, complete with cannons, an observation deck and tunnels, can still be seen. There's a small picnic area and restrooms at the base.

- **Best reason to visit Diamond Head:** To walk the trail to the summit for jaw-dropping **views**★★★—some of the best on Oahu.

Hanauma Bay Nature Preserve★★

Off Hwy. 72 in Hanauma Bay. 808-396-4229.
www.co.honolulu.hi.us/parks/facility/hanaumabay/index1.htm. Open Jun–Aug Wed–
Mon 6am–7pm (Sat until 10pm). Rest of the year Wed–Mon 6am–6pm. Closed Tue.
$5/person, (free for children ages 12 & under).

This stunningly beautiful horseshoe-shape reef, surrounded by coral sand and the sunken walls of an ancient volcano, is one of America's top beaches and one of the most popular in all Hawaii. Up to 3,000 people visit Hanauma Bay each day to swim in its warm emerald-green waters and snorkel among schools of brilliantly colored tropical fish.

Technically, the reef is now designated a State Underwater Park and Conservation District and strict conservation efforts in recent years have begun to pay off. Feeding fish is now banned at the preserve, and all visitors must watch a mandatory conservation and safety video. The park also limits the number of guests; arrive early in the morning because once the parking lot is full, you'll be turned away.

Snorkeling – The reef is tops for snorkeling year-round (masks, fins and snorkels are available for rent at the visitor center). Here, more than 150 species of fish might flitter around your fins.

Under the Sea

Don't you dare leave the islands without donning a mask and flippers and peering into the deep! Hawaii's reefs are generally smaller and younger than others in the Pacific, but alive and colorful nonetheless. There are about 680 species of fish in the islands and 40 species of reef-building corals. You're likely to see cauliflower coral, lobe coral and finger coral. Look for urchins, sea cucumbers, snails, damselfish, triggerfish, puffers, yellow tangs, snappers and spotted eagle rays. You may also spot some, like the Hawaiian cleaner wrasse and the pebbled and milletseed butterfly fish, which are only found in Hawaii.

Generally, reefs are found off the windward islands of Hawaii, Maui, Oahu and Kauai; barrier reefs can be found in Kaneohe Bay on Oahu and along the south shore of Molokai *(see Musts for Outdoor Fun)*.

Must-See Scenic Drives

See map p 106-107.

Southeast Shore★★

Begin at the town of Waikiki and go east on the H-1 Freeway to Hwy. 72.

This 30-mile loop drive along Oahu's southeast shore features the island's most spectacular scenery and some of its more popular sites. You can do this drive in a half-day, but better to take your time and plan a day for the trip. It will be crowded, typically packed with tour buses and slow-driving visitors—all the more reason to take your time. There are plenty of great stops for swimming and sightseeing along the way.

Head out of Waikiki on H-1 to Highway 72, and follow it east as it curves around the rugged coastline. Your first stop is pretty **Hanauma Bay** *(see Parks and Natural Sites and Musts for Outdoor Fun)*. This protected Marine Reserve features some of the island's best snorkeling.

As you leave the bay and circle around the Koko Head area, the coastline becomes much more rugged, and you'll have fine views of waves crashing against rocky outcrops. About 2 miles past the bay is the turn-off for the **Halona Blowhole**, where the water gushes and spouts through underwater lava tubes and tunnels. A short distance to the northeast you'll find **Sandy Beach**, popular with boogie boarders, bodysurfers and kite flyers *(see Musts for Kids)*. Across the road is **Koko Crater**. Inside the crater are the **Koko Crater Botanical Gardens★** *(see Gardens)*, a nice place to stretch your legs and take in top-of-the-crater views.

As Highway 72 winds around Makapuu Point, up the east coast of Oahu, sweeping vistas open up to the sea and Koolau Range that hugs the coastline. Ready to get out of the car again? Take the short half-hour trail to the summit of Makapuu Point with views of Rabbit Island and beautiful **Makapuu Beach** *(trailhead is located about 1.5mi north of Sandy Beach; park and walk along the service road to the lighthouse)*. Continue north and you'll pass **Sea Life Park★★** *(see Musts for Kids)* and **Waimanalo Beach**, a good place to stop for a swim.

Take the coastal route and you'll end up in the bustling town of Kailua. From here, take Pali Road (Route 61), back to Honolulu, leading across the jagged Koolau Range. A final must-stop along the way is the scenic **Pali Lookout**, with awesome mountain views.

Through the Rain Forest

If you're looking for a short drive that feels worlds away from the hustle and bustle of Honolulu take scenic **Tantalus Drive**. The two-hour excursion, minutes from downtown, takes you through a tropical preserve and the rolling foothills of the Koolau Range. Take the Wilder St. exit off H-1 and follow Wilder to Makiki St. Turn right on Makiki St. and then left on Round Top Dr.; Round Top becomes Tantalus Dr. Continue around to Makiki Heights Rd., and loop back to Makiki St.

You'll climb to about 2,000 feet and have expansive views of downtown Honolulu, Diamond Head, Waikiki and Pearl Harbor. Hikes, through rain forests and thick bamboo stands off Tantalus Drive, range from one hour to a full day. *For trail information, call the Division of Forestry and Wildlife: 808-587-0166.*

Must-See Gardens

Foster Botanical Garden★★

180 N. Vineyard Blvd., Honolulu. 808-522-7066. www.co.honolulu.hi.us/parks/hbg/fbg.htm. Open year-round daily 9am–4pm. Closed Jan 1 & Dec 25. $5.

Garden enthusiasts won't want to miss this 14-acre botanical gem on the north side of Honolulu's Chinatown, a flowery, exotic oasis smack dab in the middle of the city! And where else can you see the nearly extinct wild East African *Gigasipha macrosiphon*, with its evening-opening white flowers? Or the rare native Hawaiian *loulu* palm? Or, how about a double coconut palm that can drop 50-pound nuts? There are plenty of unusual and rare specimens here, all neatly organized according to plant groups.

The more than 150-year-old garden began when German botanist and physician William Hillebrand leased a tract of land from Queen Kalama. Some of the original trees Hillebrand planted are still standing.

Koko Crater Botanical Gardens★

Off Kealahou St. from Hwy. 72, on Koko Head. 808-522-7060. www.hawaiibotanicalgardens.com. Open year-round daily 9am–4pm.

Best part about this place? Even if you're not a gardening aficionado, you'll appreciate the dramatic crater setting. Koko Crater is a volcanic tuff cone,

created some 10,000 years ago. The 60-acre basin is home to a newly developing, hot and dry garden of desert-loving plants. Take the 1.5-mile self-guided walk through the garden, then head over to nearby Sandy Beach to cool off.

> **Touring Tip**
> Pick up the Koko Crater garden guide booklet *(free)* at the entrance before meandering the grounds. Then take one of the free and informative hour-long walking tours, held at 1pm, Monday through Friday.

Lyon Arboretum★

3860 Manoa Rd., Honolulu. 808-988-0465. Open year-round Mon–Sat 9am–3pm. Closed Sun & major holidays. $2.50.

This 193-acre nature preserve showcases more than 5,000 exotic trees and plants found in Hawaii. The woodsy oasis is crisscrossed with walking paths through stands of mountain apple, candlenut trees and taro, and along grand patches of ferns, bromeliads and magnolias. Take the trail up to Inspiration Point for pretty valley views; along the way, stop at the bo tree, a descendant of the tree that Gautama Buddha sat under for enlightenment. Just beyond the arboretum, you'll find the hiking trail to 100-foot **Manoa Falls**.

Senator Fong's Plantation★

47-285 Pulama Rd., off Hwy. 83, Kaneohe. 808-239-6775. www.fonggarden.com. Open year-round daily 10am–4pm. Closed Jan 1 & Dec 25. $14.50.

An open-air tram ride here takes you through the expansive gardens, featuring more than 70 edible varieties of fruits and nuts, 80 different types of palms, slopes of pili grass (once used to make thatch houses), an impressive collection of early Polynesian plants and 100 rare sandlewood trees. When you're not taking in the sights and scents of the flora, take a peek at the Koolau Range and the vast ocean views.

The late Senator Hiram Leong Fong started the gardens as a hobby in the early 1950s, planting exotic flower and fruit trees from around the world. Today the gardens embrace 725 acres, rising from 80 feet to 2,600 feet above sea level. Lei-making classes are offered at the visitor center.

Let Me Lei it on You!

Is there anything more symbolic of Hawaii than the traditional fresh-flower lei? (OK, there's the hula, too.) Look (and sniff!) at the best displays of leis at the stands in **Chinatown★**. Familiar favorites are still made with plumeria, ginger, orchid, ilima and carnation flowers, but you'll see more permanent varieties, too, made with nuts, herbs, seashells and dried leaves.

The origin of the lei can be traced to Hawaii's earliest settlers. The ancient Hawaiians presented leis to their gods during religious ceremonies to insure their blessings. Today, as in the past, leis are given and worn to mark memorable moments in life, special occasions and celebrations. Want to string your own necklace of flowers? Complimentary lei-making lessons are offered at many hotels and resorts throughout Hawaii.

Wahiawa Botanical Garden★

*1396 California Ave., Wahiawa. 802-421-7321. www.co.honolulu.hi.us/parks/hbg/wbg.htm.
Open year-round daily 9am–4pm. Closed Jan 1 & Dec 25.*

Take a deep breath, stop, and smell the . . .
spices! This 27-acre rain-forest garden over-
flows with West Indies spice trees (allspice,
nutmeg, ginger), palms and pom poms—all
tropical plants that require a cool, moist
environment.

Pick up a guided map *(free)* at the information desk; then walk the terraced paths
down into a shady, humid ravine. Bring your
raincoat—the area gets 52 to 80 inches of
rainfall each year.

> **Touring Tip**
>
> Why not make a day of it?
> Stop at Wahiawa Botanical
> Garden on your way to the
> north shore, where you can
> take in the surfing scene at
> **Waimea Bay**, and take the kids
> to **Waimea Valley Audubon
> Center★★** *(see Musts for
> Outdoor Fun).*

Tree Ferns – Wahiawa Botanical Garden also boasts a large collection of tree
ferns, both the Hawaiian variety and tree ferns from other tropical places, such
as Australia and Tasmania. The seeds of large, leafy Hawaiian tree ferns *(Cibo-
tium glaucum)* most likely came to the islands on the wind, millions of years
ago. These ancient plants still form the understory of many of the state's
forests.

Red, White, and Pink

Did you know that more than 5,000 varieties of hibiscus grow in Hawaii, including
a number of natives, like the hau tree with its flowers that change from yellow to
orange, and the sweet-smelling kokio keokeo, which can reach heights of up to
60 feet?

Must-See Museums

Bishop Museum and Planetarium★★★

1525 Bernice St., Honolulu. 808-847-3511. www.bishopmuseum.org. Open year-round daily 9am–5pm. Closed Dec 25. $14.95 adults, $11.95 children (ages 4-12).

If you only have time to see one museum on Oahu, make it this one. Considered one of Hawaii's finest museums, the sprawling Museum of Natural and Cultural History is the state's largest; its collection of Hawaiian and Pacific artifacts is regarded as one of the best in the world.

The museum, founded in 1889 by Charles Reed Bishop in honor of his late wife, Princess Bernice Pauahi Bishop, the last descendant of the royal Kamehameha family, was meant to house the extensive collection of Hawaiian artifacts and royal-family heirlooms of the Princess. Today it boasts more than 187,000 artifacts, documents and photographs relating to Hawaii and other Pacific island cultures.

Beyond the Exhibits: Guided Tours at Bishop Museum

For a great introduction to the Bishop Museum, catch one of the free, 15- or 20-minute guided tours, offered in Hawaiian Hall. Several tours are scheduled throughout the day. Are you interested in native plants and traditional gardening? Show up for the 25-minute tour of the museum's gardens, held twice a day. In addition, live music and dance performances are held daily and free lei-making and hula lessons are offered at the museum's Learning Activity area.

What's What at the Bishop?

Hawaiian Hall★★★ – The three-story Victorian-style gallery houses objects of Hawaiian culture from the Stone Age to the 21C. You can't miss the 55-foot sperm whale suspended from one of the ceilings (a tribute to Hawaii's whaling past) or the magnificent ceremonial robes made from the feathers of thousands of birds.

Polynesian Hall★★ – Two floors are chock-full of artifacts from Pacific cultures across Polynesia, Micronesia and Melanesia that demonstrate daily life, warfare and ceremony.

Natural History Hall★ – Housed in the Castle Building in the modern wing of the museum, this gallery is a favorite among families. You'll get an up-close look at some of Hawaii's rare, endemic birds and insects. Kids will appreciate the hands-on activities specially geared to them.

Kahili Room★ – This small gallery displays an impressive collection of *kahili,* the feather staffs traditionally used at royal ceremonies.

Jhamandas Watumull Planetarium★ – Oahu's only planetarium is a favorite among local and visiting stargazers. What's different about the sky over Hawaii? Find out for yourself in a series of changing shows, included in the museum admission *(daily at 11:30am, 12:30pm, 1pm & 3pm)*. If it's a clear day, head up to the planetarium observatory *(open daily 2:30pm–3:15pm)*.

Honolulu Academy of Arts★★

900 S. Beretania St., Honolulu. 808-536-8700. www.honoluluacademy.org. Open year-round Tue–Sat 10am–4:30pm, Sun 1pm–5pm. Closed Mon & major holidays. $7 adults (free for children ages 12 and under).

This world-class museum boasts more than 34,000 pieces of art and is internationally recognized for its extensive Asian collection—considered one of the finest in the country. Housed in an award-winning Mediterranean-style building, the collections are equally divided between Western and Asian art. More than 30 galleries surround six

landscaped courtyards here. Recently, the museum opened the Henry R. Luce Pavilion, a contemporary wing with two 4,000-square-foot galleries. The new second-floor gallery is home to the museum's permanent collection of traditional Hawaiian art.

Highlights of the Collection

Asian Art★★ – The collection consists of more than 16,000 objects from China, Japan, Korea and Southeast Asia. You'll see some 300 Japanese paintings from the 12C to the 20C. Also of note: Buddhist cave sculpture dating from the 4C to the 10C; the collection of *Scenes of Kyoto*, painted by well-known Japanese artist Kano Motohide; and author James Michener's collection of woodblock prints.

Western Art★★ – There are more than 15,000 works from European and US artists here, including paintings, sculptures, crafts, furniture, textiles and graphic works. Paintings by Paul Cézanne, Vincent Van Gogh, Claude Monet, Henri Matisse and others can be found in the European gallery. You'll also find striking contemporary canvases by Diego Rivera, Georgia O'Keeffe and Philip Guston.

Hawaiian Art★ – This gallery displays indigenous and traditional Hawaiian art and artifacts, from 18C works to contemporary sculpture, paintings and photographs.

Under the Monkey Pod Tree

Bet you worked up an appetite roaming the more than 30 galleries of the Honolulu Academy of Art. No problem. Head to the **Pavilion Café**, popular with locals, and non-museum visitors, too. The open-air eatery serves up fresh-made island dishes (like the warm Big Island goat cheese and Nalo-greens salad) against a backdrop of ferns and palms, swirling fans and teak furniture. Tables overlook gardens, waterfalls, and glass sculptures by Dale Chihuly. Pull up a seat under the shade of the 70-year-old monkey pod tree. *The café is open Tue–Sat 11:30am–2pm; call 808-532-8734 for reservations.*

Shangri La★

Tours depart from the Honolulu Academy of Arts, 900 S. Beretania St., Honolulu. 866-385-3859. www.shangrilahawaii.org. Visit by 2 ½-hour guided tour only, year-round Wed–Sat 8:30am–1:30pm. Closed Sept, Jan 1, Fourth of July, Thanksgiving Day & Dec 25. $25.

Imagine an Islamic palace in Hawaii and you have Shangri La, the private estate of Doris Duke, the wealthy only child of American tobacco baron James Duke. Built in 1937, Shangri La features Duke's eclectic collection of Islamic art, which she amassed over a span of almost 60 years. More than 3,500 objects are displayed throughout the home's exterior and interior spaces, which are exquisitely decorated with painted and gilded wood ceilings, intricate mosaic panels and bright textiles.

Touring Tip

Small, guided tours, which depart from the **Honolulu Academy of Arts**★★ *(p 121)*, are the only way to visit this architectural and artistic gem. Tours start with a look at the Arts of the Islamic World exhibition at the Honolulu Academy of Arts, followed by a 1 ½-hour walk through nearby Shangri La *(Duke's home is a 15-minute minivan ride from the museum).* Be sure to reserve your ticket well in advance.

Mission Houses Museum★★

553 S. King St., at Kawaiahao St., Honolulu. 808-531-0481. www.hawaiimuseums.org. Open year-round Tue–Sat 9am–4pm. Closed Sun, Mon & major holidays. $10.

The pieces of Hawaii's oldest Western-style structure were shipped around Cape Horn from New England and assembled here in 1821 by the first American Calvinist missionaries, with the help of the Hawaiian people. With the coming of the missionaries, Hawaii's culture changed forever. You'll learn how by taking a self-guided or guided tour of these three historic houses, which date from 1821 to 1841. Rooms brim with 19C artifacts of missionary life, including furniture, clothing, decorative arts, photographs and tools.

Polynesian Cultural Center★★

55-370 Kamehameha Hwy. (Rte. 83), Laie. 808-293-3333. www.polynesia.com. Open year-round Mon–Sat 9am–6:30pm. Closed Sun, Thanksgiving Day & Dec 25. $49 adults, $33 children (ages 3-11).

This cultural theme park, founded by the Church of Jesus Christ of Latter-day Saints (the Mormons), is Hawaii's number-one paid attraction. Located on the north shore of Oahu, about 25 miles from downtown Honolulu, the Polynesian Cultural Center features the islands of Hawaii, Samoa, Aotearoa (Maori, New Zealand), Fiji, the Marquesas, Tahiti and Tonga, spread out across a 42-acre setting. You could spend all day here, wandering the individual villages, touring island dwellings and learning about traditional skills. Hands-on activities and demonstrations are held throughout the day. For example, on Hawaii, you can discover the heritage of the hula, practice lei-making, and see how taro is harvested and cooked into poi. On the Marquesas, you can get a temporary tattoo featuring traditional artwork. On Tonga, there are drumming presentations, or try your hand at *tolo* (spear throwing).

Touring Tip

In addition to the authentic island villages, admission to the Cultural Center includes **canoe tours** on the waterways that run through the landscaped property; the **Rainbows of Paradise** water show, performed every afternoon aboard double-hulled canoes; **IMAX** theater shows; and the high-energy evening extravaganza, **Horizons: Where the Sea Meets the Sky**, featuring a cast of over 100 islanders performing traditional Polynesian songs and dances.

The Contemporary Museum★

*2411 Makiki Heights Dr., Honolulu.
808-526-0232. www.tcmhi.org. Open year-
round Tue–Sat 10am–4pm, Sun noon–4pm.
Closed Mon & major holidays. $12 adults
(free for children ages 12 and under).*

Set on 3.5 acres of sculpture and medita-
tion gardens, the Contemporary Museum
displays changing exhibitions of modern
art pieces by leading and emerging contemporary artists. It's worthwhile taking one
of the docent-led tours conducted at 1:30pm each afternoon, which offer background information on the works presented throughout the five galleries. Don't
miss the museum's centerpiece: a creative, environmental installation by David
Hockney (1983) based on his sets for *L'Enfant et les Sortileges,* Ravel's 1925 opera.

Take a Bite

Time your visit to The Contemporary Museum around lunch, so you'll have the perfect
excuse to visit the on-site **Contemporary Café**. The indoor gallery-style dining room
boasts an array of changing artwork. Or sit outside, and enjoy fresh-made salads and
sandwiches in a garden setting *(open Tue–Sat 11:30am–2:30pm, Sun noon–2:30pm; call
808-523-3362 for reservations).*

Hawaii Maritime Center★

*Pier 7, downtown Honolulu. 808-536-6373. www.holoholo.org/maritime. Open year-
round daily 8:30am–5pm. Closed Dec 25. $7.50 adults, $4.50 children (ages 6-17).*

This is one of the top places in the islands to learn about Hawaii's colorful sea-
faring past; it's both entertaining and informative for the entire family. Kids especially enjoy the humpback whale skeleton and the on-going videos of surfing
champions, including old-time surfing great, Duke Kahanamoku. There's also an

impressive 1,805-pound blue
marlin, caught off the coast
of Makaha. Grab a walkman
and a cassette for an audio
tour of the King Kalakaua
Boathouse, where you'll learn
of pirates and kings, shipwrecks and sharks.

The waterfront center, located near the Aloha Tower
(see 105), is home to the
world's only four-masted,
fully rigged ship (walk the
decks!) and a 60-foot double-
hulled sailing canoe.

Must-See Historic Sites

Iolani Palace★★

S. King & Richards Sts., Honolulu. 808-522-0832. www.iolanipalace.org. Open year-round daily 9am–4pm. Self-guided gallery tours $6; guided grand tours $20.

This rococo structure, a dominant feature in downtown Honolulu, is the only royal palace in the United States. If you're intrigued with kings and queens, join the 90-minute docent-led tour of three floors of the four-story palace, with plenty of history provided. You can also roam the galleries on your own for a peek at rare treasures and crown jewels, including the king's crown, studded with 521 diamonds, 54 pearls, 20 opals, 8 emeralds, 8 rubies, and other jewels, as well as a temple drum carved from a coconut tree and decorated with human teeth.

King David Kalakaua, back from travels in Europe, erected the palace in 1882; its last royal occupant was Queen Liliuokalani, whose government was overthrown in 1893. Across King Street stands a statue of Kamehameha the Great. A modern statue of Liliuokalani graces the other side of the palace facing the capitol.

Palace Highlights

Throne Room – Dripping with crimson and gold, the Throne Room hosted many a royal ball and reception over the years. It also served as a meeting place for the House of Representatives from 1893 to 1968, when the Palace served as the Territorial and, later, the State capitol.

State Dining Room – With its ornate, carved sliding doors and three massive sideboards, the dining room was used for State dinners. The Senate Chamber was housed in this room before the new state capitol was completed in 1969.

Coronation Pavilion – Built in 1883 for the coronation of King Kalakaua and Queen Kapiolani, the pavilion stands in the corner of the grounds *(near King & Richards Sts.)*. In more recent times, several of Hawaii's governors were inaugurated here.

Queen Emma Summer Palace

2913 Pali Hwy. 808-595-6291. www.daughtersofhawaii.org.

For another peek into the life of royalty, visit the palace where Emma, wife of King Kamehameha IV, spent her summers. Emma was of Hawaiian-British heritage and thus was an early symbol of cosmopolitanism in the isles. Royal Hawaiian and personal artifacts are displayed in her Victorian-era Nuuanu Valley retreat.

Pearl Harbor★★

6mi west of downtown Honolulu via H-1 Freeway & Kamehameha Hwy. (Rte. 90).

The infamous bay, site of the attack that hurled the United States into World War II, is Hawaii's most popular tourist attraction, drawing nearly 1.5 million visitors each year. A visit will surely stir your patriotic blood. Here on December 7, 1941, more than 2,300 servicemen were killed in a surprise early-morning Japanese air attack on the US naval fleet anchored in the bay. Eighteen ships, including six battleships and three destroyers, sank in America's greatest military disaster. President Franklin Roosevelt declared it "a date which will live in infamy" as he plunged the nation into World War II. The harbor is still surrounded by active military bases, but it also includes three must-see visitor sites.

USS Arizona Memorial★★

1 Arizona Memorial Dr., Honolulu. 808-422-0561. www.nps.gov/usar. Open year-round daily 7:30am–5pm. Closed Jan 1, Thanksgiving Day & Dec 25.

Perhaps no war memorial is more poignant than the USS *Arizona*. Floating over the hulk of a sunken battleship, the concave, 184-foot white-concrete bridge marks the permanent tomb of 1,177 sailors killed in the Pearl Harbor attack. Each victim's name is inscribed in white marble on one wall. The macabre outline of the ship's hull is visible below. Launches depart on a first-come, first-served basis from a shoreline visitor center, where historical exhibits and a 25-minute documentary film are presented. This is a very popular site; be prepared to wait in line up to an hour or more.

Visiting the USS Arizona Memorial

No matter what time of year you go, you'll run into mobs of tourists. Boat-launch tickets can run out by noon, and waits at the launch can be as long as two hours. The tickets are given on a first-come, first-served basis and each individual must pick up his/her own ticket.

Your best bet: Show up when the visitor center opens at 7:30am to pick up boat-launch tickets, then browse the exhibits and museum gift shop while you wait. If you don't want to battle traffic on the road, the **Arizona Memorial Shuttle Bus** *(808-839-0911)* picks up passengers from most major Waikiki hotels for a nominal fee. Skip the advertised boat tours of Pearl Harbor; they don't land at the visitor center or tour the USS *Arizona*.

USS Bowfin Submarine Museum & Park★

11 Arizona Memorial Dr., Honolulu. 808-423-1341. www.bowfin.org. Open year-round daily 8am–5pm (last tour of submarine at 4:30pm). Closed Jan 1, Thanksgiving Day & Dec 25. Submarine & museum tour $8 adults, $3 children (ages 4-12). Museum only $4 adults, $2 children. Children under age 4 are not permitted on the submarine, but may visit the museum and mini-theater at no charge. Tickets and trolley shuttles to the Battleship Missouri Memorial (below) are available here.

A walk through the *Bowfin*, credited with sinking 44 Japanese ships, helps define the claustrophobia of submarine missions. Visitors are given cassette players narrating their tour through the cramped spaces. The additional 10,000-square-foot on-site museum showcases submarine life with a collection of artifacts, weapons, missiles and memorabilia.

Waterfront Memorial – Honors the 52 American submarines and the more than 3,500 submariners lost during World War II.

Battleship Missouri Memorial★

11 Arizona Memorial Dr., Honolulu. Access only by shuttle bus from the USS Bowfin Submarine Museum and Park; tickets and trolley shuttles are available there. 808-423-1341. www.ussmissouri.com. Open year-round daily 9am–5pm (ticket window closes at 4pm). Closed Jan 1, Thanksgiving Day & Dec 25. Guided tour $22 adults, $14 children. Museum only $16 adults, $8 children.

This historic battleship, docked near the remains of the USS *Arizona*, features the site of the September 2, 1945 surrender that ended World War II. The six-deck ship is chock-full of models, maps, photographs and other exhibits. You can meander through the rooms, including the gunfire-control station, mess deck, galley, bakery, ship's store and sleeping area, and browse the exhibits. But you'll get more out of the visit if you sign up for the one-hour guided tour. Tour guests also get to experience a flight simulation of the assault on Iwo Jima in 1943 aboard a plane that was launched from the deck of the *Missouri*.

> **Touring Tip**
>
> History doesn't have to be boring! Have your kids pick up a free Junior Ranger booklet at the front desk of the USS *Arizona* Memorial Visitor Center. The fun-filled book, best for ages 7 to 12, guides kids through the events of the infamous attack on Pearl Harbor, with colorful photos, sketches and activities. Added bonus: They get a Junior Ranger badge when they complete the book.

National Memorial Cemetery of the Pacific★

2177 Puowaina Dr., Honolulu. 808-532-3720. www.cem.va.gov/nchp/nmcp.htm. Open year-round daily Mar–Sept 8am–6:30pm. Rest of the year daily 8am–5:30pm. Closed Federal holidays except Memorial Day & Veteran's Day.

Occupying an extinct crater known simply as The Punchbowl, the "Arlington of the Pacific" (a reference to Arlington National Cemetery in Virginia) is the final resting place for more than 40,000 US military men and others whom the government has honored. Many come to visit the graves of World War II correspondent Ernie Pyle and Hawaii astronaut Ellison Onizuka, who died in the Challenger space-shuttle disaster of 1986.

The Punchbowl – The crater in which the cemetery rests was formed between 75,000 and 100,000 years ago. Ironically, the site's Hawaiian name, *Puowaina*, translates to "Hill of Sacrifice"; ancient islanders once offered human sacrifices to the gods here.

Waikiki's Historic Resort Tours

Join Tony Bisson for the popular—and free—tour of the historic 100-year-old **Sheraton Moana Surfrider Hotel**, offered at 11am and 5pm every Monday, Wednesday and Friday *(2365 Kalakaua Ave., Honolulu; see Must Stay)*. Along with a peek at this turn-of-the-century icon—Waikiki's first beach resort—you'll hear funny insider tales of life on Oahu and of Tony's experiences as a "coin diver." Ask him about his friend who dove for a $100 bill wrapped around a quarter that was thrown into the water by Frank Sinatra.

Musts For Fun

Surfing as a Spectator Sport★★

Surf's up! No trip to Oahu would be complete without watching the rip-roaring antics and athleticism of the island's top surfers. Oahu is touted as the surfing capital of the world, renowned for its big-water beaches, high-profile championships, and famous surfing personalities. The waters off Oahu feature 600 different types of surf breaks, offering gentle breaks for beginners and formidable surf for the most experienced wave riders. For the best shows, head to Oahu's north shore.

Sunset Beach – *North of Waimea, on the north shore.* Here you'll find a pretty two-mile band of sand and some of the best surfers in the world. Throw your blanket down, take a seat, and watch the show. You're likely to see talented surfers riding powerful, 15-foot and higher waves. Technically, this entire stretch of sand is Sunset Beach, but surfers divide it up according to surf break, with names like Gas Chambers, Back Doors, Off-The-Wall, Cloud Break, Pele's Followers, and the renowned Banzai Pipeline. Oh, and the sunsets here are awesome, too.

Waimea Bay – *South of Sunset Beach, on the north shore.* The beach at Waimea boasts the longest rideable surf break in the world. Spectators crowd the sands during the winter months when the surf is at its highest. Ironically, during the summer the water is generally calm and the beach is a fine swimming spot—but if the surf is up, be careful!

Sun, Surf and Snow Cones

All that sun and surf pique your thirst? While you're on the north shore, head to **Matsumoto's** (*66-087 Kamehameha Hwy.; 808-637-4827; www.matsumotoshaveice.com*) near the town of Haleiwa for what's known as the best shave ice on the island. Mamoro Matsumoto and his wife, Helen, have been serving up shave ice here (sometimes more than 1,000 a day) since 1951. Try the local favorite: shave ice, ice cream, and red beans.

Drinks with a View

For an unforgettable birds-eye view of Waikiki Beach and downtown Honolulu, head to the **Honohono Restaurant**, perched on the 30th floor of the Sheraton Waikiki hotel *(2255 Kalakaua Ave.; 808-931-8383; www.sheraton-waikiki.com)*. No need to splurge on dinner at the pricey, upscale restaurant (unless you want to!). Instead, grab a seat at the bar, order your favorite tropical beverage, and take in the sweeping views of the beach below. There's live entertainment nightly, and dancing, too.

Take a Sunset Cruise

There are few things more romantic than a sunset cruise along the Oahu coastline. You'll slip past world-famous Diamond Head and along the sparkling Kohala Gold Coast, with the rolling Koolau mountains as a backdrop. Take your loved one out on the open deck, where you'll be caressed by balmy tropical winds and treated to a view of the postcard-pretty purple-and-pink-streaked sky. Watch the twinkling lights of Waikiki Beach and Honolulu dot the landscape, as the sun heads for the other side of the world.

Contact the **Oahu Visitors Center** *(877-525-6248; www.visit-oahu.com)* for a list of companies offering cruises. Most feature dinner and entertainment, and cost about $50 to $60.

Fabulous Freebie

There's no need to spend money on a Honolulu city tour; instead, sign up for a free walking tour, hosted by the Native Hawaii Hospitality Association. You'll hear historic legends and color-ful stories on the **Native Hawaiian Culture tour**. The two-hour excursion, conducted by a native Hawaiian, also includes a guided walk through the **Bishop Museum★★★** *(see Museums)*. On the two-hour **Queen's Tour**, you'll walk portions of the Waikiki Historic Trail. *For more information and reservations, call 808-737-6442 or visit www.waikikihistorictrail.com.*

Tea Traditions

Has all that Waikiki hustle and bustle got you frazzled? Here's a quick (and cheap) cure: participate in the traditional tea ceremony at the **Urasenke Tea House** in Waikiki *(245 Saratoga Rd.; 808-923-3059)*. The soothing, centuries-old ceremony is held from 10am to noon on Wednesday and Friday. Everyone is welcome *($3 donation suggested)*. Aaah, this is mindfulness.

Musts For Outdoor Fun

Waimea Valley Audubon Center★★

59-864 Kamehameha Hwy., Haleiwa. 808-638-9199. www.audubon.org. Open year-round daily 9:30am–5pm. Closed Jan 1 & Dec 25 (park closes at 3pm on Thanksgiving Day & Dec 31). $8 adults, $5 children (ages 4-12).

This tranquil 1,875-acre oasis, nestled in the lush Waimea Valley on Oahu's north shore, offers a peaceful escape from the concrete jungle and never-ending action of Honolulu and Waikiki Beach. It's also a great place to learn about ancient Hawaiian culture and natural history; there's a spiderweb of nature trails to meander on your own, some leading to archaeological sites.

Botanical Gardens – You could spend hours roaming the park's colorful gardens, including more than 5,000 species of plants spread across 36 themed areas and covering 150 acres. Pick up a map and pamphlet at the visitor center to help guide you through the gardens; plants from around the world, including native Hawaiian collections and rare species, are identified with small signs. Or sign up for a one-hour guided tour, offered at 2pm on Thursday and Sunday. Once-a-month full-moon night walks are sometimes offered, too.

Waimea Falls – Be sure to save time for a walk to Waimea Falls, the spectacular centerpiece of the preserve. A 3.5-mile self-guided hike leads to the 40-foot-high falls. Stand back and take a good look: do you think the falls form the shape of a woman? Some locals think so and have thus nicknamed the waters "Wahine Falls" (*wahine* is the Hawaiian word for woman). Pack your bathing suit; swimming in the crystal-clear pools is allowed when the weather and winds cooperate (lifeguards are on duty).

Luau, Anyone?

This outdoor feast—complete with a kalua pig roasted in an *imu* (underground oven)—may be the best way to hear traditional tunes and sample typical Island foods. Expect to be served poi (taro-root paste, offered fresh or fermented), *laulau* (steamed meat, fish and taro leaves wrapped in ti leaves), *lomi-lomi* (salted salmon mixed with tomatoes and onions) and *haupia* (coconut pudding).

Snorkel at Hanauma Bay★★

Off Hwy. 72, Hanauma Bay (10mi east of Wailkiki). 808-396-4229. www.co.honolulu.hi.us/parks/ facility/hanaumabay. Open Jun– Aug Wed–Mon 6am–7pm (Sat until 10pm). Rest of the year Wed–Mon 6am–6pm. Closed Tue. $5 (free for children ages 12 and under).

Crystal-clear, turquoise-blue Hanauma Bay is one of the best places in the islands for snorkeling. The underwater treasure, now a designated marine conservation district, teems with some 400,000 tropical fish (more than 150 species) that swim around the impressive reef and coral formations. Don your masks and fins (rentals are available on-site) and swim with colorful parrotfish, tangs, Moorish idols, butterfly fish and more. A snowy white beach ringing the half-mile horseshoe-shape bay, and flanking volcanic cliffs are scenic bonuses.

Marine Education Center – When you need a break from snorkeling and swimming, check out the recently opened Marine Education Center at the park, featuring programs and exhibits on the history of the bay and conservation efforts.

Touring Tip

Alas, Hanauma Bay is not an undiscovered gem. Located on the southeastern shore of Oahu, about a 30-minute drive from Honolulu, this place is hugely popular. The park now limits the number of people admitted each day; arrive early in the morning to snag a parking spot and admittance. Facilities at the beach park include restrooms, showers, concessions and equipment rentals.

Made in Hawaii

Visiting Oahu in late August? You're in luck. The annual three-day Made in Hawaii Festival showcases Hawaii-made items, created by more than 300 companies—all displayed under one roof at the Neal S. Blaisdell Center in Honolulu *(777 Ward Ave)*. There are cooking demos and live music, too. *For more information, contact the Hawaii Food Industry Association at 808-533-1292 or www.madeinhawaiifestival.com.*

Camping on Oahu

Hey, all you campers out there! Oahu has several state and county park campgrounds that sure beat the price of an upscale hotel.

State park campgrounds include the 5,228-acre **Malaekahana Beach** *(off Hwy. 83)* and the 110-acre **Kahana Valley** *(52-222 Hwy. 83, Kahana)*, both with swimming, picnic areas and hiking trails. Near Honolulu, **Keaiwa Heiau State Recreation Area** *(end of Aiea Heights Dr., Aiea)* offers rustic camping, and **Sand Island State Recreation Area** *(end of Sand Island Access Rd., off Hwy. 92, Honolulu)* offers 14 acres of camping along the coast.

Golf Oahu

Decisions, decisions. Oahu brims with top-notch golf courses, so where does a discerning duffer begin? You can't go wrong with these highly-rated links:

Ala Wai Municipal Golf Course – *404 Kapahulu Ave., Honolulu. 808-296-2000. www.co.honolulu.hi.us/des/golf/alawai.htm*. If you like company, consider this municipal course; it's in the Guinness Book of Records for being the busiest links in the world.

Hawaii Kai – *8902 Kalanianaole Hwy., Honolulu. 808-395-2358. www.hawaiikaigolf.com*. You'll revel in splendid views of the Pacific Ocean and Makapuu Cliffs at this 6,614-yard, 18-hole championship course.

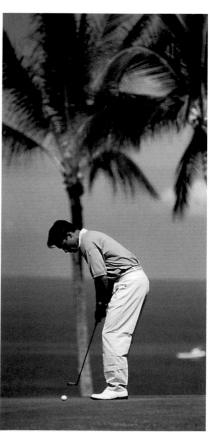

Koolau Golf Club – *45-550 Kionaole Rd., Kaneohe. 808-247-7088. www.koolau.americangolf.com.* Ready for a real challenge? The US Golf Association deems Koolau the toughest course in the country.

Koolina Golf Course – *92-1220 Aliinui Dr., Kapolei. 808-676-5300. www.koolinagolf.com.* This 6,867-yard Ted Robinson design is ranked among the top courses on the island.

Turtle Bay Resort – *57-091 Kamehameha Hwy., Kahuku. 808-293-8574. www.turtlebayresort.com.* Boasting 36 holes of championship golf, including an 18-hole course designed by Arnold Palmer and Ed Seay, Turtle Bay challenges all skill levels with five to six sets of tees on each hole.

How Did Surfing Begin?

Surfboarding, or wave riding, was an integral part of the ancient Hawaiian culture. By the time Captain Cook arrived on the islands in 1778, surf boarding was widespread, and an important aspect of sacred and religious ceremonies and practices. However, when the Europeans came to settle in the islands, Hawaiian culture, including surfing, began to die out. By the turn of the 20C, surfing had all but disappeared. It wasn't until Jack London visited Waikiki and wrote about the sport in 1907, and Alexander Hume Ford founded the Hawaiian Outrigger Canoe Club in 1908, that surfing began its modern-day resurgence.

A few years later, Duke Paoa Kahanamoku put the sport of surfing on the map for good. Duke was a famous Olympic gold-medal swimmer—and avid surfer. Known as "the fastest swimmer alive," Duke used his fame to introduce the world to surfing. Today, he's known as "the father of surfing," and you'll find tributes to him throughout the islands, including the famous Duke statue on Waikiki Beach and the popular **Duke's Canoe Club** bar and restaurant at the Outrigger Waikiki Hotel in Honolulu *(2335 Kalakaua Ave.; see Must Eat)* and on the island of Kauai *(on Kalapaki Beach, in front of the Kauai Marriott Resort; 808-246-9599; www.dukeskauai.com).*

Musts For Kids

Sea Life Park★★

41-202 Kalanianaole Hwy., Waimanalo. 866-365-7446. www.sealifeparkhawaii.com. Open year-round daily 9:30am–5pm. $24.96 adults, $12.48 children (ages 4-12).

Ever wonder what lurks under Hawaiian waters? Step into this popular attraction and you'll get a first hand—and close-up—look. The oceanfront marine park sits on scenic Makapuu Point, 20 miles outside Honolulu on the windward coast. Just inside the gates, you'll see the impressive 300,000-gallon aquarium, home to more than 2,000 species of marine life. Watch as huge schools of neon-colored tropical fish, sea turtles, eels and sharks swim by in the 18-foot-high **Hawaiian Reef Tank**. Stop by the sea lion feeding pool and the sea turtle lagoon, then make your way to the stingray exhibit, where you can watch the slinky black creatures slide through the water—and touch them, if you wish.

Entertaining dolphin and sea lion shows are presented throughout the day, and the park offers a number of special tours. Have you always wanted to train dolphins? Would you like to swim alongside a school of stingrays? Here's your chance; behind-the-scene programs are offered daily (for an extra fee).

Swim Little Turtles, Swim!

The sea turtle lagoon at the Sea Life Park on Oahu doubles as a breeding sanctuary for threatened Hawaiian green sea turtles. To date, 2,200 hatchlings have been produced in the park lagoon and released into the wild.

The cold-blooded reptile gets its name from the color of its body fat, which turns green from the algae it eats. Once plentiful on the islands and heavily hunted by natives, the Hawaiian green sea turtle is now protected by law. Over 90 percent of the nesting of these island reptiles now occurs inside the National Wildlife Refuge at French Frigate Shoals.

Honolulu Zoo★

In Kapiolani Park, 151 Kapahulu Ave. (between Diamond Head & Waikiki), Honolulu. 808-971-7171. www.honoluluzoo.org. Open year-round daily 9am–4:30pm. Closed Jan 1 & Dec 25. $6 adults, $1 children (ages 1-6).

Kids and animals—this is one combination where you can't go wrong! Make a beeline for the Diamond Head side of town to this small but sure-to-please zoo, home to more than 1,200 animals. The zoo stretches over 42 flat acres in Kapiolani Park; you can see the entire place in half a day— then, off to the beach! Kids and adults alike vote the **Kabuni Reserve** as their favorite area. This African Savannah habitat covers 12 acres, where you can walk along a path and peer at free-roaming zebra, rhinos, lions, hippos, giraffes, chimps and more. Don't miss the tropical forest, the Galapagos tortoises, and the reptile house. Chances are you haven't spotted Hawaii's state bird in the wild, but you'll see them here; rare nene birds *(see p 62)* waddle around the zoo, chirping happily.

Kualoa Ranch★

49-560 Kamehameha Hwy., Kaaawa. 808-237-7321. www.kualoa.com. Open year-round daily 8am–5pm. Closed Jan 1 & Dec 25. Ranch and movie set tour, $15. Other prices vary, depending on activity.

The ropin', the ridin', the shootin'—yee haw! Play cowpoke for a day at this authentic working ranch, sitting on 4,000 acres on Oahu's north shore, about an hour from Honolulu. The property is stunning, encompassing three mountains and two valleys, spreading from steep mountain cliffs to the seashore. Of course, your kids won't care much about the views, but they will enjoy horseback riding (pony rides for ages 3-7), ATV trail rides, kayak trips to Secret Island, and ranch tours. If the scenery looks familiar, it's because Kualoa Ranch has been used as a backdrop for several movies, including *Jurassic Park, Mighty Joe, Pearl Harbor, Windtalkers*, and *Along Came Polly*.

Go Fly A Kite

Why not combine a day at the beach with some kite flying? **Sandy Beach** on Oahu's east shore is considered the kite-flying capital of the islands. Look up and you'll see blue skies, wispy clouds, and a riot of colorful wings and tails. There's plenty of action in the water, here, too. The wild shore break and big swells make it a favorite among body boarders and surfers. Bring a picnic and enjoy the show!

Waikiki Aquarium★

*In Kapiolani Park, 2777 Kalakaua Ave., Honolulu. 808-923-9741.
http://waquarium.otted.hawaii.edu. Open year-round daily 9am–4:30pm.
Closed Dec 25; limited hours Jan 1 & Thanksgiving Day. $9 adults, $4 youth (ages 13-17),
$2 children (ages 5-12).*

Dating back to 1904, the second-oldest public aquarium in the country showcases more than 2,500 underwater animals at its location on the Diamond Head end of Waikiki Beach. Here, you'll see slinky sea jellies, skinny moray eels, living corals, and giant, two-foot-long clams, the largest in the world. Kids love the **Hunters on the Reef** exhibit, where they get a close look at hungry reef sharks circling the tank. The tide-pool area and the outdoor tank, home to a couple of endangered and oh-so-cute monk seals, are also popular.

Take in a show at the Sea Visions Theater (several are held daily), or sign up for day and night reef walks, behind-the-scenes programs, and diving and snorkeling trips.

Some Fish With Your Meal

Mealtime at the **Oceanarium Restaurant** at the Pacific Beach Hotel in Honolulu *(2490 Kalakaua Ave.; 808-922-1233; www.pacificbeachhotel.com)* is sure to entertain your little ones. The restaurant's centerpiece is a three-story, 280,000-gallon aquarium, showcasing more than 400 fish. Divers feed the fish during lunch and dinner hours for added excitement. Can anyone find the spotted eagle ray?

Hawaii Children's Discovery Center

*111 Ohe St., Honolulu. 808-524-5437. www.discoverycenter
hawaii.org. Open year-round Tue–Fri 9am–1pm, weekends 10am–3pm. Closed Mon, Sept 7–20, Jan 1, Easter
Sunday & Dec 25. $8 adults, $6.75 children (ages 2-17).*

If you have little ones in tow and need to get out of the sun for a while, check out the Discovery Center, located across the street from Kakaako Waterfront Park. You'll find four galleries of please-touch exhibits where kids can pretend to be firefighters, bankers or mechanics, make rainbows, and learn about other cultures. There's even a special play area for the under-five set.

Must Go: Performing Arts

Hawaii Opera Theatre

987 Waimanu St., Honolulu. 800-836-7372. Box Office: 808-596-7858. www.hawaiiopera.org. Season runs Jan–March. Ticket prices vary.

Grand opera in the middle of the Pacific? You bet. The Hawaii Opera Theatre, HOT for short, has never been hotter! Recent productions (*La Bohème, The Merry Widow, The Flying Dutchman*) held at the 2,000-seat **Neil S. Blaisdell Concert Hall** *(777 Ward Ave.)*, have received international recognition. Of special note: The concert hall's lyric captioning system allows the audience to follow the story line in English.

Hawaii Theatre

1130 Bethel St., Honolulu. Box Office: 808-528-0506. www.hawaiitheatre.com.

You'll find top-notch music, theater, film and dance performances at Honolulu's historic Hawaii Theater. Built in 1922, the 1,400-seat hall, dubbed the "Pride of the Pacific," has been a landmark venue in downtown Honolulu for more than eight decades. The theater reigned as a grand movie palace from the 1930s to 50s. By the 1980s, however, the venue sat derelict and decaying until a group of citizens stepped in to save it. Hawaii Theatre reopened in 1996 after a six-year restoration, returned to its former Beaux-Arts glory, and its acoustics kicked-up with modern technology and design. The lovely Lionel Walden mural, the *Glorification of Diana*, now restored, still decorates the proscenium arch above the stage.

One-hour guided tours, highlighting the architecture and history of the performance hall, are offered weekly; tours include a demonstration of the theater's impressive Robert Morton pipe organ.

Touring Tip

The best way to tap into local culture: time your visit to coincide with an "Only in Hawaii" event. Tops in this category include the annual Merrie Monarch Festival on the Big Island, the Ki Ho'alu Slack Key Guitar and Ukulele Concert series on Kauai, and the Friday concerts by the Royal Hawaiian Band *(opposite)* on the grounds of Iolani Palace on Oahu. *See Calendar of Events for other options.*

Honolulu Symphony Orchestra

777 Ward Ave., Honolulu. 809-792-2000. Box Office: 808-591-2211.
www.honolulusymphony.com. Season runs Sept–May. Season, half-season,
and single tickets available.

Founded in 1900, this well-regarded group is the oldest American orchestra
west of the Rockies. Director Samuel Wong woos top international artists to
the Neal S. Blaisdell Concert Hall, to perform classical works by Bernstein,
Dvorak, Mozart, Gershwin and others. The symphony also pays tribute to the
cultural roots of Hawaii, working the Chinese lute and Japanese taiko drums
into the repertoire.

The grammy-nominated Honolulu Symphony Pops blends an exciting mix of
classical and pop music, bringing in guest stars such as Burt Bacharach, Diane
Reeves, Arturo Sandoval and Kealii Reichel.

Royal Hawaiian Band

If you happen to be king and like music, what do you do? You create a band, by royal
decree. That's what King Kamehameha III did in 1836, and the band plays on. Today the
Royal Hawaiian Band is an agency of the city and county of Honolulu and the only
full-time municipal band in the US. For a delightful earful of traditional island music,
check out the band's free concerts, held Fridays from noon to 1pm at the Coronation
Pavilion at **Iolani Palace**★★ *(S. King & Richard Sts.; see Historic Sites).* The band
also plays several times a week at various locations throughout the city. *For more
information and a schedule of appearances, call 808-922-5331 or check online at
www.royalhawaiianband.com.*

Must Shop

Chinatown★

West of Nuuanu Ave., between Ala Moana & Vineyard Blvds., Honolulu. 808-521-4934. www.chinatownhi.com. Outside vendors open year-round daily, 8:30am–5pm.

This fascinating 15-block historic enclave—said to be the oldest Chinatown in the country—is a colorful, eclectic place to roam, shop and eat. The ethnic neighborhood, dating back more than 120 years, was once worn down and seedy. Today, the revitalized district buzzes with energy and brims with local color and culture. Browse the sidewalk markets that overflow with exotic fruits, flowers (this is *the* place to buy a lei!) and foodstuffs.

When hunger strikes, stop at **Legend Seafood Restaurant** (*100 N. Beretania St.; 808-532-1868*) for some of the best dim sum you'll find in the islands.

Celebrate Chinatown – To really experience Chinatown, visit during one of the neighborhood's annual festivals. Here are a few to choose from:

- **Night in Chinatown** – Kick off the Chinese New Year at this annual street fair *(on Mauakea St., from Beretania St. to King St.)*, which features food, arts and crafts, music and dancing.

- **Narcissus Festival** – *808-533-31818 or www.ccchi.org/narcissus/index.html.* Started in 1950 to showcase Chinese art and culture, the Narcissus Festival is the oldest ethnic festival in Hawaii. The celebration is held in conjunction with the Chinese lunar New Year.

- **Dragon Boat Festival** – *808-595-6417 or www.idealhawaii.com.* Dragon boat races are the main reason to attend this traditional summertime event, held to drive off evil spirits. Crews in colorfully painted dragon-headed canoes challenge each other to the rhythm of beating drums.

Best Source for Aloha Wear

Established in 1963, **Hilo Hattie** (*808-535-6500; www.hilohatties.com*), with stores scattered throughout the islands, remains one of the best places to buy Aloha wear and island-made fashions. For the widest selection and prices, visit the flagship store and manufacturing facility in Honolulu *(700 N. Nimitz Hwy.)*. It's open from 8am to 6pm, 365 days a year.

Ala Moana Shopping Center

1450 Ala Moana Blvd., Waikiki. 808-946-2811. www.alamoana.com. Open year-round Mon–Sat 9:30am–9pm, Sun 10am–7pm. Closed Dec 25.

Hawaii's largest open-air mall boasts more than 240 stores. Located in the heart of Waikiki, overlooking Ala Moana Beach Park, this shopping venue is always bustling. Serious shoppers will find retail biggies like Macy's and Neiman Marcus, as well as a collection of top-name designers—Escada, DKNY, Prada, Gucci, and Hermès. There are also several stores specializing in Hawaiian-made products and island wear.

Even if you're not looking to buy, this is a great place to hang out. The outdoor space is opulently landscaped, and there are plenty of places to grab a bite to eat, from the food court to fine dining. Take in some free entertainment while you're at the mall; more than 500 performances and special events are held here throughout the year.

Take a Trolley

You want to shop, but the rest of your group wants to sunbathe. Go ahead, leave them the car and hop on one of the island's trolleys. The open-air trolleys travel from major hotels to the big malls in Honolulu and Waikiki, stopping at top attractions along the way. For schedules and routes, contact The Trolley Company *(800-824-8804; www.waikikitrolley.com)*. A one-day pass costs $25 and offers unlimited on-and-off boarding. You can pick up a **Waikiki Trolley Map Guide** at the Royal Hawaiian and Ala Moana malls, as well as at many hotels.

Aloha Stadium Swap Meet

Aloha Stadium, 99-500 Salt Lake Blvd., Honolulu. 808-488-0924. www.alohastadium.hawaii. gov/events/swapmeet.html. Open year-round Wed, Sat & Sun 6am–3pm. Closed Dec 25, and at 1pm on days when University of Hawaii football games are scheduled.

If you're looking for a bargain and consider haggling a sport, don't miss this popular outdoor flea market held outside the University of Hawaii's Aloha football stadium. Hordes of people gather around the stalls of vendors, bargaining for arts and crafts, souvenirs, housewares and knick-knacks. It's a fun atmosphere and a great place to rub elbows with the locals.

Aloha Tower Marketplace

Pier 9, downtown Honolulu. 808-528-5700. www.alohatower.com. Retail shops open Mon–Sat 9am–9pm, Sun 9am–6pm. Special holiday hours apply on Thanksgiving Day & Dec 25.

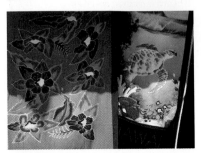

You can't miss this entertainment, dining and shopping complex, wrapped around the imposing **Aloha Tower★** landmark *(see Cities/Honolulu)*. And you can't beat the location, sitting on downtown Honolulu's pretty oceanfront harbor.

This is a popular place to hang out, pick up souvenirs and sundries, and grab a bite to eat. Stores run the gamut from gift, apparel, home furnishings and jewelry shops. With its array of casual restaurants and bars, the marketplace is a lively place both day and night.

Sweet Souvenirs

If you're craving those chocolate-covered macadamia nuts, visit the **Menehune Mac Factory Gift Center** *(707-A Waiakamilo Rd.; 808-841-3344; www.menehunemac.com)*. Buy some for munching immediately (who can resist?), then stock up on handmade chocolates, kaiulani spices, Hawaiian pasta and island-made jams and jellies to take home.

Royal Hawaiian Shopping Center

2201 Kalakaua Ave., Waikiki. 808-922-0588. www.royalhawaiianshoppingcenter.com. Open year-round daily 10am–10pm. www.shopwaikiki.com. Special holiday hours apply on Thanksgiving Day & Dec 25.

Located in the heart of Waikiki, within walking distance of most major hotels, this is one of Hawaii's largest malls, stretching over two blocks with more than 150 shops. Whatever you want, you'll find it here, from tacky to tony. Upscale boutiques are scattered among souvenir shops, arts and crafts, sundries and convenience stores.

Check out the free hula, ukulele and lei-making lessons, a big draw at Royal Hawaiian center. Why not learn a traditional island craft, while the others are spending their vacation money? Torch-lighting ceremonies and Polynesian cultural shows are also held throughout the week.

Before You Leave the Royal Hawaiian

. . . Venture up Nuuanu Street, north of Hotel Street, where you'll find a collection of contemporary art galleries. This newly revived neighborhood, dubbed **NoHo** (for North of Hotel Street) by the locals, is fast-becoming the hottest art scene in town.

Must Be Seen: Nightlife

Barefoot Bar at Duke's Waikiki

2335 Kalakauna Ave., Waikiki Beach. 808-922-2268. www.dukeswaikiki.com.

This classic beach-boy bar, named in honor of surfing legend Duke Kahanamoku, overlooks busy Waikiki Beach. The koa-wood-paneled room is chock-full of surfing memorabilia, including an outrigger canoe, antique surfboards and posters. It's a fun, casual vibe, with live Hawaiian entertainment nightly. For late-night noshing, there's a bar menu available until midnight with pizza, sandwiches, salads and burgers.

Chai's Island Bistro

Aloha Tower Marketplace, Pier 9, downtown Honolulu. 808-585-0011. www.chaisislandbistro.com.

Combine fabulous Hawaiian regional and Pacific Rim food with live, local entertainment and you have the winning combination of this upscale night spot on Waikiki Beach. Crowds flock to Chai's nightly to hear the hottest new musicians in Hawaii. Come later on Saturday night *(10pm–2am)* for DJ tunes, dancing, and free pupu (the Hawaiian term for appetizers).

A Night on the Town—Without the Kids

Looking for a little adult alone-time? The **Hawaii Tourist Network** *(800-833-4609; www.tourismpartners.org/hawaii)* has a group of qualified nannies and experienced babysitters available. All sitters are 21 years or older and certified in child/infant CPR and basic first-aid. You can schedule a sitter up to two months in advance, but you can often book sitters at the last minute, too. Cost is $25 an hour *(3-hour minimum)*; discounted daily rates are available.

Mai Tai Bar

1450 Ala Moana Blvd., in the Ala Moana Shopping Center, Honolulu. 808-947-2900. www.maitaibar.com.

You'll find plenty of action at this popular bar, perched over the Ala Moana Shopping Center *(see p 141)*. It's a great place to hear live music, and locals cram the airy, tropical bar during late afternoon Happy Hour. Sink into a cushy couch and sip one of their signature mai tais—made with three types of rum and fresh-squeezed fruit juices—as you listen to island rhythms.

Ocean Club

500 Ala Moana Blvd., downtown Honolulu. 808-531-8444. www.oceanclubonline.com.

The ultra-sleek Ocean Club, sporting rich mahogany woods, tile floors and steel accents, is one of Honolulu's hottest venues for Happy-Hour noshing (when the fresh pupu items go for half-price) and late-night dancing. A sophisticated group gathers early; when the DJ starts spinning hip hop later in the evening, the bar draws an under-30 crowd. Dancing goes on until 4am.

Wave Waikiki

1877 Kalakaua Ave., downtown Honolulu. 808-941-0424. www.wavewaikiki.com.

Dress up or dress down, anything goes at this perennially popular downtown club (located across from the Convention Center). This premier night spot, with two levels and two bars, is one of Oahu's oldest and best. There's lots of action every night of the week, featuring a mix of live local and international entertainment, DJ spins, and special promotions and events such as the Halloween weekend Monster Mash, featuring a $1,000 prize for the best costume.

Don Ho

A name that's synonymous with nightlife in Hawaii, Don Ho has been entertaining audiences for more than 40 years. The Honolulu native, famous for his crooning voice and "talk story," got his start playing Duke's Waikiki in 1962. He went national four years later, opening at Hollywood's Cocoanut Grove in 1966. Since then, "Hawaii's living legend" has delighted live audiences in New York and Las Vegas, as well as TV audiences (remember "Tiny Bubbles?"). While you're on Oahu, you can catch his show *(call for schedule)* at the **Waikiki Beachcomber Hotel** *(2300 Kalakaua Ave., Honolulu; 808-923-3981 or 877-693-6646; www.donho.com).*

Must Be Pampered: Spas

Abhasa Waikiki Spa

Royal Hawaiian Hotel, 2259 Kanalaua Ave., Honolulu. 808-922-8200. www.abhasa.com.

Housed within the "Pink Palace" on Waikiki Beach, Abhasa Spa specializes in Ayurvedic treatments. Trust this ancient wellness philosophy from India to set your karma straight. Indulge in hydro-color light therapy, a water treatment where healing colors and water jets are customized to your aura. Or strengthen your immune system with an Ayurveda herbal body treatment. Don't want to miss that beautiful day? Take your massage in an outside tent, nestled in the palm gardens with the soothing sound of the surf in the background.

Ihilani Spa

JW Marriott Ihilani Resort at Ko Olina, 92-1001 Olani St., Kapolei. 808-679-0079. www.ihilani.com.

Ihilani means "heavenly splendor," an apt name for this 35,000-square-foot sanctuary on Oahu's sunny western shore. Spend a few hours here (go ahead,

make it a day!), getting a green-tea detoxifying wrap or a seaweed mask, followed by a four-handed lomilomi massage. The spa is known for its authentic thalasso therapy, a seawater-jet massage, coupled with pure colored light designed to de-stress body and mind. In between treatments, you can relax in steam rooms and saunas, take a lap in the pool, or a plunge into one of the Roman baths (bathing suits optional).

Mandara Spa at Kalia Tower

Hilton Hawaiian Village Beach Resort, 2005 Kalia Rd., Honolulu. 808-949-4321. www.hiltonhawaiianvillage.com.

The Mandara chain operates more than 50 spas around the world. On Oahu, the spa takes on a Balinese and Hawaiian décor and tone, featuring a blend of Asian, European and Hawaiian therapies. There are 25 private rooms tucked into the tower wing's fourth floor at the Hilton Hawaiian Village Beach Resort, where you can revel in a host of exotic treatments, like the macadamia nut and chocolate body scrub or the vanilla and Pikake facial. Bring a close friend or your spouse and book a couple's suite; then relax together at the outdoor infinity-pool area.

Na Hoola Spa

Hyatt Regency Waikiki, 2424 Kalakaua Ave., Honolulu. 808-921-6097. www.hyattwaikiki.com.

This two-story, 10,000-square-foot spa, the largest on Waikiki, offers a peaceful oasis from the bustling beach scene below. You'll find 19 treatment rooms as well as a sauna, steam showers, and a couple's massage room—everything you need to ease your tired bones. Feeling a bit jet-lagged? Take a signature Hawaiian sea-salt jet bath. If your skin's feeling parched from the tropical sun, consider the spa's Polynesian body scrub, done with Hawaiian sea salt and kukui-nut oil.

Lanai★

Visitor information: 800-947-4774 or www.visitlanai.net.

Billing itself as the "most enticing" island, tiny Lanai is central in the chain, with Molokai and Maui to the north and Kahoolawe to the east. (Ferry service to Lanai is available from Lahaina on Maui's west coast.) Formed by a single volcano, Lanai boasts stretches of white sandy beaches, pristine bays and cool, pine-shrouded mountaintops. A series of gulches snakes down the island's east side. To the west, you'll see towering sea cliffs—some 1,000-feet tall—rising from remote Kaumalapau Harbor.

Fast Facts
• Measuring 18 miles long and 13 miles wide, Lanai is Hawaii's sixth-largest island.
• Only 3,000 people live on Lanai.
• Pineapple king James Dole purchased Lanai in 1922 for $1.1 million.
• Today about 96% of the island of Lanai is privately owned and developed as an upscale resort.
• You won't find a single traffic light on the island of Lanai.

If you're adventurous, a four-wheel-drive vehicle will take you across some of the island's undeveloped 80,000 acres of countryside and through tropical jungles. Scuba divers come to explore the legendary **Cathedral Ledges**★ *(see Musts for Outdoor Fun)*, while adventurers head up the **Munro Trail**★★ *(see Scenic Drives)* to 3,370-foot Lanaihale, the island's highest peak. In truth, though, most people come here to be pampered at the island's two luxury resorts, the **Lodge at Koele** and the **Manele Bay Hotel** *(see Must Stay)*.

Demons, Demons Everywhere

Legend has it that Lanai was once an evil place, overrun by demons. It was not until the demons were driven out by Kaululaau, the exiled son of a West Maui king, that people finally came to live on Lanai.

After Boston businessman James Dole purchased the island in 1922, Lanai became home to the world's largest pineapple plantation. **Lanai City** was built in 1924 by the Hawaiian Pineapple Company, later known as Dole Food Company. Nestled on the top of a 1,620-foot mountain plateau, Lanai City now contains the majority of the island's 3,000 residents. Yet it remains, like the rest of the island, small, quaint and very laid-back.

The Hawaiian corporation of Castle & Cooke later bought the pineapple plantation, retaining Dole's name. When market demand for Lanai pineapples plummeted in the 1990s, the company turned to high-end tourism, plowing under thousands of acres of the former pineapple plantation and developing the land with two posh hotels and two golf courses. Those in search of seclusion and upscale sybaritic pleasures will find them on Lanai.

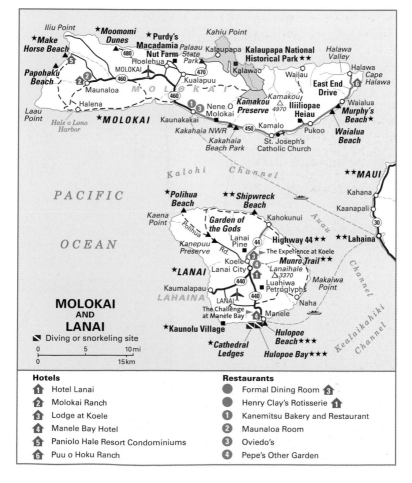

Hotels	Restaurants
1 Hotel Lanai	Formal Dining Room
2 Molokai Ranch	Henry Clay's Rotisserie
3 Lodge at Koele	1 Kanemitsu Bakery and Restaurant
4 Manele Bay Hotel	2 Maunaloa Room
5 Paniolo Hale Resort Condominiums	3 Oviedo's
6 Puu o Hoku Ranch	4 Pepe's Other Garden

Must-See Beaches

Hulopoe Beach★★★

Hulopoe Beach is located next to the Manele Bay Hotel off Manele Rd./Hwy. 440 on the south end of the island.

Considered one of the top beaches in the US, this popular stretch of white sand on Lanai's south shore draws crowds of swimmers, sunbathers and snorkelers. (Daily excursion boats from Maui land here.) The crystal-clear waters and shallow offshore reefs make it one of the best places in the islands to snorkel *(see Musts for Outdoor Fun)*. To the left of the beach is **Puu Pehe Rock**, also known as Sweetheart Rock. (Ask a local to tell you the Sweetheart Rock story; *see sidebar below*). Facilities include restrooms, showers and a picnic area with grills.

Sweetheart Rock

The legend goes that this rock takes its name from a tragic incident. Long ago, a Lanai warrior kidnapped a young, beautiful Maui girl and hid her on this rock. While the warrior was away, a storm blew in and washed the girl into the roiling surf, where she drowned. Heartbroken, the warrior flung himself from the cliff into his own watery grave.

Shipwreck Beach★★

At the end of Keomuku Rd. (Rte. 44), 8mi northeast of Lanai City.

This is a great place to walk, search for shells and driftwood, take in the salt air, and listen to the rhythmic hiss of the surf. The beach lines the island's northeast shore, stretching from Kahokunui at the end of Highway 44 to Polihua Beach to the northwest. Ancient Hawaiians called this eight-mile span of beach Kaiolohia, or "choppy seas."

Today it's the site of a number of shipwrecks, beginning with American and British ships in the early 1800s. You'll still see remnants of ship hulls and other debris here; one of the most prominent is the rusting hulk of a World War II vessel, forever grounded on the reef offshore. The water isn't great for swimming—it's too muddy and rough—but nature lovers will enjoy the wild, pristine surroundings.

Rock Art

While you're in the area of Shipwreck Beach, be sure to go see the petroglyphs, or rock carvings, at the end of Highway 44 *(when the paved road ends, take the north branch sand road all the way to the end)*. Follow the trail, marked with white paint on the rocks, to a cluster of stones—many of which are etched with ancient drawings. You'll see lots of primitive images of men, women and children engaged in a variety of activities, such as surfing, fishing and hunting. Dogs, brought to the islands by the first Polynesians, and deer, brought from India in the mid-1800s, are also depicted.

Polihua Beach★

On the north coast, at the end of dirt Polihua Rd., beyond the Garden of the Gods (for directions, see Gardens).

Polihua, meaning "eggs nest" or "bay of eggs," was named for the large numbers of sea turtles that once nested on this beach. After nearly becoming extinct, the sea turtles are starting to return to Polihua to nest—if you do see them, please remember to keep your distance. Forget about swimming here—the waters are too dangerous—but the wild, rugged character of the beach, with its crashing surf and solitude, is worth the drive to Lanai's north coast.

Must-See Natural Sites

Petroglyph Sites

Without a written language, ancient Hawaiians used rock carvings—known as **petroglyphs**—to record their experiences. Tiny Lanai is home to three ancient petroglyph sites. For driving directions to these sites, contact Destination Lanai *(800-947-4774 or www.visitlanai.net)*.

- At the end of a dirt road on the northwestern tip of the island, you'll find **Kaena Point,** Lanai's largest *heiau* (ancient place of worship).

- On the island's south shore, west of **Hulopoe Beach**★★★ *(see Beaches),* are the ruins of **Kaunolu Village**★, an ancient Hawaiian fishing village abandoned in the mid-19C. Here you can see the remains of Halulu Heiau, and a variety of petroglyphs on the surrounding boulders and rock walls.

- On a hillside overlooking the Palawai Basin are the **Luahiwa petroglyphs**, Lanai's largest concentration of ancient rock drawings, or *kaha kii*, carved in a number of large boulders scattered in the field *(off Hwy. 440, south of Lanai City).*

Must-See Scenic Drives

See map p 147.

Highway 44★★

Begin in Lanai City, and take Hwy. 44 north.

This eight-mile drive, along Lanai's northeast coast, packs a lot of splendid scenery into its short distance. Also called Keomuku Road, the paved, two-lane byway, one of only two paved highways on Lanai, heads north out of Lanai City, past the Lodge at Keole. You'll enter a neon-green rain forest, backed by misty mountains. Along the way, there are turn-offs for the **Munro Trail**★★ *(opposite)* and the **Garden of the Gods** *(see Gardens).* The road makes a final descent toward scenic **Shipwreck Beach**★★ *(see Beaches).* This is a great spot to get out and explore; you'll find remnants of old shipwrecks and fabulous coastal scenery here.

Rent a Jeep

You'll need to rent a hefty, four-wheel-drive vehicle at the airport to explore the back (and muddy!) roads of Lanai. Is the off-road/back-road scenery worth the extra cost of a jeep? You bet; you won't see much of the island from its limited paved roads.

Munro Trail★★

Off Hwy. 44, near the Lodge at Koele.

If you've rented a four-wheel-drive vehicle (and you should), don't miss driving this bumpy dirt road to Lanai's highest point. The Munro Trail, located off Highway 44, is one of Lanai's most popular driving excursions, with exceptional views from its 3,370-foot summit. The trail is named after George Munro, who planted the tall Cook Pines in the early 1900s along the ridge of the mountains. The trees were planted to draw water from the clouds, releasing it into the underground aqueducts, thus providing fresh water for the island.

The seven-mile trail zigzags up Lanaihale Mountain, then back down to the Palawai Basin, with lots of lookouts along the way. Chances are, it will be drizzling in the cloud-shrouded mountains, which only adds to the ambience.

Touring Tip

Be sure to check on the condition of the unpaved roads of Munro Trail and to the Garden of the Gods *(see Gardens)* before driving on them. When you're driving on Munro Trail, stay on the main road; it's easy to get lost on the spider web of trails and dirt roads leading off the beaten path.

When in Hawaii . . .

. . . Do as the Hawaiians do. Ancient Hawaiians revered nature, and respect for the land still holds a strong place in the lives of islanders. Treat all property with respect while visiting, especially sacred sites and natural areas. Don't touch anything, or leave litter behind. Other local customs include removing shoes before entering a private home, and obeying the speed limit (this is an easy-going place!). Don't pat children on the head, as the head is considered to be a sacred part of the body. Is it okay to say "aloha" if you're not Hawaiian? Sure, everybody does (aloha works for both "hello" and "goodbye"). Mahalo ("thank you") is handy, too.

Must-See Gardens

Garden of the Gods

225 B3 Polihua Rd., 6mi northwest of Lanai City. (Polihua Rd. starts just beyond the Lodge at Koele.) 866-268-7459. www.hawaiiweb.com. Open year-round daily 24 hours.

This isn't your typical garden! You won't find lush greenery here; instead you'll see a rugged, lunar-like landscape of randomly scattered volcanic boulders. Visit at sunrise or sunset, when the gold-tinged sky seems to illuminate the rocks from within. Seems like the perfect place for a UFO landing.

> ### Touring Tip
> The road to reach the garden, Polihua Road, is a rutted dirt trail; you'll need a four-wheel-drive vehicle to navigate it. Call before you go; if there's been a recent rain, the road may be closed. Allow about an hour for your visit, and make sure you have plenty of gas before setting out—there are no facilities along this route.

Must-See Historic Sites

Kaunolu Village★

On the southwest coast. From Lanai City, take Hwy. 440 toward Kaumalapau; turn left onto Kaupili Rd. and go south to Kaunolu Trail.

Ready for an adventure? Put on your walking shoes and rent a hefty four-wheel-drive vehicle for this trek to an old fishing village on Lanai's southwest coast. The area is said to contain one of the best collections of ancient Hawaiian ruins in the islands. If you look hard enough, you'll find crumbled house foundations and ruins of the Halulu Heiau temple. But you won't have any problem spotting the impressive 1,000-foot-high sea cliffs. Look for Kahekili's Jump at the top of the stone wall, where early Hawaiian warriors would amuse the chief by jumping off the 90-foot-high ledge. Today it's the site of cliff-diving competitions.

> ### Dining Hawaiian-style
> The hottest trend in fine dining on the islands is Hawaiian Regional Cuisine, where the islands' top chefs marry local ingredients to cultural influences in a culinary fusion of tastes. This new cuisine relies heavily on fresh local fish such as ahi (yellowfin tuna) and mahi-mahi (dolphin fish). So much for the days when pineapple-and-ham-topped pizza defined Hawaiian food! Island fruit is always in fashion, from passion fruit and mangoes to the sweetest little "sugarloaf" pineapples. Of course, you'll finish off any meal with a cup of Kona coffee, grown on plantations in Kona, on the Big Island, and considered to be the world standard for excellent coffee.

Musts For Fun

Drive the Backroads

If you really want to see the best of Lanai's scenery, you'll have to brave its bumpy backroads. Stay on the road more traveled and you'll miss the heart of this tiny island. In fact, only 30 miles of Lanai's 141 square miles are paved; the rest are open for the adventurous to explore.

Lanai offers more than 100 miles of unpaved, rough roads to travel, with spectacular views and remote vistas. Four-wheel-drive rental vehicles and road maps are available at the airport. Don't miss a trip through the **Kanepuu Preserve**, about five miles northwest of Lanai City *(Polihua Rd,, the dirt route leading to the preserve, is just beyond the Lodge at Koele)*. The 590-acre preserve boasts a large collection of native Hawaiian plants.

Continue about a mile on the Polihua Road to the Garden of the Gods *(opposite)*, a bizarre stand of nature-sculpted rock formations. From here, strap on those seat belts and follow the dusty, dirty, rock-strewn road across the island to windswept **Polihua Beach★** *(see Beaches)*, a favorite sea turtle nesting ground on the north shore. You won't be disappointed: the beach here is wild, rugged and hauntingly beautiful.

Pull! Aim! Fire!

If you're looking for a unique experience (or just want to bone up on your rifle shooting), check out the **Sporting Clays at Lanai Pine** *(Hwy. 44, North Central Lanai; 808-563-4600)*. Located on the picturesque plains of Mahana, on the north side of the island, this 14-station clay-shooting course welcomes both first-timers and experienced shooters. If you've never tried clay shooting, this is the place. A two-hour introductory session, including instruction, costs about $75; you'll be hitting those targets in no time!

Musts For Outdoor Fun

Snorkeling at Hulopoe Bay★★★

Hulopoe Bay is located next to the Manele Bay Hotel off Manele Rd./Hwy. 440 (7mi south of Lanai City). The adjacent beach park has rest rooms and showers.

Ultra-clear waters and abundant (and friendly!) fish make Hulopoe Bay on Lanai's south shore one of the best snorkeling spots in the islands. The protected marine conservation area features a shallow reef just offshore and lots of large tide pools, creating some great marine animal-watching opportunities.

Head to the rocky sides of the beach for the best snorkeling; here, you'll find plenty of neon-colored coral and reef fish. If you arrive at Hulopoe early in the morning, you may see spinner dolphins frolicking offshore.

Cliff Diving

Legend has it that Kahekili, chief of Lanai during the 18C, challenged his followers by leaping 90 feet off the sacred cliffs at Kaunolu into the waters of the Pacific Ocean. For decades, *lele kawa* (cliff diving) was an honored Hawaiian tradition, a way for ancient island warriors to prove their courage and loyalty, and to honor the gods.

Today, Lanai, considered the birthplace of cliff diving, plays host to the **Red Bull World Cliff-Diving Championships** every August, when the best cliff divers compete for the international title on Kaunolu Point on the island's south shore.

Scuba Diving at Cathedral Ledges★

Off the western edge of Holupoe Bay, next to the Manele Bay Hotel off Hwy. 440 (7mi south of Lanai City).

Green sea turtles, white-tipped reef sharks, spinner dolphins, octopi, eagle rays, hundreds of rare tropical fish, and more; the waters surrounding Lanai swim with marine life, a natural aquarium that draws scuba divers from around the country. Divers flock here to explore underwater ledges, arches, caves and lava tubes, home to thousands of neon-colored fish, sea creatures and reef corals.

A popular place to dive is the Cathedrals, a large underwater amphitheater resting 60 feet below the water's surface, just outside the western edge of Holupoe Bay. Light shines through the openings of this massive lava formation, creating the effect of a cathedral. Bright colors streak the lava walls and eels hide in the crevices.

What If I Want A Guide?

The Cathedrals dive is relatively easy, drawing both novice and more advanced divers; it's one of the most popular dives in the islands. If you want to take a guided dive, **Trilogy**, based on Maui, offers several diving excursions to Lanai *(departs from Lahaina Harbor on the west coast of Maui; 888-628-4800; www.sailtrilogy.com).*

Golf Lanai

Lanai's two resort courses, The Experience at Koele and The Challenge at Manele Bay, have both received oodles of accolades and are consistently ranked as two of the top resort courses in the country, if not the world. (In 2003, *Condé Nast Traveler* ranked The Experience at Koele the number-one golf resort in the world.)

The Challenge at Manele Bay – *Manele Bay Hotel, 7mi south of Lanai City on Manele Rd./Hwy. 440. 808-565-2222. www.manelebayhotel.com.* Take the Challenge at this Jack Nicklaus-designed course, stretching across gorges and ravines with sweeping ocean vistas from every hole. Three holes perch on the cliffs of Hulopoe Bay, using the Pacific Ocean as a water hazard!

The Experience at Koele – *The Lodge at Koele, .5mi north of Lanai City on Hwy. 430. 808-565-4653. www.lodgeatkoele.com.* Greg Norman laid out this 163-acre course, which meanders around large stands of distinctive Cook pines and eucalyptus trees, seven lakes, and several cascading streams, with mountain and ocean views, to boot.

Musts For Kids

Outdoor Adventures

Lanai's 140 square miles of sandy shoreline, secluded bays, green valleys, lofty plateaus and dense forests make for some great recreation—perfect for outdoor enthusiasts and adventurous families. Of course, you'll want to get out and play!

• **Take a hike** through the forest and valleys of the island's pretty uplands. Parents will appreciate the lofty scenery of the sheer valley walls and the open vistas, with the islands of Maui and Molokai on the horizon. Kids will enjoy running along the trail, through the leafy, enchanted forest. A guided

5-mile tour is offered each morning at the Lodge at Koele *(.5mi north of Lanai City on Hwy. 430; see Must Stay)*. Private hikes are also available.

• Sign up for a **guided horse back ride** through the countryside. Equestrians young and old will enjoy this excursion; even the little tykes can hop in the saddle for a gentle ride around the corral. *Call the stables at the Lodge at Koele for more information and reservations: 808-565-7300.*

Pilialoha Children's Program

Manele Bay Hotel (7mi south of Lanai City on Hwy. 440) and the Lodge at Koele (.5mi north of Lanai City on Hwy. 430). Reservations required: 808-565-2398. www.manelebayhotel.com or www.lodgeatkoele.com. See Must Stay.

Sure, time with mom and dad is great but, let's face it, kids love to be with other kids. Give them a break (okay, and you, too!) by signing them up for the Pilialoha Children's Program, offered through both the Manele Bay Hotel and the Lodge at Koele, Lanai's two resorts.

Pilialoha means "close friendship," and your kids are bound to make new friends while engaged in such activities as visits to the island's pineapple fields and petroglyph sites, Hawaiian arts and crafts, hiking, snorkeling and bike rides. There's wind-down time, too, when children listen to books on tape, play games or watch movies. The daily program costs $60 a day, $40 for half-day sessions. Evening hours are also offered on Tuesday and Friday *(5pm–10pm)*; the $55 fee includes dinner.

Must Be Pampered: Spas

The Spa at Manele

At the Manele Bay Hotel, Manele Bay (7mi south of Lanai City on Manele Rd./Hwy. 440). 808-565-7700. www.manelebayhotel.com.

Now this is the life: reserve the open-air cabana at the ultra-luxe spa at Manele Bay Hotel for your personal massage. The private outdoor room is tucked in a corner between the resort's too-blue pool and the open seas, where you can listen to the sound of the surf while the therapist kneads your tired muscles (no piped-in nature CDs needed, here!). If you prefer, there's also the Garden Hale outdoor room, set amidst lush greenery, exotic flowers, and cascading waterfalls. Why not try a Pohaku Wela (stone) outdoor massage, overlooking a waterfall, followed by a rain-forest shower?

From Poi to Pineapple: Eating Hawaiian-style

Talk about a melting pot! Seems like many Hawaiian food treats incorporate a dollop of several cultures and a dash of island ingredients. One example: Spam musubi, which consists of sticky rice topped by Spam and wrapped in dried seaweed. Introduced to Hawaii by the military during World War II, good old Spam (spiced ham in a can) remains a favorite here. Hawaiians eat more of the stuff than anyone else in the world!

The ubiquitous plate lunch, a local favorite at roadside stands, consists of white rice, pasta salad, and an entrée—perhaps Chinese-style chicken in soy sauce, Japanese teriyaki, curry stew, fried fish, or even an American hamburger. Another dish that was borrowed from a different culture but comes with a Hawaiian twist is **saimin**, a Japanese noodle soup. Called ramen on the mainland, this souped-up version contains a soup base of seaweed, dried shrimp, mushrooms and fish shavings.

Poi is uniquely Hawaiian. Made out of pounded taro root, this purplish, pasty stuff is said to have special healing properties. There's not much of a flavor to it, and the texture is a little odd, but it's worth a taste, just to say you tried it. If you're not tempted by poi, you may well want to sample **shave ice**, an old-fashioned treat from the days when islanders would shave ice into powder and flavor it with fruit juice. (Remember, it's shave ice, not shaved ice!)

Molokai★

Visitor information: 808-553-5221 or www.molokai-hawaii.com.

Set in the center of the island chain, unspoiled Molokai is a slice of Old Hawaii. This 38-mile-long island was once the province of *kahuna* (priests) whose religious practices included human sacrifice. The island was considered sacred then. Now a grove of kukui trees (sacred themselves) marks the burial site of Lani Kauli, one of the most powerful kahunas.

Fast Facts
• Molokai measures 38 miles long and 10 miles wide.
• The world's tallest ocean cliffs loom above Molokai's north shore.
• Molokai is home to 7,000 residents and the state's highest percentage of native Hawaiians.
• The island, site of a leper colony from 1866 to 1969, was long shunned by visitors.

Molokai was also the home of Father Damien, the Belgian Roman Catholic priest who devoted his life to caring for the victims of Hansen's Disease (aka leprosy). His place of exile is now the site of **Kalaupapa National Historical Park★★** *(see Historic Sites)* reachable by foot, small plane or mule.

In more recent years, the island was a sleepy community of ranches and pineapple plantations. Since the Del Monte plantation closed in the early 1980s, unemployment has been an issue for Molokai's residents. Still, an easy-going independence pervades on "the friendly isle," as Molokai calls itself.

The downside to Molokai (or the upside, depending on your point of view) is that there's not much in the way of posh restaurants, boutiques or nightclubs. You'll be clued in to that fact when you arrive: a popular T-shirt reads, "Molokai Night Life." Pictured below the heading? Nothing!

Touring Tip
Visitors to Molokai will find a wide range of outdoor activities, such as hiking, snorkeling and kayaking—and no waiting; crowds and lines are nonexistent.

Must-See Beaches

Make Horse Beach★

Off Kaluakoi Rd., western Molokai. To reach the beach, walk down the dirt road at the Paniolo Hale parking lot.

Make means "dead" in Hawaiian, but you won't find any dead horses on this beach—just three lovely crescents of sand, separated by volcanic rock.

Murphy's Beach★

Mile marker 20, Kamehameha Hwy. (Rte. 450), in eastern Molokai. Parking on the south side of the highway, just beyond mile marker. No restrooms or showers on-site.

Murphy's Beach, or 20 Mile Beach as it's also known, makes an excellent snorkeling spot, thanks to the barrier reef that runs alongside it.

Papohaku Beach

Kaluakoi Rd., 5mi northwest of Maunaloa, western Molokai. The beach has three access points from Kaluakoi Rd.; all are marked with signs.

Nearly 3 miles long, and up to 60 yards wide, Papohaku has more surface area than any other beach in the islands. This broad, gorgeous stretch of sand is backed by dunes and lapped by turquoise waters—wonderful for sunbathing but not good for swimming or snorkeling, since riptides and rogue surf threaten.

Waialua Beach

Mile marker 19, Kamehameha Hwy. (Rte. 450), in eastern Molokai. Limited parking. Enter near the western edge of the beach, along the highway, to avoid trespassing.

This beach is a real social scene by Molokai standards, and it's also a good swimming spot. Families come here to snorkel, swim and sunbathe, and you'll likely see kids jumping off the bridge into Waialua Stream. There are no restrooms or showers on-site.

Hula, Anyone?

According to ancient legend, the goddess Laka first danced the hula on a hill in Molokai, thus making the island the birthplace of the hula. This certainly seems plausible in May, when the **Ka Hula Piko** festival brings scores of hula groups and musicians from the other islands. Held on the shores of Papohaku Beach Park, the festival, whose name translates to "Center of the Dance," celebrates the different forms of traditional hula, accompanied by arts and crafts exhibits, Hawaiian games and music. *For schedules and information, call 808-552-2800 or check online at www.molokaievents.com.*

Must-See Natural Sites

Moomomi Dunes★

Hwy 480, 3mi past Hoolehua town.

Set on the northwest coast of the island, this wild and windswept landscape is managed by the Nature Conservancy of Hawaii. The 920-acre property is a haven for wildlife watchers looking for native shorebirds like sanderlings and golden plovers, and the colony of endangered Hawaiian monk seals—often spotted sunbathing on the golden-sand beach. The Nature Conservancy runs guided hikes here, but perhaps the best way to enjoy this pristine area is simply to roam, explore, and take in the vastness of the raging ocean and salt-splashed dunes.

Must-See Scenic Drives

See map p 147.

East End Drive (Kamehameha V Highway)

Hwy. 450, along the southeastern and eastern shoreline, from Kaunakakai east to Halawa. 27mi one way (allow a day for round-trip).

Old fishponds, good birding and historic sites add to the pleasure of this drive, which skirts Molokai's mountains on one side and the Pacific Ocean on the other. If you have yet to see the endangered nene (Hawaiian goose), **Nene O Molokai** *(at mile marker 4; 808-553-5992; visit by appointment only)* is a worthwhile stop. They raise Hawaii's state bird for release into the wild here; call for an appointment for a free tour.

Back heading east on East End Drive, you'll soon reach **Kakahaia Beach Park**, a national wildlife refuge that's a haven for local birds. At mile marker 10, look for **St. Joseph's Catholic Church**, built by Father Damien in 1876 and marked by a statue of the famous priest. About 15 miles east stands **Iliiliopae Heiau** *(opposite)*, a 13C temple that's the oldest on the island. After a series of wild twists and hill climbs, the road emerges at **Halawa Valley**, Molokai's most breathtaking spot, set off by velvety green hillsides and sparkling waterfalls.

Must-See Historic Sites

Kalaupapa National Historical Park★★

Access is by small plane or private boat—or for the adventurous, by foot or by mule ride (reservations: 808-567-6088 or 800-567-7550; $165/person). A 3.2mi trail with 26 switchbacks begins at Palaau State Park (Rte. 470, 10mi north of Kaunakakai). There is no road access between Kalaupapa and the rest of Molokai. 808-567-6802. www.nps.gov/kala. Open year-round daily by invitation only (free) or by tour ($40; no tours Sun). Ages 16 and up only.

This unique site encompasses a 13.6-square-mile peninsula separated from the rest of Molokai by a 1,600-foot cliff. To create an isolated colony for victims of Hansen's Disease (leprosy), native Molokaians were relocated from the beautiful windswept promontory in 1865, to be replaced the following year by banished lepers. In 1873 Father Damien de Veuster, a saintly Belgian priest, arrived to live and work (and die, in  1889) among the infected. His original St. Philomena's Roman Catholic Church stands above the ruins of the village of Kalawao. Forty or so elderly leprosy patients, who pose no health threat to adult visitors, continue to live at Kalaupapa. Not permitted to raise children, they shower their affections on scores of dogs and cats.

Iliiliopae Heiau

Mile marker 15, Hwy. 450, Pukoo. Park on the grassy area west of the bridge on the mountain side of the road.

This is the second-largest temple in Hawaii, and a highly sacred site, now accessed via private property. Stay on the path, follow the small signs reading "heiau," and hike up the hill to this ancient temple. It was used for human sacrifice and as a gathering place for *kahunas* (priests) from the islands. They say the temple was built in a single night, and that it was originally twice the size it is now.

Musts For Outdoor Fun

Hike Kamakou Preserve

In east central Molokai. Maps and directions are available from the Nature Conservancy office at 23 Pueo Pl. (off Hwy 460, 3mi west of Kaunakakai). 808-553-5236. www.nature.org/hawaii. Open year-round Mon–Fri 7:30am–3pm.

Jewel of Molokai, the 22,774-acre Kamakou Preserve is home to more than 250 species of Hawaiian plants. The peak of the preserve, about 5,000 feet above sea level, is the highest point on the island. This beautiful plot of land was donated by Molokai Ranch to the Nature Conservancy. The conservancy runs guided hikes through the rain forest *(one day a month; call or check online for schedule)*, and they can drive you directly to trailheads from their office *(above)*. If you do it yourself, you'll need a four-wheel-drive vehicle just to reach the preserve, and you'll need to park and walk from the entrance to the preserve and **Waikolu Lookout** (the main trailhead). It's notoriously easy to get stuck in the mud around here, and that will definitely cut into your hiking time.

Waikolu means "three waters" in Hawaiian, and you'll quickly figure out why: waterfalls are everywhere. The elevation at the lookout is 3,700 feet, although rain and clouds often affect visibility. Check in with the Nature Conservancy before you go, so you'll be updated on trail conditions; routes are well-marked and boardwalks make this enterprise less muddy than expected. The main trail in the preserve is **Pepeopae Trail**, which begins about 3 miles past the Waikolu Lookout. On this path, you'll traverse a lovely bog and lush vegetation, and end up at **Pelekunu Valley Overlook**.

Will You Ferry Me?

Want to ferry from Maui to Molokai? The *Molokai Princess (808-667-6165 or 866-307-6524; www.molokaiferry.com)* offers service between Lahaina and Kaunakakai Harbor, departing from Lahaina Harbor on Maui at 6:30am *(Mon–Sat)*. You can spend the day exploring Molokai and return to Maui in late afternoon—just in time for dinner at the oceanfront **Hula Grill**, north of Lahaina in Kaanapali *(see Must Eat)*.

Musts For Fun

Purdy's Macadamia Nut Farm★

Lihi Pali Ave., Kualapuu. 808-567-6001. Open year-round Tue–Fri 9:30am–3:30pm, Sat 10am–2pm, weather permitting.

Don't plan to just dash in for a bag of Hawaii's best, home-roasted macadamia nuts. Chances are, you'll be accosted—in a charming way—by Tuddie Purdy, who greets visitors at his family's 80-year-old macadamia-nut orchard. He'll coax you to come look at the trees on the five-acre farm, and will lend you a hammer to crack open some nuts, so you can help yourself, as he'll urge you to do. He'll also share the island's most delectable treat—slices of fresh coconut, slathered in macadamia honey—and share his take on living on Molokai, should you happen to ask.

Molokai Hoe Canoe Race

Considered Molokai's biggest annual social and athletic event, the 41-mile race across the treacherous waters of the Kaiwi Channel to Oahu ranks as the world championship of long-distance outrigger-canoe racing. The contest, held in October, starts at the rocky harbor of Hale o Lono, on the southwest coast of Molokai, and ends at Duke Kahanamoku Beach in front of the Hilton Hawaiian Village in Waikiki. What began as an interisland race with three teams in 1952, has mushroomed into a popular event that lures as many as 100 teams of racers from around the world each year.

Carved from the islands' plentiful hardwood trees and designed to maintain stability in the Pacific's swells, outrigger canoes were essential to the life of ancient Hawaiians, who used the craft for transportation and as vehicles in times of war. Hawaiians celebrated the completion of a canoe with religious ceremonies and feasts; each individual vessel was believed to have its own destiny. *For more information, call 808-259-7112 or visit www.holoholo.org.*

At present, these islands are off-limits to visitors without an invitation. For map, see inside front cover.

Kahoolawe

The island of Kahoolawe, smallest of Hawaii's eight major islands, has a colorful past. It has served as a penal colony for Catholics, then a ranch, then it was a base for US Army military exercises. After the attack on Pearl Harbor in 1941, the US Navy took over, and began using it for bombing practice. Nearly every instrument of war used by the US military and its allies since World War II has bombarded this island, where unexploded munitions still lurk on the beaches and in the offshore waters. The island was returned to Hawaii, with much fanfare and blowing of conch-shell horns, in 1994. A clean-up plan was launched, and much of the island is now deemed safe for controlled visits, but access is strictly limited. Looks like it will be a while before Kahoolawe is truly open to the public.

Niihau

Meanwhile, Kauai tourists hear whispers of Hawaii's "Forbidden Island," Niihau. Set 17 miles off the west coast of Kauai, this privately-owned island has no paved roads and no electricity. The 250 or so inhabitants are mostly native islanders who live a traditional Hawaiian lifestyle. Also at home on the coast of Niihau are monk seals, the largest colony in the major Hawaiian Islands.

Niihau was once a ranching outpost. Now this arid island stays afloat financially by serving as a base for support services for NASA and the US Navy, and by operating helicopter tours and safaris. Hunters can bag plentiful Polynesian boar and feral sheep, and, on a limited basis, Barbary sheep, eland and oryx antelope.

Touring Tip

For the lowdown on tours and hunting safaris to Niihau, as well as other island information, your best bet is to call the **Niihau Helicopters** office *(808-335-3500 or 877-441-3500; www.hawaiian.net/~niihauisland/heli.html).*

A Wealth of Shells

Niihau is famous for its shell jewelry. This island is the only place where the tiny, lustrous pupu shells are gathered. Local kahelelani shells are fashioned into exquisite pieces, which can fetch thousands of dollars. A Niihau shell lei is displayed in the British Museum as a memento of Captain Cook's first visit to the Hawaiian Islands. Making shell leis is often a shared family occupation here.

Hawaiian Culture

About 19 percent of Hawaii's population call themselves Hawaiian, although the number with pure Hawaiian blood may be less than 1 percent—perhaps about 10,000. Many Hawaiians died in the 19C from diseases introduced by European settlers. Over the past 150 years, native islanders intermarried easily, especially with Caucasians (*haoles* in Hawaiian) and Chinese. But the natives' influence on local culture goes far beyond their numbers. Some of the best-known aspects of Hawaiian culture—music, dance, food and the welcoming aloha attitude—have been absorbed by all those who live in Hawaii.

For at least 1,000 years, the Polynesian Hawaiians lived alone in the islands. They came in great double-hulled canoes—first from the Marquesas Islands between AD 500 and 750, later from Tahiti about 1100—and built houses of thatched grass. Their lives revolved around fishing, cultivating taro (a starchy edible root) and yams, gathering fruit and raising pigs. With their sophisticated knowledge of astronomy, the early peoples calculated the effect of the seasons on farming and harvesting. They imbued birds, fish and inanimate objects with supernatural powers; things that were sacred were labeled as *kapu*, or forbidden.

As the centuries passed, stories of their former lands became mere songs and lore. Hawaiians retained the basic spoken Polynesian language, adapting it to their own needs. After 1820, American missionaries transliterated Hawaiian to make it a written language, reducing the number of consonants to just seven—h, k, l, m, n, p and w. The Hawaiian language today is regularly spoken in daily life only on the private island of Niihau. Hawaiian locals speak either standard English or a type of pidgin composed mainly of English words, but with unusual inflections and numerous Chinese, Japanese and Filipino words stirred into the conversation.

Many other cultural aspects were developed after contact with the West. From Spanish-speaking cowboys (*paniolo*) on the Big Island, Hawaiians learned guitar; they loosened the strings to change the tuning and invented the "slack-key" style of playing. When Portuguese immigrants arrived in the late 19C, Hawaiians learned to play the four-stringed *braga*, renaming it the ukulele. This instrument, along with a drum, was played to accompany the hula. Originally performed only by men as part of an ancient religious ritual, hula evolved into a graceful dance for women. Grass skirts were a 20C import from Micronesia; dancers were traditionally clad in ti leaves.

The venues listed below were selected for their ambience, location and/or value for money. Rates indicate the average cost of an appetizer, an entrée and a dessert for one person (not including tax, gratuity or beverages). Most restaurants are open daily (except where noted) and accept major credit cards. Call for information regarding reservations, dress code and opening hours.

$$$$	**Over $50**	**$$**	**$15–$30**
$$$	**$30–$50**	**$**	**Under $15**

Big Island

Donatoni's $$$ Italian

At the Hilton Waikoloa Village Resort, 425 Waikoloa Beach Dr., Waikoloa. Dinner only. 808-886-1234. www.hiltonwaikoloavillage.com.

To get the full romantic effect of Donatoni's, cruise to the restaurant by boat from the hotel lobby. Once there, you'll dine on a garden terrace with ocean views, on seductive dishes like shrimp and scallops nestled in pasta with a to-die-for cream sauce, or fusilli with artichokes and pancetta.

Huggo's $$$ Seafood

75-5828 Kahakai Rd., Kailua-Kona. 808-329-1493. www.huggos.com.

This place is a local institution, complete with sherbet-hued sunsets and technicolor cocktails that only enhance the food—think seared ahi, pasta with vegetables and wild mushrooms, and chicken cooked in ti leaves. The thatched bar, Huggo's on the Rocks, is an island hot spot for noshing on pupu (appetizers) and dancing at the water's edge.

Merriman's $$$ Hawaiian Regional

Kawaihae Rd., Opelu Plaza, Waimea. 808-885-6822. www.merrimanshawaii.com.

Owner Peter Merriman is one of Hawaii's superstar chefs, and a real master at creating cutting-edge dishes out of fresh local ingredients. Lamb comes from

nearby Kahua Ranch, and it's roasted with plum sauce and served with papaya-mint relish. Wok-charred ahi is a signature dish, as is Merriman's Caesar salad, to which he adds sashimi, Pahoa corn and shrimp fritters.

Aloha Angel Cafe $$ Hawaiian

79-7384 Mamalahoa Hwy., Kainaliu. No dinner Mon & Tue. 808-322-3383.
www.alohaangelcafe.com.

Visit this hip little cafe at the Aloha Theatre for breakfast or lunch, and sit on the breezy lanai. Take in views of coffee fields that slope to the sea while you feast on thick sandwiches (try the fresh ahi) stuffed between whole-wheat buns, or tasty burritos and omelets. All go down well with fresh-fruit smoothies. Organic produce, local ingredients and home-baked desserts are mainstays here. Dinner is served indoors.

Kilauea Lodge Restaurant $$ Continental

Old Volcano Rd., Volcano Village. 808-967-7366. www.kilauealodge.com.

Cozy, rustic Kilauea Lodge is an inviting stop on a cool night in Volcano, especially when there are logs crackling in the fireplace. This is the fine-dining option near Kilauea volcano, with classic entrées featuring game (antelope flambé) and hasenpfeffer (rabbit braised in wine), along with vegetarian offerings and great soups.

Oodles of Noodles $$ Pasta

75-1027 Henry St., Crossroads Shopping Center, Kailua-Kona. 808-329-9222.

Carbs of all cultures meet in happy harmony here, from saimin to spaghetti, udon to orzo. If you love slurping noodles, you'll be in heaven at Oodles of Noodles. The room is cute and bright, and the noodles are as gourmet as they get: think tuna casserole made with wok-seared ahi. Design your own dish, or choose one of their fabulous concoctions, perhaps fettucine with grilled chicken, corn and cilantro.

Ken's House of Pancakes
$ American

1730 Kamehameha Ave., Hilo. Open 24 hours daily. 808-935-8711.

"K-Hop," as the locals call it, is an old-fashioned coffee shop, featuring liver and onions, French toast, hash, and, of course, perfectly golden pancakes—all served with a side order of local color. Favorites include shredded kalua pig on a hoagie, French toast made with sweet Portuguese bread, and coconut-custard pie. Come Sunday for "all-you-can-eat" spaghetti night.

Kimo's Family Buffet
$ American

Kona Bay Hotel, 75-5739 Alii Dr., Kailua-Kona. Closed Mon. 808-329-1393.

Got hearty eaters or hungry kids in tow? This local favorite will be a welcome find. Twice daily, they offer an island-style, all-you-can-eat buffet at bargain prices. Mornings, you'll find the usual suspects, like baked goods and omelets; come dinnertime, they offer a full salad bar and a mix of family-pleasing entrées, some Asian, some Hawaiian, some basic American.

Lava Rock Café
$ American

Old Volcano Hwy., next to Kilauea General Store in Volcano Village. No dinner Sun & Mon. 808-967-8526. http://volcanovillage.com/LavaRock.htm.

This knotty-pine roadhouse is a happy oasis en route to the volcano, and you can make it one-stop shopping: grab beverages, sunscreen and other necessities at the adjacent general store. The menu is a grab bag of teriyaki chicken, fajitas, and T-bone steaks (plus a good grilled mahi-mahi), followed by killer desserts like mango cheesecake. They also pack a mean hiker's lunch, with hefty sandwiches, chili and even fried chicken.

Tex Drive In
$ International

On Hwy. 19, Honokaa. 808-775-0598. www.texdrivein.com.

The major attraction at Tex's: a Portuguese specialty called *malasadas*, best described as sort of a gourmet donut hole. Rolled in sugar, these delectable goodies come filled with gooey stuff like pineapple-papaya preserves. These make a terrific breakfast, as the bevy of early-bird regulars will attest. The rest of the menu is a mix of ethnic favorites from around the globe, from your basic burger to kalua pork to Korean chicken. Try the homemade sweet-potato chips.

What's Shakin' $ Health Food

27-999 Old Mamalahoa Hwy., Pepeekeo. Open daily 10am–5pm. 808-964-3080.

Set along scenic Pepeekeo Drive *(see Big Island/Scenic Drives)*, this unassuming wooden house is a must-stop, if just for a fresh-fruit smoothie. These are among the best you'll ever taste, featuring delectable blends of fruits from the owner's farm. Try the Papaya Paradise, with pineapple, papaya, banana and coconut. Lunch items rely on organic local ingredients and they won't disappoint. Entrées like the Blue Hawaii, a blue-corn tamale with homemade salsa, come with fresh fruit and a crunchy green salad topped with sesame dressing.

Maui

Nick's Fish Market $$$$ Seafood

Fairmont Kea Lani Hotel, 4100 Wailea Alanui. Dinner only. 808-879-7224. www.fairmontkealani.com.

The service here is absolutely impeccable—the staff will actually ask, "Would you like to relax with some menus right now?" and you'll be unobtrusively served by several people. All of this would seem like so much posturing, except that the food is simply exquisite. Fresh fish and lobster are perfectly prepared and artfully presented. The lamb simply melts in your mouth. The room is lovely, too, perched above the pool with stars overhead; cool art-glass lighting adds a warm amber glow.

Hula Grill $$$ Hawaiian Regional

Whalers Village, 2435 Kaanapali Pkwy., Kaanapali. 808-667-6636. www.hulagrill.com.

Chef Peter Merriman divides his time between Hula Grill and Merriman's on the Big Island, and it's clear he has another hit on his hands. Set on the beach, with live hula (of course!), the Hula Grill has a great vibe, and the signature Merriman touch with seafood. Fresh fish is grilled on wood or paired with a choice of sauces and salsas, and some of the smallest dishes make the biggest splash (crab-macadamia-nut wontons, anyone?). Save room for the gourmet ice-cream sandwich, with creamy vanilla stuffed between giant chunks of chocolate-macadamia-nut brownies.

Mama's Fish House $$$ Seafood

799 Poho Pl., 1.5mi east of Paia. 808-579-8488. www.mamasfishhouse.com.

You can't beat the ambience here: Mama's is a converted beach house set in a coconut grove, all decked out in Polynesian décor. Tables are adorned in tapas-print cloths, and hinged windows are propped open to let in the sea breeze. This place wouldn't have lasted 30 years, though, if the food didn't match the surroundings—and it does. Stand-out dishes include Tahitian *poisson cru*, an appetizer of ono (a local fish) marinated in lime and coconut milk. Selections of fresh island fish always include at least four different preparations.

KKO (Kai Ku Ono) $$ American

2511 Kihei Rd., Kihei. 808-879-1954.

Breakfast on the deck is an appealing option here (the beach is across the street): try the breakfast casserole, a tasty, cheesy mixture of scrambled eggs, potatoes, Maui onions, bell peppers and bacon, topped with cheddar and baked to bubbly perfection. If you've been tempted to try taro, this is the place—the Maui taro burger is tasty and non-threatening. Dinner brings choices like mango barbecue ribs and the evening's fresh fish, crusted with macadamia nuts and served with a brown-butter lemon sauce.

Longhi's $$ Seafood

888 Front St., Lahaina (second location in Wailea, at the Shops at Wailea). 808-667-2288. www.longhis.com.

Park yourself on the second floor of this La-haina landmark and enjoy great views of the sunset. Readers of the *Maui News* picked Longhi's as the "best overall restaurant," and you're likely to agree with them. Stick with the seafood selections and you'll fare best: fried calamari, mahi-mahi with macadamia-nut crust and mango chutney, or shrimp marinara. Desserts are an absolute must here; try Caramel Knowledge for the name alone!

Anthony's Coffee Co. $ American

90 Hana Hwy., Paia. Open daily 5:30am–6pm. 808-579-8340 or 800-882-6509. www.anthonyscoffee.com.

Breakfast and lunch are the way to go here. Anthony's roasts their own coffee, and they sell it by the pound and by the cup, including pure Kona and their own special blends. For a hearty way to start your day, try kalua pork Benedict or the breakfast wrap (eggs, tomato, cheese, rice, bacon); you'll want to go lighter if you can't resist a pineapple-coconut muffin (and you shouldn't!) Anthony's makes an awesome picnic lunch, too, with hefty sandwiches that don't fall apart, served with a side salad, if you choose. (The sign says, "Shirts and shoes please," but bikini tops and bare chests rule.)

Jawz Fish Tacos $ Mexican

Across the street from Makena Beach, Makena. 808-874-8226.

The original Jawz was, and still is, a wood-shingled taco truck, parked across from Makena Beach. They make wonderful fish tacos with pink sauce (what-ever is in that sauce, it sure is good!) and terrific smoothies. **Jawz Fish Tacos Island Style Grill** *(1279 S. Kihei Rd., in the Azeka Mauka Shopping Center, Kihei; 808-874-8226)* offers the same great tacos, burritos and salads, plus Maui's largest salsa bar. Top your taco with roasted habanero-pepper salsa, made with pineapple and carrots. Now that's salsa!

Kauai

Café Hanalei

$$$$ Pacific Rim

5520 Ka Haku Rd., Princeville. 808-826-9644. www.princeville.com.

Dining at this intimate open-air, terraced space at the elegant Princeville resort *(see Must Stay)*, overlooking the stunning Hanalei Bay, Bali Hai and the shimmering waters of the Pacific Ocean, is one of the most romantic dining experiences on Kauai. Combine it with innovative, expertly prepared food, and you have a meal you won't soon forget. Signature dishes on the often-changing menu include a duet of duck confit and crispy duck breast served with yama sweet-potato brulée. Try the opulent Friday-night seafood buffet or the popular Sunday brunch.

Tidepools

$$$$ Hawaiian

1571 Poipu Bay, Hyatt Regency Kauai, Koloa. Dinner only. 808-742-1234. www.kauai.hyatt.com.

Love is in the air at this open-air, thatched-roof dining room, suspended over exotic koi ponds and cascading waterfalls. Gas-lit lanterns twinkle in the surrounding tropical gardens and candles flicker as diners feast on appetizers like tempura slipper lobsters, and coconut-lobster soup with Tahitian vanilla-bean crème. From there, move on to Kauai-spiced opah stuffed with lump crabmeat, shiitake mushrooms and asparagus, or roasted rack of lamb served with eggplant and goat-cheese risotto.

Beach House

$$$ Pacific Rim

5022 Lawai Rd., Koloa. Dinner only. 808-742-1424. www.the-beach-house.com.

Combine a stunning ocean view with award-winning Pacific Rim food and you have one of Kauai's favorite special-occasion restaurants. The chef sometimes gets carried way with complicated combos but you can't go wrong with the signature dishes: wasabi-crusted snapper with lilikoi lemongrass butter, kiawe-grilled filet mignon or the lemongrass-and-kaffir-lime-crusted sea scallops. Begin your meal with shiitake-crusted mussels or the ahi taster, and end with the kahlua-taro cheesecake.

Gaylord's

$$$ Hawaiian

2087 Kaumualii Hwy., Lihue. 808-245-9593. www.gaylordskauai.com.

This gracious, open-air dining room, overlooking 35 acres of gardens and fields, was once a 1930s plantation home. Since 1986, the Wallace family has been serving Kauai islanders and visitors plates of fresh fish, top-quality steaks and traditional Hawaiian fare. Relax in wicker chairs, bumped up to white-linen-draped tables, and order ahi served with purple sweet potatoes and green Thai coconut-milk sauce, flame-broiled moonfish with champagne vinegar and cucumber sauce, or blackened prime rib with wasabi horseradish. Go Tuesday or Thursday evening for the traditional Hawaiian luau.

A Pacific Cafe
$$$ Pacific Rim

4-831 Kuhio Hwy. (Hwy. 56), in Kauai Village Shopping Center, Kapaa. Dinner only.
808-822-0013. www.apacificcafe.com.

Don't let the strip-mall location of this award-winning restaurant put you off. Pacific Cafe, serving a creative blend of European and Pacific Rim cuisine, is considered one of the top dining experiences in the islands. The dining room sports a clean, sophisticated design, with black lacquered chairs, wood tables, and bamboo placemats. In the centerpiece open kitchen, chef Jean-Marie Josselin and his staff create mouthwatering dishes like sashimi tempura, wok-charred mahi-mahi with garlic-sesame crust and lime-ginger sauce, and potato-crusted onaga. Meat-eaters favor the Mongolian-style rack of lamb.

Roy's Poipu Bar & Grill
$$$ Hawaiian

2360 Kiahuna Plantation Dr., Poipu. 808-742-5000. www.roys-restaurants.com.

Renowned Chef Roy Yamaguchi brings his signature—and award-winning—Hawaiian fusion cuisine to this sleek dining room in the Poipu Shopping Center. You'll find all his favorite dishes here, including the opakapaka smothered in macadamia-nut sauce, roasted duck with passion fruit, blackened ahi, wood-grilled Szechuan-spiced ribs, and hibachi salmon.

Kintaro's
$$ Japanese

4-370 Kuhio Hwy. (Rte. 56), Wailua. 808-822-3341.

Quite simply, this no-frills restaurant located on Highway 56 on Kauai's east side is the best place for sushi on the island. Its large, cavernous dining rooms are nearly always full with loyal locals and savvy visitors. Service is fast, friendly and efficient; the sushi is wonderfully fresh. There are full plates of Japanese entrées but most folks make a meal of their favorite sushi and dim sum offerings. Chefs perform at some tables, slicing, dicing and cooking meats and vegetables tableside.

Ono Family Restaurant
$ American

4-1292 Kuhio Hwy., Kapaa. 808-822-1710.

What's not to like about a place that serves meatloaf and eggs for breakfast? This family-owned, longtime island favorite is a great place for breakfast and lunch. You'll find more than 15 omelet choices and a variety of special egg dishes, along with hotcakes and specialty coffees and fruit smoothies. For lunch, there's the usual lineup of sandwiches and burgers, plus Oriental stir frys, Portuguese-style pork platters, and fish and chips—all at prices that won't bust the budget.

Oahu

Alan Wong's Restaurant $$$$ Hawaiian Regional

1857 S. King St., 3rd floor, Honolulu. Dinner only. 808-949-2526. www.alanwongs.com.

Arguably the best restaurant in Hawaii, Alan Wong's continues to rack up well-deserved accolades. The dining room's design is clean, crisp and inviting, with neutral walls, white tablecloths and an open kitchen. Start with appetizers like baked Kona lobster mousse wrapped in nori with crab-avocado stuffing, or crispy won ton ahi poke balls with wasabi sauce. For entrées, try the macadamia-nut-coconut-crusted lamb chops or the mahi-mahi with wasabi cream. Save room for the house-made macadamia-nut crunch bars. Five-course *($65)* and seven-course *($85)* tasting menus are available nightly.

Chef Mavro $$$$ French

1969 S. King St., Honolulu. Dinner only. Closed Mon. 808-944-4714. www.chefmavro.com.

One of the finest restaurants on Oahu, Chef Mavro serves up unique fusion dishes, combining French haute cuisine with fresh Hawaiian ingredients. Owner-chef George Mavrothalassitis, a native of southern France, has won acclaim for his tasting menus that pair each item with wine *(three courses, $81; four courses, $98; six courses, $134; prices are less without wine)*. Prawn salad with hummus and cumin, sautéed foie gras with red currant-balsamic glaze and carmelized Maui onions, and sesame-crusted *uku* (snapper) with lotus root and enoki mushrooms are just a few of the dishes you might find on the ever-changing menu. As you'd expect, the service is top-notch.

John Dominis Restaurant $$$$ Seafood

43 Ahui St., Honolulu. Dinner & Sun brunch only. 808-523-0955. www.johndominis.com.

Nothing says "special occasion" like a meal at this Oahu landmark, which has been serving Honolulu diners since 1979. The view overlooking Diamond Head is spectacular; inside, a koi pond snakes through the dining room. John Dominis is known for offering some of the freshest fish in town; you can choose from five different preparations for each one. Favorite dishes made with island fish include Szechwan-style moi with spicy sweet-and-sour sauce, Cajun-style seared opakupaka, grilled miso salmon, and wok-fried onaga. For carnivores, there's a selection of steaks and fowl.

La Mer $$$$ French

2199 Kalia Rd., in the Halekulani Hotel, Honolulu. Dinner only. 808-923-2311. www.halekulani.com.

Itching to dress up? Want to splurge? This formal restaurant (jackets or long-sleeved dress shirts required for men), located in the elegant Halekulani Hotel *(see Must Stay)*, offers the best in haute cuisine. The food, combining French techniques with fresh Hawaiian ingredients, matches the spectacular setting overlooking Waikiki beach. Chef Yves Garnier offers up creative twists on classics, like the crispy onago fillet with truffle jus and fried basil, roasted salmon and salmon tartare with mustard sauce, milk-fed veal with Roquefort, and a trio of Kobe beef filets.

Chai's Island Bistro $$$ Pacific Rim

Aloha Tower Marketplace, Pier 9, Honolulu. 808-585-0011. www.chaisislandbistro.com.

Chef Chai Chaowasaree has built a loyal following, who crave his innovative Pacific-Rim cuisine. This relaxed, energetic eatery, with indoor and outdoor seating and live entertainment, offers a variety of creative dishes made with fresh local ingredients. Start with the Japanese eggplant and zucchini soufflé or crispy duck spring rolls. For entrées, you'll find a wide selection that changes seasonally. Try the spicy garlic and pepper frog legs, the Asian pesto sake-steamed whole moi, or the pork chop stuffed with sautéed wild mushroom and ricotta cheese. For dessert, don't miss the white-chocolate truffle topped with raspberry-guava purée.

Duke's Canoe Club $$$ Hawaiian

2335 Kalakaua Ave., Honolulu. 808-922-2268. www.dukeswaikiki.com.

You won't go away hungry at this restaurant, named in honor of Duke Kahanamoku, the father of surfing. Known for its hefty steak and fresh seafood dishes and lively bar *(see Oahu Nightlife)*, the place is always bustling. The dining room is beach-bar casual—it sits on Waikiki Beach with great ocean views—and is filled with surfing memorabilia. Pupu includes spicy sugarcane shrimp or macadamia-nut and crab won tons. Then it's on to prime steaks, mango-glazed barbecue ribs, and fresh fish dishes, each offered with a variety of preparations and sauces. All dinners come with Duke's legendary salad bar.

Indigo $$$ Asian

1121 Nuuanu Ave., Honolulu. Closed Sun & Mon. 808-521-2900. www.indigo-hawaii.com.

Owner-chef Glenn Chu, raised in the Manoa Valley, has designed an eclectic menu that consistently earns Honolulu's best dining awards. The warmly decorated dining room, near old Chinatown, features Indonesian hand-carved wood paneling, Chinese lanterns, tropical plants and bamboo accents. You'll have a tough time narrowing down your choice from the diverse entrée menu that includes moi roasted in a banana leaf, black-mustard-and-pepper-crusted ahi steak, and braised ginger-ham shanks. A gong announces the chocolate volcano dessert. The restaurant's Green Room lounge is a popular local watering hole.

Roy's Restaurant $$$ Hawaiian

6600 Kalanianaole Hwy., Honolulu. 808-396-7697. www.roys-restaurants.com.

Renowned Chef Roy Yamaguchi and his talented staff fire up dishes like opakapaka smothered in macadamia-nut sauce, roasted duck with passion fruit, blackened ahi, wood-grilled Szechuan-spiced ribs, hibachi salmon and more. The first of Roy's 30 restaurants around the world, this two-level dining room, with its open kitchen and energetic vibe, overlooks the Pacific Ocean.

Sam Choy's Diamond Head Restaurant $$$ Hawaiian

449 Kapahulu Ave., Honolulu. Dinner & Sun brunch only. 808-732-8645.
www.samchoy.com.

Sam Choy's flagship restaurant is the setting for the popular local cooking show *Sam Choy's Kitchen,* and a longtime local favorite. Bring the family and your appetite; the restaurant is friendly and unpretentious, and the servings are large. The extensive selection of Choy classics includes seafood laulau with mahi-mahi, shrimp, scallops and vegetables wrapped in ti leaves; Asian veal ossobuco; red-wine-braised short ribs; and the signature bouillabaisse. There are vegetarian dishes, too, and a Sunday brunch buffet that always draws a crowd.

Sansei Seafood Restaurant & Sushi Bar $$$ Japanese

2552 Kalakaua Ave., Waikiki Beach Marriott Resort, Waikiki. Dinner only. 808-931-6286.
www.sanseihawaii.com.

If you're looking for fresh, creatively prepared seafood and sushi, you'll find it at this lively eatery, tucked in the popular Waikiki Beach Marriott Resort. Try the award-winning Japanese calamari salad, Asian rockshrimp cake, mango-crab-salad roll or tea-duck egg roll. Large plates feature specialties like panko-crusted ahi wrapped in arugula, and shichimi-seasoned beef tenderloin served over Japanese udon noodles. The sushi menu is one of the best you'll find on the islands!

Don Ho's Island Grill $$ Hawaiian

Aloha Tower Marketplace, Pier 9, Honolulu. 808-528-0807. www.donho.com/grill.

The beach-bar atmosphere is lively, the food fresh and filling at this casual harborside restaurant. You'll find pupu, burgers and sandwiches (the shredded pork seasoned with Hawaiian salt is a favorite). Thin-crust "surfboard" pizzas are served atop a mini surfboard balanced on two cans of pineapple; try the Chinatown (chicken Char-Siu sausage, cilantro pesto and sweet peppers) or the North Shore Hang Ten (rockshrimp, sweet peppers and macadamia-nut pesto). Entrées include the signature sautéed miso butterfish and Molokai lobster fried rice. The restaurant, owned by Don Ho *(see p 144),* is decorated with the performer's mementos, posters and photos.

Keo's in Waikiki $$ Laotian-Thai

2028 Kuhio Ave., Honolulu. 808-951-9355. www.keosthaicuisine.com.

As Hawaii's preeminent Thai chef, Keo Sananikone has done much to help popularize Thai cuisine in America. Of his five local restaurants, this is nearest to major hotels (it's open for breakfast, lunch and dinner daily). The extensive menu lists starters like crispy noodles, summer rolls, and papaya salad; main courses include curry dishes, seafood selections (try the Indonesian shrimp in peanut sauce or the crispy mahi-mahi) and house specialties like grilled country game hen or Bangkok duck.

Ahi's Restaurant $ Seafood

53-146 Kamehameha Hwy., Punaluu, on the windward coast. Closed Sun. 808-293-5650.

Heading to the windward coast? Don't miss a stop at this friendly, family-owned restaurant. Come as you are for their heaping platters of shrimp—scampi-style, cocktail-style, tempura or deep-fried—topped with spicy sauce. Can't decide? Try the sampler platter for about $10. Fish dishes reign here; all are fresh and prepared with a minimum of fussiness. If you're a mai tai fan, order one of Ahi's generously portioned concoctions. Expect to wait in line; Ahi's doesn't take reservations, and tables fill up fast, especially on Saturday.

Big City Diner $ Asian

3569 Waialae Ave., Honolulu. 808-738-8855.

You can't beat this casual diner in Honolulu's Kaimuki neighborhood for its big portions and easy-on-the-wallet prices. It features an interesting mix of dishes, including kim chee rice, pulehu steak, guava-coated ribs, panko-crusted calamari steak, and spicy tempura. Entrées come with choice of rice and either soup or salad. Don't leave without tasting the gooey double-chocolate bread pudding.

Rainbow Drive-In $ Hawaiian

3308 Kanaina Ave., Honolulu. 808-737-0177.

There are some things that inspire cravings. Such is the case for the Rainbow Diner's made-from-scratch chili, at least according to hordes of local Oahu residents. See for yourself, but don't stop with a mere bowl. Order up one of the classic mixed-plate lunches, too—a heaping dish of barbe-cued meat, fish, chicken or pork, piled high with scoops of the requisite macaroni salad and rice.

Lanai

Formal Dining Room at the Lodge at Koele $$$$ New American

1 Keamoku Dr., Lanai City. Dinner only. 808-565-3800 or 800-450-3704.
www.lodgeatkoele.com.

As the name implies, this top-end restaurant at the Lodge at Koele *(see Must Stay)*, offers an elegant dining experience, noted for its high-quality cuisine and impeccable service. The stately dining room is bathed in soft light from flickering candles and a glowing log fire. On the menu you'll find well-executed classics, including steaks, lobster, fish and Hawaiian regional specialties—all at hefty prices.

Henry Clay's Rotisserie

$$$ Creole

828 Lanai Ave., at the Hotel Lanai, Lanai City. Dinner only. 877-665-2624. www.hotellanai.com.

Chef Henry Clay, a native of New Orleans, brings his culinary heritage (and spicy recipes!) to Lanai at this down-home restaurant at the Hotel Lanai *(see Must Stay)*. The casual eatery is a lively place, a favorite among locals and visitors alike. Heaping platters of Rajun Cajun Clay's shrimp, Almost Grandma's gumbo, and the moist, mouth-watering herb-marinated rotisserie chicken are top sellers.

Pepe's Other Garden

$ American

Corner of 8th & Houston Sts., Lanai City. 808-565-9628.

This tiny, bright bistro is the perfect place to stop for an overstuffed sandwich or burrito, organic salads, and homemade breads and soups. Their picnic lunches are popular with the hiking, biking, on-the-go crowd. At night, there are tasty, fresh-made pizzas, too, and you can bring your own bottle of wine.

Molokai

Maunaloa Room

$$$ Hawaiian Regional

100 Maunaloa Hwy., at the lodge at Molokai Ranch, Maunaloa. 808-660-2725. www.molokairanch.com.

Molokai's top choice for fine dining is way out at 54,000-acre Molokai Ranch *(see Must Stay)*, a working ranch with a posh lodge. The menu leans toward eclectic Hawaiian fare, and doesn't take itself too seriously. Irresistible choices include mai tai mahi-mahi (with rum syrup) and an oozing-with-chocolate Molten Lava cake—an apt dessert to have in the land of volcanoes.

Kanemitsu Bakery & Restaurant

$ Hawaiian

79 Ala Malama St., Kaunakakai. Open Mon & Wed–Sun 5:30am–6:30pm. Closed Tue. 808-553-5855.

This bakery is a great place to buy Molokai's distinctive French bread. You can buy the popular bread straight from the oven to go or nibble on it here, while you hang out with the regular breakfast crowd and eavesdrop on the local scuttlebutt. Besides bread, hearty diner fare rules at Kanemitsu Bakery— think burgers, sandwiches and fried chicken.

Oviedo's

$ Filipino

145 Ala Malama St., Kaunakakai. Open daily 10:30am–5:30pm. 808-533-5014.

Home-cooked Filipino specialties draw diners to this no-frills lunch stand, for delicious stews made with chicken and papaya, adobos, and more adventurous fare—pig's feet and tripe stew, anyone? There are a few tables inside, but most locals just stop in to chat with the owner and order lunch to go.

The properties listed below were selected for their ambience, location and/or value for money. Prices reflect the average cost for a standard double room for two people. Many hotels offer special discount packages; ask about them when you make your reservations. Price ranges quoted do not reflect the Hawaii hotel tax of 11.4%.

$$$$$	Over $350	$$	$100–$175
$$$$	$250–$350	$	Under $100
$$$	$175–$250		

Big Island

Kona Village Resort $$$$$ 125 rooms

Queen Kaahumanu Hwy., Kailua-Kona. 808-325-5555. www.konavillage.com.

This Polynesian-style resort is a world unto itself. Hammocks sway beneath coconut palms beside thatched-roof beachfront cottages. Well-appointed *hales*, or houses, have no phones, televisions or radios to remind you of the outside world; if you don't want to be disturbed, just place a coconut outside your door. Kids and parents kayak and windsurf by day and enjoy luaus in the oceanview restaurant by night.

Mauna Kea Beach Hotel $$$$$ 310 rooms

62-100 Mauna Kea Beach Dr., Kohala Coast. 808-882-7222 or 800-882-6060. www.maunakeabeachhotel.com.

The beach on Kaunaoa Bay is spectacular, the golf courses are award-winning, and the rooms are airy and large. An added bonus here: Laurence Rockefeller's collection of Asian and Pacific art—more than 1,600 pieces—adorns the hotel and its grounds. No wonder some families have been returning here for generations, even as newer, sleeker properties have sprouted up in the neighborhood.

Fairmont Orchid $$$$ 540 rooms

One North Kaniku Dr., Kohala Coast. 808-885-2000. www.fairmont.com.

Set on 32 acres of a sheltered lagoon, the Fairmont Orchid offers a hushed elegance. Guest rooms are in the process of a Hawaiian-style makeover, with island artwork, block-cut native wall coverings, and palm-leaf pillow shams. The Fairmont has also moved to chemical-free cleansers and organic landscaping. Willow Stream Spa *(see Big Island/Must Be Pampered)* offers outdoor massage. A children's program, water-sports equipment rentals, and a bevy of restaurants round out the amenities.

Four Seasons Hualalai $$$$ 243 rooms

100 Kaupulehu Dr., Kaupulehu-Kona. 808-325-8019. www.fourseasons.com.

An intimate, bungalow-style resort on the water, this lush tropical retreat melts easily into the natural environment. Guests can swim in a saltwater pool (one of four oceanfront pools here) or cool off in outdoor rock showers after a round of golf or a spa treatment. Each room has its own private lanai and ocean views; over-size bath towels, down duvets and thick terry robes are just a few of the luxuries. And did we mention the wonderful spa *(see Big Island/Must Be Pampered)*?

Hilton Waikoloa Village $$$$ 1,240 rooms

425 Waikoloa Beach Dr., Waikoloa. 808-886-1234. www.hiltonwaikoloavillage.com.

The Big Island's answer to Walt Disney World®, this waterfront resort whisks you to your room via monorail or boat. Seven million dollars' worth of artwork is displayed on the property, including a one-mile museum walkway. You can swim with dolphins, slide down a 175-foot waterslide, kayak in a lagoon—the activities are seemingly endless!
Executive chef Wilhelm Pirngruber shows a masterful touch in the kitchen, too—**Donatoni's** *(see Must Eat)* and **Kamuela Provision Co.** **($$$$)** are the all-stars in a lineup of the hotel's nine restaurants.

Waikoloa Beach Marriott Resort $$$ 555 rooms

69-275 Waikoloa Beach Dr., Waikoloa. 808-886-1234 or 888-924-5656.
www.waikoloabeachmarriott.com.

Pale, earthy tones predominate at this property, where you'll find loads of amenities (including a spa, a water-sports program and children's activities) in slightly less posh digs than neighboring properties; the room rate is lower, as well. Outdoors is where the Waikoloa Beach Marriott really shines—it's set on Anaehoomalu Bay on the Kohala coast, a super playground for all sorts of water activities, including swimming, snorkeling, kayaking and windsurfing.

Kilauea Lodge $$ 14 rooms, 3 cottages

Old Volcano Rd., Volcano. 808-967-7366. www.kilauealodge.com.

Unless you're camping, this is your best bet for sleeping in the shadow of the Kilauea volcano (the lodge is located a mile from Hawaii Volcanoes National Park). Formerly a YMCA camp (c.1938), this high-ceilinged, rustic lodge is a cozy, inviting place to stay on a cool night (and aren't they all, here?). Some rooms have fireplaces, and all are adorned with fresh flowers. Rates include a full breakfast. The on-property restaurant offers fine dining with an Old World, European flavor.

Namakani Paio Cabins $ 10 cabins

3mi west of Hawaii Volcanoes National Park entrance on Rte. 11, Volcano. 808-967-7321.

These simple cabins can sleep four people, and are a great value at just $50 per unit. You get a lot more for your money than you do at the Volcano House Hotel (located in the national park), where four times that price gets you plain-Jane motel-style digs. Cabins (and campsites) are reserved through the Volcano House, where you'll also pick up linens and sleeping bags for the cabins. You might want to bring your own fleece blanket to ward off the chill. Each cabin comes with a grill, a picnic table and access to the campground's restrooms.

Maui

Fairmont Kea Lani $$$$$ 450 rooms

4100 Wailea Alanui Dr., Wailea. 808-875-4100 or 800-659-4100. www.fairmont.com.

Service is a true art form here, where valets literally sprint to your car to open the door for you, and guests— male and female—are greeted with fresh leis. It's all about quiet luxury, from the marble bathtubs to the pale-on-pale décor. The hotel is bright white and almost Grecian, set against the cerulean blue of sea and sky. At night, the Kea Lani really sparkles, thanks to well-placed torch lights. Don't miss a treatment at the hotel's Spa Kea Lani *(see Maui/Must Be Pampered)*, or a meal at **Nick's Fish Market** *(see Must Eat)*. The Fairmont's casual, poolside pizza restaurant is a good option, too.

Hotel Hana-Maui $$$$$ 69 rooms

5021 Hana Hwy., Hana. 808-248-8211. www.hotelhanamaui.com.

Bungalow-style suites and plantation cottages blend into the landscape here, where Hana Bay provides a spectacular backdrop. A gentle, New Age spirit pervades this property, which is brought to you by the same folks who opened the Post Ranch Inn on the cliffs of Big Sur, in California. You'd expect daily yoga classes in a place that emphasizes wellness and healing, and you'd be right! They offer an on-site spa, Hawaiian cultural activities and—a real plus—close proximity to the Haleakala volcano for hiking and horseback riding.

Hyatt Regency Maui $$$$ 806 rooms

200 Nohea Kai Dr., Lahaina. 808-661-1234. www.maui.hyatt.com.

This luxury-level beach resort really has it all: fabulous Kaanapali Beach right outside its door, an oceanfront spa, two world-class golf courses, and Camp Hyatt, so parents can enjoy it all while the kids are happily engaged. Keiki (kids) Lagoon is a popular spot, with its dancing fountains and sea-creature motif. Active types meet on the beach on Wednesday, Friday and Saturday at 8am for Beach Boot Camp, with the resort's fitness instructor. The hotel also owns a catamaran; few guests can resist the allure of a sunset sail, with the islands of Lanai and Molokai shimmering in the distance. Given the location, and the resort's popularity with families, this isn't the place to go for a serene escape, but there's lots of action and a lively vibe.

Inn at Mama's Fish House $$$ 6 cottages

*799 Poho Place, Paia. 808-579-9764 or 800-860-4852. www.mamasfishhouse.com.
Three-night minimum stay.*

Psst . . . behind Mama's Fish House restaurant stand six pleasant little cottages with tile floors and lanais, TVs, grills and—the best feature—access to the beach. Oh, yes, and guests get a 20 percent discount at the restaurant! Cottages include four two-bedroom units and two one-bedroom units. This isn't the place to go for a secluded, romantic getaway—there's not a lot of privacy here—but the inn has a fiercely loyal clientele, who feel they've stumbled upon a true gem among Maui's lodgings.

Lahaina Inn $$ 12 rooms

127 Lahainaluna Rd., Lahaina. 808-661-0577. www.lahainainn.com.

Once a whaling town, Lahaina offers a charming counterpoint to the luxury hotels on much of Maui. This fine old inn is stuffed with antique wooden furniture and more than a couple of tall tales. Rooms are individually decorated with Hawaiian quilts and flower-print wallpaper, and guest can mingle in the living room, where board games and cards are available. Another bonus: the food here is terrific.

Kauai

Hyatt Regency Kauai $$$$$ 602 rooms

1571 Poipu Rd., Koloa. 808-742-1234 or 800-554-9288. www.kauai.hyatt.com.

The grounds surrounding this upscale resort on the south shore are over-the-top beautiful, with a series of swimming pools (for children and adults) snaking through tropical gardens and cascades and waterfalls tumbling down the tiered levels. Enjoy a cocktail in one of the thatched-roof, open-air bars overlooking the sprawling golf course and the Pacific Ocean. Rooms have views of the ocean, hotel lagoons, gardens or the Haupu Mountains. On-site restaurants include the award-winning **Toppers ($$$$)**, and the resort's Anara Spa is considered one of the best in the US *(see Kauai/Must Be Pampered)*.

Princeville Resort $$$$$ 252 rooms

5520 Ka Haku Rd., Princeville. 808-826-9644 or 800-826-4400. www.princeville.com.

Considered one of the premier properties in the islands, Princeville Resort commands a dramatic view of Hanalei Bay and famous Bali Hai. Tucked away on Kauai's pristine north shore, the small hotel was built on the side of a bluff, overlooking the beginnings of the rugged **Na Pali Coast**★★★. Guests gather in the opulent lobby to sit and enjoy the views from its soaring windows; entertainment and drinks are offered in the lobby's Library Room. Every activity under the sun is available here, including excursions to the Na Pali Coast, golf at two championship courses *(see Kauai Musts for Outdoor Fun)*, and services at the spa. Dining is world-class at **Café Hanalei** *(see Must Eat)* and **La Cascata ($$$$)**.

Kauai Marriott Resort

$$$$ 356 rooms

Kalapaki Beach, Lihue. 808-245-5050 or 800-220-2925. www.marriotthawaii.com.

This lush 800-acre resort is set on 1.4 miles of south shore sandy beach, and surrounded by 51 acres of tropical gardens and two championship golf courses. The outdoor public spaces are impressive, with fine art, Asian-style statuary and sculpture, and exotic flowers. Considered one of the finest on the island, the 24,000-square-foot pool features waterfalls and hidden hot tubs. Rooms, though spacious, are basic, decorated in pastel tones, most with a garden, pool or ocean view. Four restaurants and lounges and two golf courses complete the amenities here.

Sheraton Kauai Resort

$$$$ 412 rooms

2440 Hoonani Rd., Poipu Beach. 808-742-1661 or 800-782-9488. www.sheraton-kauai.com.

The Sheraton's location, on the shores of Poipu Beach, is its main selling point. A cluster of low-slung buildings hugs the shores of the sandy white beach, with fine swimming and snorkeling at their doorstep. Reserve a room in the Beach or Ocean wings, where views all face the sea; Garden Wing rooms across the street are less desirable. There are separate swimming pools for kids and adults, a beachside activity center, and an open-air, oceanfront bar that's popular with guests as well as beachcombers.

Hanalei Bay Resort

$$$ 134 suites

5380 Honoiki Rd., Princeville. 808-826-6522 or 800-827-4427. www.hanaleibayresort.com.

Set on the north shore, next to the famed Princeville Resort, this all-suite property is perfect for vacationers looking for a get-away-from-it-all destination resort. Suites offer plenty of room, with wicker furnishings, kitchenettes or full kitchens, and a value-conscious price tag. The property commands picturesque views overlooking Hanalei Bay and a crescent of sandy beach. Tennis courts, poolside massages, and two pools—one featuring a waterfall and an open-air Jacuzzi—complete the package.

Radisson Kauai

$$$ 345 rooms

4331 Kauai Beach Dr., Lihue. 808-245-1955 or 888-805-3843. www.radissonkauai.com.

Situated on Kauai's sunny east shore, fronting a three-mile-long sandy beach, this moderately priced resort attracts families and vacationing couples. Newly remodeled rooms feature dark woods and floral fabrics, with views of the ocean, gardens or pools. This casual, friendly hotel boasts four pools and a thatched-roof beachside lounge area (where the popular manager's complimentary cocktail party is held each evening). Radisson offers a variety of money-saving package deals throughout the year.

Waimea Plantation Cottages
$$ 44 cottages

9400 Kaumualii Hwy., Waimea. 808-338-1625 or 800-992-4632. www.waimea-plantation.com.

Waimea Plantation's charming early-20C sugar-workers' bungalows stretch among 27 acres of coconut groves along a black-sand beach on Kauai's west side. Units with full kitchens and televisions are perfect for families, and hammocks for two invite long naps by the sea. An unexpected perk: complimentary broadband wireless Internet access.

Oahu

Halekulani Hotel
$$$$$ 456 rooms

2199 Kalia Rd., Honolulu. 808-923-2311 or 800-367-2343. www.halekulani.com.

One of the top hotels in the world, the graceful Halekulani presides over the shores of Waikiki Beach like an aging grand dame. Since 1917, this top-notch hotel has been a mecca for the rich and famous, who come for its Waikiki beach location and top-drawer service. Rooms have elegant furnishings and amenities, like marble vanities, deep soaking tubs, entertainment centers and wireless Internet access, not to mention views overlooking the Pacific Ocean from towers as lofty as the clientele. For dining, both **La Mer** *(see Must Eat)* and **Orchid's ($$$$)** are worth a visit.

J.W. Marriott Ihilani Resort & Spa
$$$$$ 423 rooms

92-1001 Olani St., Kapolei. 808-679-0079 or 800-626-4446. www.ihilani.com.

This sleek, ultra-deluxe destination resort sits on 640 secluded oceanfront acres, 23 miles outside Waikiki Beach and downtown Honolulu. Nesting on Oahu's sunny western shore, the 17-story hotel overlooks pristine beaches, turquoise-colored lagoons and open ocean. Rooms are decorated in contemporary teak furnishings and feature in-room CD players, high-tech sound systems, and marble baths; most have sweeping ocean views and private lanais. There's no need to set foot off the property: on-site you'll find a 35,000-square-foot spa *(see Oahu/Must Be Pampered)*, an 18-hole golf course, a fitness club, pools and four restaurants, including award-winning **Roy's Restaurant** *(see Must Eat)*.

Kahala Mandarin Oriental
$$$$$ 70 rooms

5000 Kahala Ave., Honolulu. 808-739-8888 or 800-367-2525. www.mandarin-oriental.com.

Quiet, serene and luxurious describes this luscious resort tucked away on a secluded bay, 10 minutes from Waikiki. The elegant oceanfront hotel features six restaurants, a full-service spa, a fitness center, a dive shop and an impressive 26,000-square-foot, dolphin-inhabited lagoon (guests can sign up for the hotel's swim-with-a-dolphin program). Rooms blend Old Hawaiian décor with Asian accents, including mahogany furniture, teak parquet floors and grass-cloth wall coverings.

Royal Hawaiian

$$$$$ 527 rooms

2259 Kalakaua Ave., Honolulu. 808-923-7311 or 800-782-9488. www.royal-hawaiian.com.

The sprawling, storied Pink Palace of the Pacific was a Hollywood playground when the Moorish-style hotel was built in 1927; today it retains its chic Art Deco-era sensibility. The Waikiki beachfront property offers activities galore, including water sports, golf, shopping and sightseeing tours, boat cruises and more. Luaus with Polynesian dances are staged weekly. Families favor the Royal Hawaiian for its supervised children's program, special activities for teens, and the on-site, Abhasa Waikiki Spa *(see Oahu/Must Be Pampered)* for mom and dad. The mai tai cocktail is said to have been first created in the bar of the same name here, still a popular spot for sunset cocktail hour.

Sheraton Moana Surfrider

$$$$$ 791 rooms

2365 Kalakaua Ave., Waikiki Beach. 808-922-3111 or 800-782-9488. www.sheraton-hawaii.com.

Dubbed the "first Lady of Waikiki," this 1901 landmark is the island's oldest hotel. The large oceanfront property combines Old Hawaiian charm with modern-day touches. The open-air lobby, boasting expansive Waikiki Beach views, makes a lasting first impression. Rooms in the newer tower sections are the most spacious. If you're looking for Old Hawaii ambience, reserve a room in the Banyan wing. Accommodations here are smaller but full of charm, decorated with antiques and rare koa-wood and custom furnishings.

Hilton Hawaiian Village Beach Resort & Spa

$$$$ 2,998 rooms

2005 Kalia Rd., Honolulu. 808-949-4321 or 800-774-1500. www.hawaiianvillage.hilton.com.

One of the world's largest oceanfront hotels stretches over 22 acres and features six separate guest towers. Hilton Hawaiian Village includes more than 90 fine shops, 22 restaurants and lounges, and a fitness center and Mandara Spa *(see Oahu/Must Be Pampered)*. The immaculate grounds wrap around a lagoon, with roaming wildlife and leafy botanical gardens; the beachfront pool is the largest on the island. Bali-by-the-Sea and the Golden Dragon offer fine dining, and the acclaimed **Bishop Museum**★★★ *(see Oahu/Museums)* has a branch in the new Kalia Tower.

Hyatt Regency Waikiki
$$$$ 1,230 rooms

2424 Kalakaua Ave., Honolulu. 808-923-1234 or 800-233-1234. www.hyattwaikiki.com.

Located across the street from Kuhio Beach and near Kapiolani Park, this large-scale resort is a lively spot. The open-air lobby, with its tumbling waterfalls, live music and the often-hopping Harry's Bar, is the center of action. Guest rooms, with private lanais, are modestly sized and decorated with light colors. There's also a 10,000-square-foot Na Hoola Spa *(see Oahu/Must Be Pampered)* and fitness center, an oceanfront pool, supervised children's programs and activities galore.

Outrigger Waikiki on the Beach
$$$$ 525 rooms

2335 Kalakaua Ave., Honolulu. 808-923-0711 or 800-688-7444. www.outrigger.com.

This busy, beachfront hotel is a perennial favorite among Oahu vacationers. Light and contemporary rooms are basic but the property commands a top spot on bustling Waikiki Beach. Guests here can choose among a host of water sports, boat cruises, and shopping options. The Outrigger is also home to The Society of Seven concert show and Duke's Canoe Club, one of Oahu's most popular bars *(see Oahu/Nightlife)*.

Ala Moana Hotel
$$$ 1,219 rooms

410 Atkinson Dr., Honolulu. 808-955-4811 or 800-367-6025. www.alamoanahotel.com.

Across from the Hawaii Convention Center, overlooking pretty Ala Moana Beach Park, this landmark high rise is popular with businesspeople and families looking for quality at a decent price. The towering 36-story hotel, with a fitness center, restaurants and bars, is also connected to the popular Ala Moana Shopping Center *(see Oahu/Must Shop)*. Rooms are decorated with light, airy island colors and have private lanais, most with mountain or ocean views.

Aston Waikiki Beach
$$$ 716 rooms

2570 Kalakaua Ave., Honolulu. 877-997-6667 or 800-877-7666. www.astonwaikiki.com.

After a major renovation, this two-tower high rise is fast becoming one of the "best-value" properties in Honolulu (in 2004, *Travel and Leisure* magazine ranked it among the 50 best affordable beach resorts in the world). Located just off Waikiki Beach and within walking distance of major downtown sites and attractions, the hotel has gone from dowdy and non-distinctive to hip and lively. Room décor, including wild colors and bead curtains, appeals to young families and couples. **Tiki's Grill and Bar ($$$)**, located on the second floor of the hotel, is a popular dining venue and a hangout for locals and visitors.

Hawaii Prince Hotel $$$ 512 rooms

100 Holomoana St., Honolulu. 808-956-1111 or 800-321-6248. www.hawaiiprincehotel.com.

Business travelers, golfers and vacationers who appreciate big-city elegance flock to this modern property. Twin 350-foot-high towers of glass, steel and slate overlook the Ala Wai Yacht Harbor, within walking distance of the Hawaii Convention Center and popular Ala Moana Shopping Center *(see Oahu/Must Shop)*. Guests have privileges at the property's championship 27-hole golf course, designed by Arnold Palmer; the Hawaiian Prince is the only hotel in Waikiki with its own course. Rooms have floor-to-ceiling windows with ocean views. Hotel restaurants include the elegant **Prince Court ($$$)**, and **Hakone ($$$)**, offering some of the best Japanese food in town.

Waikiki Parc Hotel $$$ 298 rooms

2233 Helumoa Rd., Honolulu. 808-921-7272. www.parchotel.com.

Just off the Waikiki Beach (across the street from Oahu's famous Halekulani resort), this property offers the services and amenities of a top-end resort hotel without the beachfront price tag. Rooms are bright and airy, decorated in light pastel colors with tropical accents. There's a fitness center, two restaurants, and a pool overlooking the ocean. When you make your reservations, ask about special promotions and package deals.

Manoa Valley Inn $$ 7 rooms, 1 cottage

2001 Vancouver Dr., Honolulu. 808-947-6019. www.manoavalleyinn.com.

A 1912 post-Victorian inn, set in a lush neighborhood near the University of Hawaii, this charming bed-and-breakfast was restored in the late 1970s. Now filled with period antiques, Moana Valley Inn features rooms decked out with four-poster beds; some share bathroom facilities. It offers travelers an economic—and homey— alternative to Honolulu's concrete high rises.

Waikiki Joy Hotel $$ 94 rooms

320 Lewers St., Honolulu. 808-923-2300 or 877-997-6667. www.waikikijoyhotel.com.

Within walking distance of Waikiki Beach, the stylish boutique hotel provides a quiet, serene oasis from the hustle and bustle of downtown Honolulu. Spacious rooms have elegant touches, such as marble-tile entryways, in-room Jacuzzis, private lanais and state-of-the-art sound systems. All come equipped with small refrigerators; suites have full kitchens. You'll also find a fitness center, a restaurant and a swimming pool on-site. This is a great value for those who don't mind being off the beach.

Lanai

Lodge at Koele
$$$$$ 102 rooms

1 Keamoku Dr., Lanai City. 808-565-7300 (resort information); 808-565-3800 or 800-450-3704 (reservations). www.lodgeatkoele.com.

Discerning travelers looking for peace and pampering (and willing to pay the high price for it) favor this upscale, country-style lodge, set in Lanai's uplands among towering Cook pines and banyan trees. The lodge's great room features two massive stone fireplaces (said to be the largest in Hawaii), overstuffed chairs and sofas, and an interesting array of antiques, sculpture and artwork. Rooms have four-poster beds draped in crisp, fine linens, marble baths and private lanais. Activities include horseback riding (the lodge has its own stables), mountain biking, hiking, four-wheel-drive excursions, children's programs and more. The Experience at Koele golf course is ranked as one of the top in the country *(see Lanai/Musts for Outdoor Fun)*, and the **Formal Dining Room** offers wonderful New American cuisine *(see Must Eat)*. Be sure to ask about special promotions and packages offered throughout the year.

Manele Bay Hotel
$$$$$ 249 rooms

1 Manele Rd., Lanai City. 808-565-7700 (resort information); 808-565-3800 or 800-450-3704 (reservations). www.manelebayhotel.com.

Tucked along the shores of Lanai's pristine Hulopoe Beach, the elegant oceanfront resort offers impeccable service and peaceful, luxurious surroundings. The sister resort to the Lodge at Koele (both are owned by the same company) boasts rooms surrounded by tropical gardens and waterfalls. All have private balconies, plush linens, marble baths and four-poster beds. Favorite activities include snorkeling in the tide pools at Hulopoe Bay, a designated marine conservation area; golfing at the top-ranked Challenge at Manele course *(see Lanai/Musts for Outdoor Fun)*; private boat excursions; tennis and hiking. Guests may also take advantage of the hedonistic spa *(see Lanai/Must Be Pampered)*. True to its name, which means "heavenly splendor," **Ihilani** restaurant (**$$$**) serves scrumptious Mediterranean fare.

Hotel Lanai
$$ 10 rooms, 1 cottage

828 Lanai Ave., Lanai City. 808-565-7211 or 877-665-2624. www.hotellanai.com.

This charming, 1923 house, located in quaint Lanai City, offers an economic and intimate option for lodging on the island of Lanai. Built by James Dole as housing for Dole Plantation executives, the restored plantation guest house provides small but pleasant rooms, with hardwood floors, ceiling fans, colorful country quilts and private baths. You'll want to dine, as many islanders do, at the hotel's **Henry Clay's Rotisserie** *(see Must Eat)*.

Molokai

Molokai Ranch
$$$$ 62 rooms

100 Maunaloa Hwy., Maunaloa. 808-552-2741 or 888-627-8082. www.molokairanch.com.

There are two ways to go here: rooms in the small luxury lodge or the beach village, a series of unique canvas bungalows that are open to sun and sea on platform decks and run on solar energy. Call the latter "upscale camping"—it's a cool concept and much more comfortable than it sounds! A restaurant pavilion is set alongside the crashing surf. The 1940s-era ranch/lodge boasts a spa, billiards lounge, and plush, fat sofas that are perfect for curling up with a good book. The staff here will arrange as much activity as you wish, from hiking and biking to snorkeling and shooting clays.

Paniolo Hale Resort Condominiums
$$ 77 condominiums

Lio Place, Maunaloa. 800-367-2984. www.molokai-vacation-rental.com.
Two-night minimum stay.

Perched on a rocky ledge in the hilltop village of Maunaloa, the Paniolo Hale condo complex offers beautiful beach views and simply furnished studios or two-room condominiums. Guests here have privileges at the neighboring 18-hole Kaluakoi Golf Course, and Papohaku Beach, with its three miles of white sand, lies adjacent to the resort.

Puu o Hoku Ranch
$$ 15 rooms, 2 cottages

Kamehameha V Hwy., near Halawa. 808-558-9109. www.puuohoku.com.

Named "Hill of Stars" in Hawaiian, this 14,000-acre ranch, on Molokai's wild east end, welcomes *paniolo* (cowboy) wannabes to enjoy a splendid landscape of sand and sea in simple but pretty rooms decked out in wicker and colorful prints, each with its own kitchen, in the historic lodge. They also offer two large, secluded two-bedroom cottages with fully equipped kitchens and views that seem to go on forever; cottages make the perfect accommodations for two couples or families. Ask about the guided horseback rides (on trails or on the beach) at this working cattle ranch.

The following abbreviations may appear in this Index:
NHP National Historical Park; NHS National Historical
Site; NP National Park; NWR National Wildlife Reserve;
SHP State Historic Park; SP State Park, SRA State
Recreation Area.

Accommodations 17
Airports 13
Akaka Falls SP, Hawaii 33
Alexander & Baldwin Sugar Museum, Maui 66
Allerton Botanical Garden, Kauai 93
Aloha Tower, Oahu 105, 142
Aloha Tower Marketplace, Oahu 105, 142
Bali Hai, Kauai 96
Banzai Pipeline, Oahu 111
Battleship Missouri Memorial, Oahu 127
Beaches 26, 60, 82, 109, 148, 159
Big Beach, Maui 60
Biking 68
Bishop Museum and Planetarium, Oahu 119, 131
Byodo-In Temple, Oahu 17
Calendar of Events 8
Camping 63, 98, 133
Captain Cook, Hawaii 46
Car Rental 14, 150
Cathedral Ledges, Lanai 146, 154
Chain of Craters Road, Hawaii 30, 35, 36, 37
Children's Garden, Kauai 100
Chinatown, Oahu 117, 140
Cities, Oahu 105
Cliff Diving 154
Climate 12
Contemporary Museum, Oahu 124
Cook, Captain James 21, 46
Crater Rim Drive, Hawaii 30, 35
Cruises 14, 130
Devastation Trail, Hawaii 36
Diamond Head, Oahu 112
Disabled Travelers 11
Dolphins 51
East End Drive (Kamehameha V Highway), Molokai 160
Establishment Day, Hawaii 42
Fern Grotto, Kauai 88
Ferries 80, 162
Festivals 8, 45, 52, 159, 163
Flumin' Da Ditch, Hawaii 50
Foreign Visitors 15
Foster Botanical Garden, Oahu 116
Garden of Eden Arboretum & Botanical Garden, Maui 66
Garden of the Gods, Lanai 150, 152
Gardens 40, 67, 92, 116, 152
Golf 99, 133, 155
Green Sand Beach, Hawaii 27
Grove Farm Homestead, Kauai 94
Haena Beach Park, Kauai 92
Halawa Valley, Molokai 160
Haleakala, Maui 57, 68
Haleakala NP, Maui 62, 64
Halemaumau Crater, Hawaii 30, 35, 47
Hana, Maui 66
Hana Highway, Maui 64, 65

Hanakoa Valley, Kauai 97
Hanalei, Kauai 91
Hanalei Bay, Kauai 81, 82, 92, 95
Hanauma Bay Beach Park, Oahu 110
Hanauma Bay Nature Preserve, Oahu 113, 114, 132
Hapuna Beach SRA, Hawaii 26
Hawaii, The Big Island 22
Hawaiian Cuisine 152, 157
Hawaiian Culture 165
Hawaiian Music 78
Hawaii Children's Discovery Center, Oahu 137
Hawaii Maritime Center, Oahu 124
Hawaii Opera Theatre, Oahu 138
Hawaii State Capitol, Oahu 105
Hawaii Theatre, Oahu 138
Hawaii Visitor and Convention Bureau, Oahu 10
Hawaii Tropical Botanical Garden, Hawaii 38, 40
Hawaii Volcanoes NP, Hawaii 22, 29, 50
Helicopter Tours 51, 95
Highway 44, Lanai 150
Hiking 32, 37, 50, 63, 70, 86, 97, 156, 162
Hilo, Hawaii 23
Historic Sites 42, 67, 94, 125, 152, 161
History 20
Ho, Don 144
Honolulu, Oahu 104, 105
Honolulu Academy of Arts, Oahu 105, 121
Honolulu Symphony Orchestra, Oahu 139
Honolulu Zoo, Oahu 108, 136
Hookipa Beach Park, Maui 61, 72
Horseback riding, Lanai 156
Hotels 34, 128, 178
Hula 52, 69, 159
Hulihee Palace, Hawaii 43
Hulopoe Beach, Lanai 148, 150
Iao Needle, Maui 64
Iao Valley SP, Maui 64
Iliiliopae Heiau, Molokai 160, 161
International Market Place, Oahu 109
Iolani Palace, Oahu 104, 105, 125, 139
Ironman Triathlon, Hawaii 48
Isaac Hale Park, Hawaii 35
Kaanapali Beach, Maui 60
Kaena Point, Lanai 150
Kahana Valley, Oahu 133
Kahanamoku, Duke 108, 124, 134, 143
Kalahaku Overlook, Maui 63
Kahilu Theatre, Hawaii 52
Kahoolawe 164
Kailua Beach Park, Oahu 110
Kakahaia Beach Park, Molokai 160
Kalalau Lookout, Kauai 90
Kalalau Trail, Kauai 80, 85, 97
Kalalau Valley, Kauai 97
Kalaupapa NHP, Molokai 158, 161
Kaloko-Honokohau NHP, Hawaii 44
Kamakou Preserve, Molokai 162
Kamehameha I, King 21, 23, 104
Kanepuu Preserve, Lanai 153

Kapaa, Kauai 81
Kapiolani Park, Oahu 108
Kau Desert, Hawaii 30
Kauai 80
Kauai Museum, Kauai 94
Kaumahina State Wayside Park, Maui 66
Kaunaoa Beach (Mauna Kea Beach), Hawaii 26
Kaunolu Village, Lanai 150, 152
Kawaiahao Church, Oahu 105
Kayaking 88
Keaiwa Heiau SRA, Oahu 133
Kealakekua Bay SHP, Hawaii 46, 51
Kee Beach, Kauai 84, 92, 100
Keoneheehee Trail, Maui 70
Kilauea Iki, Hawaii 35, 36, 50
Kilauea Point NWR, Kauai 88, 91, 100
Kilauea Volcano, Hawaii 22, 30
Kilauea Visitor Center, Hawaii 30, 63
Kipahula Visitor Center, Maui 63
Kipuka Puaulu, Hawaii 38
Kiteboarding 72
Kite flying 136
Kohala Coast, Hawaii 22, 34
Kokee Natural History Museum, Kauai 86, 90
Kokee SP, Kauai 86, 89, 98
Koko Crater Botanical Gardens, Oahu 114, 116
Koko Crater, Oahu 114
Kualoa Ranch, Oahu 136
Kula Botanical Gardens, Maui 67
Lahaina, Maui 57, 74
Lanai 146
Lanai City, Lanai 147
Lanikai Beach, Oahu 111
Lapakahi SHP, Hawaii 44
Laupahoehoe Point Beach, Hawaii 27
Lava Tree State Monument, Hawaii 39
Leatherman, Stephen P. 26, 61
Leis 13, 117
Lihue, Kauai 81, 95
Liliuokalani, Queen 41
Liliuokalani Gardens, Hawaii 41
Limahuli Garden, Kauai 92
Lindbergh, Charles 64
Luahiwa petroglyphs, Lanai 150
Luaus 93, 131
Lumahai Beach, Kauai 92
Lydgate Park Beach, Kauai 100
Lyman Museum & Mission House, Hawaii 45
Lyon Arboretum, Oahu 116
Makapuu Beach, Oahu 115
Make Horse Beach, Molokai 159
Malaekahana Beach, Oahu 133
Malama Trail, Hawaii 34
Mana Hale, Hawaii 44
Manoa Falls, Oahu 116
Marine Education Center, Oahu 132
Marriage in Hawaii 17
Maui 56
Maui Arts and Cultural Center, Maui 74

Maui Ocean Center, Maui 73
Maui Tropical Plantation, Maui 68
Mauna Kea, Hawaii 22, 33, 48
Mauna Loa, Hawaii 22, 31, 47
Mauna Loa Road, Hawaii 38
Mauna Loa Trail, Hawaii 32
McBryde Botanical Garden, Kauai 93
Menehune Fishpond, Kauai 94
Menehunes 94
Mission Houses Museum, Oahu 105, 122
Molokai 158
Molokai Hoe Canoe Race, Molokai 163
Molokini Island, Maui 71
Monk Seals 83
Munro Trail, Lanai 146, 150, 151
Mookini Heiau, Hawaii 43
Moomomi Dunes, Molokai 160
Mt. Waialeale, Kauai 80
Murphy's Beach, Molokai 159
Museums 47, 66, 94, 119
Musts for Fun 68, 95, 129, 153, 163
Musts for Kids 52, 73, 100, 135, 156
Musts for Outdoor Fun 48, 70, 97, 131, 154, 162
Na Aina Kai Botanical Gardens, Kauai 100
Nakalele Point, Maui 64
Nani Mau Gardens, Hawaii 41
Na Pali Coast, Kauai 80, 85, 90, 92, 95, 97
National Memorial Cemetery of the Pacific, Oahu 128
Natural Sites 150, 160
Neil S. Blaisdell Concert Hall, Oahu 138
Nene bird 162
Nightlife 54, 78, 102, 143
Niihau 164
North Shore, Kauai 91
North Shore Beaches, Oahu 111
Oahu 104
Oheo Gulch, Maui 64
Onomea Foot Trail, Hawaii 38
Paia, Maui 65, 75
Papohaku Beach, Molokai 159
Parker Ranch, Hawaii 17, 43
Parks and Natural Sites 29, 62, 85, 112
Pawai Bay, Hawaii 51
Pearl Harbor, Oahu 21, 126
Pele 32
Pepeekeo Scenic Drive, Hawaii 38, 40
Pepeopae Trail, Molokai 162
Performing Arts 52, 74, 138
Petroglyphs 149, 150
Piilanihale Heiau, Maui 67
Pilialoha Children's Program, Lanai 156
Pipiwai Trail, Maui 70
Poipu, Kauai 81, 95
Poipu Beach Park, Kauai 83, 100
Polihale Beach, Kauai 84
Polihale SP, Kauai 84, 98
Polihua Beach, Lanai 149, 153
Polynesian Cultural Center, Oahu 123
Practical Information 10

Princeville, Kauai 81
Public Transportation 14
Punaluu Black Sand Beach, Hawaii 28
Purdy's Macadamia Nut Farm, Molokai 163
Puuhonua o Honaunau NHP 42
Puukohola Heiau NHS, Hawaii 45
Puuopelu, Hawaii 44
Puu Pehe Rock (Sweetheart Rock), Lanai 148
Queen Emma Summer Palace, Oahu 125
Rainbow Falls, Hawaii 23, 34
Red Bull World Cliff-Diving Championships, Lanai 9, 154
Red Road, Hawaii 39
Restaurants 166
Royal Hawaiian Band, Oahu 139
Royal Kona Museum & Coffee Mill, Hawaii 46, 47
Sand Island SRA, Oahu 133
Sandy Beach, Oahu 114, 136
Scenic Drives 35, 65, 89, 114, 150, 160
Scuba Diving 49, 154
Sea Life Park, Oahu 115, 135
Sea Turtles 72, 135
Secret Beach, Kauai 82
Senator Fong's Plantation, Oahu 117
Senior Citizens 11
Shangri La, Oahu 122
Shipwreck Beach, Lanai 148, 150
Shopping 53, 74, 101, 140
Silversword 63
Skiing on Mauna Kea, Hawaii 33
Smith's Tropical Paradise, Kauai 93
Snorkeling 44, 49, 51, 71, 100, 113, 132, 154
Southeast Shore, Oahu 114
Spas 55, 79, 103, 144, 157
Sporting Clays, Lanai 153
Spouting Horn, Kauai 83
St. Joseph's Catholic Church, Molokai 160
Stargazing, Hawaii 48
Sunset Beach, Oahu 111, 129
Surfing 60, 71, 129, 134
Surf shops 75
Swim with Rays, Hawaii 49
Taxis 14
Tedeschi Vineyards, Maui 69
Thomas A. Jaggar Museum, Hawaii 30, 35, 47
Thurston Lava Tube, Hawaii 36, 52
Tunnels Beach, Kauai 92
Urasenke Tea House, Oahu 130
USS Arizona Memorial, Oahu 104, 126
USS Bowfin Submarine Museum & Park, Oahu 127
Visitors Bureaus 10, 95
Wahiawa Botanical Garden, Oahu 118
Waialua Beach, Molokai 159
Waianapanapa SP, Maui 66
Waikiki, Oahu 104, 108
Waikiki Aquarium, Oahu 108, 137
Waikiki Beach, Oahu 109
Wailea Beach, Maui 61
Wailua, Kauai 81
Waimanalo Beach, Oahu 115

Waimea Bay, Oahu 111, 129
Waimea Canyon, Kauai 80, 95, 98
Waimea Canyon Drive, Kauai 87, 89
Waimea Canyon SP, Kauai 87
Waimea Falls, Oahu 131
Waimea Valley Audubon Center, Oahu 131
Waimoku Falls, Maui 70
Waipio Valley, Hawaii 22
Whale-Watching 61, 71, 73
Whalers Village, Maui 60, 73, 77
Windsurfing 72
World Botanical Garden, Hawaii 40

Photo Credits